QUICK & EASY
MICROWAVE
COOKING

QUICK & EASY
MICROWAVE
COOKING

DI BUSSCHAU

PHOTOGRAPHY BY ANTHONY JOHNSON

ACKNOWLEDGEMENTS

The publishers would like to thank Sharp Electronics for the loan of a microwave
oven during the course of photography.

First published in 1996 by
New Holland (Publishers) Ltd
London • Cape Town • Sydney • Singapore

24 Nutford Place, London W1H 6DQ, UK
PO Box 1144, Cape Town 8000, South Africa
3/2 Aquatic Drive, Frenchs Forest, NSW 2086, Australia

ISBN 1 85368 545 3 (hb)
ISBN 1 85368 543 7 (pb)

PROJECT MANAGER: Jenny Barrett
EDITORS: Jenny Barrett, Thea Coetzee and Elizabeth Frost
DESIGNER: Petal Palmer
COVER DESIGNER: Petal Palmer
TYPESETTERS: Suzanne Fortescue and Damian Gibbs
PHOTOGRAPHER: Anthony Johnson★
STYLIST: Vo Pollard★

★ except page 31: photographer Mike Robinson and
stylists Helen Lindsey-Clark and Di Busschau

Reproduction by Hirt & Carter (Pty) Ltd
Printed by Times Offset (M) Sdn. Bhd.

CONTENTS

INTRODUCTION

Everybody enjoys eating, but many people equate healthy food with boring food. I believe very strongly, however, that a meal that is nutritious can be just as appealing and delicious as a meal lacking the proper nutrients, and that the basis of healthy eating is wholesome and nutritious home-made food.

I also operate on the principle that fresh is best. Our lives have become increasingly busy and we are more dependent on processed, refined, packaged and preserved foods than ever before. More and more, we exclude raw or whole foods from our diet. And very often our 'fresh' foods have been subjected to spraying, refrigeration, irradiation, and so on, so that by the time we eat our food it has lost many of the essential nutrients it is supposed to provide. Many of life's rituals, like birthdays, bar mitzvahs, courtship, weddings, anniversaries, even funerals, are centred around sweets, cakes and other rich, high-calorie foods. Some people eat for psychological reasons — out of boredom, frustration, anger or unhappiness, for example — while others develop eating disorders. In order to lead healthier lives we need to eat more healthily. This requires a conscious re-evaluation of our shopping and eating habits. Fad diets are now getting kicked out of the back door as they deserve and being replaced with the age-old philosophy of 'everything in moderation'.

A balanced diet, with lots of raw, whole foods and with cooked food correctly prepared and combined in the right way, will help us achieve that desired and most important goal of 'a sound mind in a healthy body'. This does not mean that we have to become slaves in the kitchen. On the contrary, much of our food intake should be in the form of fresh, raw fruit and vegetables, which can be simply prepared. As for

cooked food, the microwave certainly helps me to achieve my goal of healthy eating without tying me down to the kitchen! The nutritional content of the food is retained far more effectively than when food is cooked conventionally. This is especially the case with vegetables, as little water is used and their goodness therefore does not get thrown out with the cooking water. They also retain their fresh raw colour well, so look more appealing than conventionally cooked vegetables. In addition, with the aid of a browning dish, little or no fat is needed to make delicious 'fried' food! And for the cook in a hurry, microwaving is also often a far quicker way of preparing food. Just imagine being able to cook your Sunday roast in under half an hour!

For several practical reasons, the microwave is a real boon to the modern compact kitchen. Even the largest models take up less space than a conventional oven, and since the microwave can safely be plugged into any socket, it can be positioned anywhere in the kitchen where there is an accessible power point. It is cheaper to run, as microwaving uses little energy compared with heating elements, as well as taking less time. It also provides a cleaner way of cooking as the whole cooking process is enclosed, and because there is no direct heat within the microwave, messes that do occur do not get baked in nearly as quickly and are thus far easier to clean off than in a conventional oven. For the same reason, the kitchen does not get overheated and becomes a more pleasant environment to work in. For open-plan kitchens, it offers the advantage of minimizing unwanted kitchen odours. And because the microwave turns off automatically, you do not have to rush back into the kitchen the minute your food is ready.

CONTAINERS

I have three ovenproof glass bowls — small, medium and large (1 litre, 2 litre and 3 litre capacity respectively) — which I use frequently. In many of the recipes I have specified the size and type of dish to be used.

Most dishes and containers can be used in the microwave, with the exception of:
♦ crockery with silver rims;
♦ ordinary Tupperware;
♦ plastic that is not pliable (as with certain plastic jugs);
♦ metal containers.

For combination ovens, use ovenproof dishes and those brands of plasticware that are manufactured specifically to withstand temperatures of up to 210 °C.

SERVINGS

The number of servings is indicated on each recipe. If you wish to increase the number of servings, increase the cooking time proportionately, then subtract ⅓ of the number you arrive at; for example, if a baked potato takes 4 minutes, 3 potatoes will take 8 minutes ([4 x 3] − 4 = 8). To decrease quantities, decrease the cooking time and add ⅓ of the total.

BROWNING DISH

This dish is to the microwave what the frying pan is to the hob. Mica in the base of the dish absorbs microwave energy, making the base very hot. It then sears and browns any food that comes into contact with it. The browning dish should be preheated according to the manufacturer's instructions. Depending on its size, it should have a maximum preheating time of about 8 minutes. Meat should be patted dry, flavoured with herbs or spices and placed immediately in the dish. The dish should not be removed from the oven until cooking is complete as its base must remain very hot to brown the food, and it must therefore not make contact with any cool surface. The use of fat in the browning dish depends on personal preference, but it can be omitted.

COOKING ON A RACK

When cooking a dish such as a quiche, where you don't want to end up with a soft, undercooked base, place the dish on a slightly raised rack. This enables the microwaves to cook from underneath the dish.

COVERING FOOD

Generally, for moist cooking (as with vegetables), the food should be covered securely with a lid or pierced cling film. For dry cooking (as with cakes), the food should not be covered.

DEFROSTING

All food should be completely defrosted before being cooked in the microwave. It is safer to defrost food quickly in the microwave than over a period of time at room temperature as there is less chance of harmful bacteria building up. Also, important nutrients, flavour and moisture are not lost when food is defrosted quickly. Remember that food should be turned or shielded when defrosting to ensure that it defrosts evenly, and that it will continue defrosting while standing.

INGREDIENTS

♦ Depending on your cholesterol count or personal preference, butter may be replaced with margarine in all recipes. They have the same quantity of fat and the same calorie-count — both should be used sparingly if you are trying to stick to a healthy diet. Softening butter makes it easier to spread, and it is then easier to use less; if it hard, simply microwave the required amount on High for a few seconds at a time until it is softer, taking care not to let it melt. Low-fat spreads can also be used instead in some cases for a more slimming alternative.

♦ Where cream is suggested, plain yoghurt may be substituted — it does not curdle in the microwave as long as it is cooked at a relatively low power level. If possible, add yoghurt right at the end.

♦ The smooth cottage cheese used in these recipes is known as curd cheese in some countries.

♦ Eggs should never be boiled in the microwave, as they are liable to explode.

♦ For the same reason, prick the skins of whole vegetables such as potatoes, butternut squash and aubergines and the membranes of chicken livers.

♦ If you prefer to avoid using cornflour and flour when thickening a stew or casserole, purée some of the cooked vegetables in the stew and return to the dish.

♦ Freshly chopped herbs and freshly ground spices are best for flavour, but dried herbs and spices are more convenient to use. Substitute 5 ml/1 teaspoon dried herbs for 15 ml/1 tablespoon fresh.

♦ As gelatine is an animal product, strict vegetarians may wish to substitute agar-agar (made from seaweed) or arrowroot, which is particularly suitable for thickening fruit sauces and gives a clear, transparent colour. Use less arrowroot or agar-agar than you would gelatine, for example, 7.5 ml/1½ teaspoons arrowroot or 10 ml/2 teaspoons agar-agar to set 600 ml/1 pint liquid instead of 15 ml/1 tablespoon gelatine.

♦ Although only microwaving instructions are given in the text, parts of the recipes, such as boiling pasta or rice, can easily be done on the hob while you prepare other parts of the meal in the microwave; this can save time and may mean that no reheating will be necessary.

COMBINATION OVENS

These ovens use both convection and microwave energy and have become very popular because they give excellent results. Some use convection and microwave energy simultaneously, other types alternate them. Much shorter cooking times are required with the former.

A quartz grill is now a feature of most combination ovens and some compact microwaves, adding a new dimension to microwave cooking. It can be used on its own or with either microwave power or convection.

COOKING AND STANDING TIMES

Cooking times vary according to the wattage and make of the microwave. All the cooking times given in this book are therefore approximate. These recipes were tested in a 650 watt microwave, so if yours has a higher wattage, it is best to use a shorter cooking time initially and then cook for a little longer if necessary.

Food continues to cook for a short time after being removed from a microwave. This is known as standing time. In those recipes where this is an essential part of the cooking process, it is specified.

APPROXIMATE MASS PER 250 ML/9 FL OZ (1 CUP)

Breadcrumbs, dry	120 g	4 oz
Breadcrumbs, fresh	60 g	2 oz
Bulgur wheat	180 g	6½ oz
Butter	230 g	8 oz
Carrots, grated	125 g	4½ oz
Cheese, grated		
Cheddar	100 g	3½ oz
cottage/cream	250 g	9 oz
Gruyère	120 g	4 oz
mozzarella	125 g	4½ oz
Parmesan	100 g	3½ oz
Chickpeas, dry	190 g	6½ oz
Chickpeas, cooked	150 g	5½ oz
Coconut	80 g	2½ oz
Cornflakes, crushed	60 g	2 oz
Cornflakes, whole	30 g	1 oz
Celery, sliced	100 g	3½ oz
Cucumber, chopped	100 g	3½ oz
Dried fruit	150 g	5½ oz
Flour	120 g	4 oz
Millet, dry	230 g	8 oz
Millet, cooked	170 g	6 oz
Minced beef	250 g	9 oz
Nuts, chopped	150 g	5½ oz
Nuts, whole	100 g	3½ oz
Oats	150 g	5½ oz
Okra, sliced	75 g	2½ oz
Potatoes, grated	125 g	4½ oz
Rice, dry	220 g	8 oz
Rice, cooked	160 g	5½ oz
Sesame seeds	150 g	5½ oz
Sugar	200 g	7 oz
Sunflower seeds	150 g	5½ oz
Wheat germ	80 g	2¾ oz

SAFETY

Extensive research has shown that there are no harmful or long-term effects on health associated with the use of the microwave oven. All microwave ovens have an inbuilt safety mechanism which ensures that the oven will not operate while the door is open; never tamper with this mechanism.

MICROWAVE POWER LEVELS

Instead of temperature settings, as on a conventional oven, microwaves operate by means of variable power levels that control the speed at which the food cooks. Unfortunately the terms used to describe these different levels are not standardized, and are expressed by different manufacturers in words, in numerals or as a percentage of the total wattage. The following is merely a guide:

POWER LEVEL	% POWER
Low	25
Defrost	30
Medium-Low	40
Medium	50
Medium-High	60–70
High	100

There is no exact formula for adjusting cooking times when using microwaves of a different power level to the one specified. If the recipes have been tested in a 650 watt microwave, as in this book, and yours is, for example 700 watts, it is suggested that you take off 10 seconds for every minute and then check the food. Conversely, if your microwave oven is less powerful, you will need to cook the food a little longer.

Most manufacturers supply detailed instructions for specific models; they usually also have a cookery advice service staffed by experienced home economists who will be able to tell you what adjustments to make.

Microwaves are frequently used to heat the ready-made dishes that are widely available in supermarkets. In the UK, for example, some of these are now labelled Heating Category A, B and so on to indicate the microwave power level, in an attempt to introduce standardized descriptions in the EC.

CHAPTER ONE

BREAKFASTS

BREAKFAST is the most important meal of the day. Don't cut it out, especially if you're dieting, otherwise you'll be hungry for the rest of the day and snacking will be a great temptation. Fruit, wholegrain cereals and eggs will all give you a good, healthy start to the day.

DRIED FRUIT COMPOTE

250 g/9 oz mixed dried fruit
250 ml/9 fl oz apple juice
250 ml/9 fl oz water
10 ml/2 teaspoons lemon juice
5 ml/1 teaspoon grated lemon zest

Microwave all ingredients in a small bowl, covered, on High for 6 minutes, stirring after 3 minutes. Serve warm or chilled. SERVES 4.

VARIATION: Serve with a jug of low-fat plain yoghurt.

FRUITY OAT BRAN

Oat bran is a particularly good porridge for a low-fat diet. Add wheat germ for vitamin E.

250 ml/9 fl oz low-fat milk
50 g/1¾ oz oat bran
30 ml/2 tablespoons wheat germ
pinch of salt
1 Granny Smith apple, peeled, cored and
  roughly chopped
15 ml/1 tablespoon sultanas
honey or brown sugar to serve

Microwave the milk, oat bran and wheat germ in a medium-sized glass bowl on High for 3–4 minutes, stirring every minute. Stir the chopped apple and sultanas into the porridge and microwave on High for 1½ minutes, until thick. Add salt to taste. Serve hot with a spoonful of honey or brown sugar. SERVES 2.

VARIATION: Omit the fruit and make plain oat bran. Serve it with low-fat plain yoghurt and with chopped dates sprinkled on top.

EGGS FLORENTINE

250 g/9 oz frozen chopped spinach, thawed
  and drained
45 ml/3 tablespoons low-fat plain yoghurt
salt and freshly ground black pepper to taste
pinch of nutmeg
4 eggs, at room temperature

Mix the spinach, yoghurt, seasoning and nutmeg together. Divide among four ramekin dishes. Microwave on Medium for 2 minutes. Break an egg into each ramekin. Prick the yolks twice with a cocktail stick. Cover with cling film, pierced. Place in a circle on the outer edge of the turntable. Microwave on Medium-High for 3–4 minutes. (One egg will take about 45 seconds, 2 eggs will take about 1½ minutes.) Leave to stand for 1 minute, then serve. SERVES 4.

APPLE 'N' OATS PORRIDGE

75 g/2½ oz oats
30 ml/2 tablespoons wheat germ
250 ml/9 fl oz low-fat milk
pinch of salt
75 ml/2½ fl oz puréed stewed apples
pinch of ground cinnamon
10 ml/2 teaspoons clear honey

Microwave the oats, wheat germ, milk and salt in a medium-sized glass bowl on High for 4–5 minutes, stirring twice. Stir in the apple purée and cinnamon. Pour the porridge into serving bowls and drizzle over just enough honey to sweeten. SERVES 2.

HINT: Although fresh is always best, if you don't have stewed apples at hand and don't have the time to prepare them, use unsweetened bottled apple sauce instead.

Dried Fruit Compote (page 10), Refreshing Lemon Drink (this page), Fruity Oat Bran (page 10) and Eggs Florentine (page 10).

CORN MEAL PORRIDGE WITH APRICOTS

  60 g/2 oz yellow corn meal
  pinch of salt
  125 ml/4½ fl oz cold water
  375 ml/13 fl oz boiling water
  125 ml/4½ fl oz low-fat milk
  6 dried apricots, roughly chopped

Mix the corn meal, salt and cold water into a paste in a medium-sized glass bowl. Gradually add the boiling water, combining ingredients with a balloon whisk, then whisk in the milk. Microwave on Medium-High for about 6 minutes, stirring often, until the porridge thickens. Divide between two bowls, top with the dried apricots, and serve with a little brown sugar and low-fat milk. SERVES 2.

REFRESHING LEMON DRINK

  10 ml/2 teaspoons grated lemon zest
  300 g/11 oz sugar
  125 ml/4½ fl oz water
  375 ml/13 fl oz freshly squeezed lemon
    juice (see Hint, page 123)

Combine zest, sugar and water in a large glass bowl. Microwave on High for 6–8 minutes until boiling, stirring twice to dissolve sugar. Add lemon juice and mix. Cool. Bottle and refrigerate.

To serve, pour 60–75 ml/2–2½ fl oz syrup into a tall glass and top up with cold water or soda water and ice. Garnish with a lemon slice. For a jugful, add 1.25 litres/2¼ pints of cold water or soda water to 250 ml/9 fl oz lemon mixture. Add ice cubes and stir. SERVES 12.

CHEESY HAM AND EGG PUFFS

These are delicious, look wonderful and are easy to prepare!

2 thin slices ham
30 ml/2 tablespoons grated Cheddar cheese
2 eggs, beaten
30 ml/2 tablespoons plain yoghurt
salt and freshly ground black pepper to taste
15 ml/1 tablespoon chopped parsley
pinch of paprika

Line two greased ramekins with ham. Sprinkle with half the cheese. Mix eggs and yoghurt thoroughly, add seasoning and pour the mixture into the ramekins. Sprinkle with the remaining cheese, the parsley and paprika. Microwave on Medium–High for 4–5 minutes — until the centre has set. Serve hot. SERVES 2.

VARIATION: Use smoked salmon slices instead of ham for a special occasion.

SCRAMBLED EGGS

3 eggs, lightly beaten
45 ml/3 tablespoons milk or single cream
15 ml/1 tablespoon butter, melted (see Hint, page 13)
salt and freshly ground black pepper to taste

Mix eggs and milk or cream and add to butter. Microwave on Medium–High for 2–3 minutes, drawing the outer edge to the centre with a wooden spoon every 30 seconds. The eggs should be just set with some liquid showing, as cooking continues during standing time. Leave to stand for a minute, season and serve. SERVES 2.

NOTE: For one person, use 1 egg, 5 ml/1 teaspoon butter and about 15 ml/1 tablespoon milk or cream. Microwave on Medium–High for about 1-1½ minutes.

VARIATION: As an optional luxury, add some chopped smoked salmon to the eggs and milk before cooking.

Scrambled Eggs (this page) and Cheesy Ham and Egg Puffs (this page).

FLUFFY CHEESE OMELETTE

3 eggs, separated
30 ml/2 tablespoons milk or single cream
pinch of cayenne pepper
15 ml/1 tablespoon butter
60 g/2 oz Cheddar cheese, grated

Preheat a browning dish on High for 3 minutes. Beat egg yolks lightly with milk or cream and cayenne pepper. Beat egg whites until stiff but not dry; fold into egg yolks gently with a metal spoon. Add butter to the browning dish, swirling it around to coat the base. Pour in the egg mixture, spreading it quickly to fill the base. Microwave on High for 1½ minutes. Sprinkle with cheese or add a filling (see below), fold the omelette over in half, and serve. SERVES 2.

NOTE: If you are cooking for one, use 1 large egg, 10 ml/2 teaspoons milk or cream, 5 ml/1 teaspoon butter and about 45 ml/3 tablespoons cheese. Cook on High for about 45 seconds.

SUGGESTED FILLINGS:
♦ 50 g/1¾ oz cooked ham or bacon, diced.
♦ 1 small tomato, diced, ½ onion, chopped, 50 g/1¾ oz mushrooms, chopped, and 15 ml/1 tablespoon butter. Microwave in a small bowl on High for 3 minutes.

HINT
To melt 10–30 ml/2 teaspoons–2 tablespoons butter, place it in a bowl and microwave on High for about 10–30 seconds.

GRAPEFRUIT BREAKFAST SPECIAL

1 grapefruit, halved and pips removed
10 ml/2 teaspoons honey or soft brown sugar
2.5 ml/½ teaspoon ground cinnamon
30 ml/2 tablespoons chunky cottage cheese
20 ml/4 teaspoons toasted wheat germ (see Note)

Loosen segments of grapefruit with a knife and remove pith. Spread flesh with honey or sprinkle with sugar. Dust with cinnamon. Put grapefruit on a plate and microwave on High for 2–3 minutes. Place a dollop of cottage cheese in the centre of each half, sprinkle with wheat germ and serve. SERVES 2.

NOTE: To toast wheat germ, spread 20 ml/4 teaspoons wheat germ over the base of a preheated browning dish. Microwave on High for 30 seconds, stirring thoroughly after 15 seconds.

STEWED DRIED FRUIT

125 g/4½ oz mixed dried fruit
250 ml/9 fl oz fruit juice of your choice
1 stick cinnamon (optional)

Soak the fruit in the juice with the cinnamon, if using, for 1 hour. Microwave, covered, on High for about 4 minutes. Leave to stand for 5 minutes. Remove the cinnamon and serve hot or cold. SERVES 2.

POACHED EGGS IN MUSHROOMS

2 large flat mushrooms
15 ml/1 tablespoon butter, melted (see Hint, left)
10 ml/2 teaspoons butter
5 ml/1 teaspoon curry powder
1 small onion, finely chopped
10 ml/2 teaspoons plain flour
pinch of salt
125 ml/4½ fl oz milk
10 ml/2 teaspoons lemon juice
15 ml/1 tablespoon water
2.5 ml/½ teaspoon vinegar
2 eggs

Remove stems from mushrooms and hollow out the centres slightly. Brush mushrooms on both sides with the 15 ml/1 tablespoon melted butter. Place on a plate and microwave on High for 1½ minutes.

Place the 10 ml/2 teaspoons butter in a small glass bowl and microwave on High for 20–30 seconds. Stir in curry powder and onion, then microwave on High for 3 minutes. Stir in flour, salt and milk, and microwave on High for 3 minutes, stirring after 2 minutes. Add lemon juice.

Divide the water and vinegar between two ramekins and microwave on High for 40 seconds, until boiling. Break an egg gently into each ramekin and pierce each yolk twice with a sharp cocktail stick. Cover the ramekins with pierced cling film. Microwave on Medium-High for 1½ minutes (rotate the dishes during cooking time if your microwave does not have a turntable), or until the eggs are poached as you like them. Drain off the water.

Gently place the eggs in the hollows of the mushroom caps and cover with the curry sauce. Microwave on Medium-High for a few seconds to heat through. Serve at once, while hot. SERVES 2.

VARIATION: To make a cheese sauce, use a pinch of mustard powder instead of curry powder. Omit the onion. Stir in grated Cheddar cheese to taste instead of the lemon juice.

CHAPTER TWO

SOUPS AND STARTERS

Soup makes a delicious, wholesome meal on its own for nourishing lunches or light suppers — or a simple starter to a more elaborate dinner. Alternatively, try serving a few tasty dips with crudités or savoury biscuits for an informal, leisurely appetizer.

CREAM OF CELERY SOUP

1 head of celery, chopped
1 onion, chopped
2 potatoes, peeled and diced
750 ml/1¼ pints hot Vegetable Stock (page 26)
pinch of ground mace
1 bouquet garni (sprig of parsley, bayleaf and
  sprig of sage tied together; see page 80)
100 ml/3½ fl oz low-fat plain yoghurt (optional)

Microwave all ingredients except yoghurt on High for 35–40 minutes. Remove bouquet garni. Process to a smooth texture. If desired, add yoghurt and microwave for 3–4 minutes on High to reheat soup. SERVES 4.

CABBAGE, APPLE & TOMATO SOUP

3 large tomatoes, roughly chopped
125 ml/4½ fl oz water
200 g/7 oz cabbage, shredded
1 onion, chopped
3 Granny Smith apples, peeled and diced
5 ml/1 teaspoon brown sugar
pinch each of salt and nutmeg
1 litre/1¾ pints Vegetable Stock (page 26)

Microwave tomatoes and water, covered, for 6 minutes on High. Press through a sieve. Add all remaining ingredients, cover and microwave on High for 5 minutes and on Medium for 20 minutes. SERVES 4.

HINT
For a healthier dish, leave vegetables such as potatoes and carrots unpeeled, as the skin contains many important nutrients.

VICHYSSOISE

3 leeks, thinly sliced
15 ml/1 tablespoon butter
500 g/1 lb 2 oz potatoes, peeled and diced
1.5 litres/2¾ pints hot Chicken Stock (page 21)
salt and freshly ground black pepper to taste
150 ml/¼ pint low-fat plain yoghurt
15 ml/1 tablespoon snipped chives

Combine the leeks and butter in a deep dish and microwave on High for 5 minutes, stirring twice. Add the potatoes and 500 ml/18 fl oz of the stock. Cover and microwave on High for 10 minutes until the potatoes are soft. Add remaining stock, then purée soup in a processor. Season. Refrigerate for 3 hours, stir in the yoghurt and sprinkle with snipped chives. Alternatively, cover and reheat on High for 6 minutes until boiling, then stir in the yoghurt, sprinkle with chives and serve hot. SERVES 4.

LENTIL, BARLEY AND BEAN SOUP

60 g/2 oz pearl barley
100 g/3½ oz red split lentils,
  washed and drained
100 g/3½ oz haricot beans
1 leek, sliced
3 sticks celery, sliced
1 carrot, sliced
50 g/1¾ oz chopped parsley
2 litres/3½ pints hot Vegetable Stock (page 26)

Place barley, lentils and beans in a bowl. Cover with boiling water and leave overnight. Drain and rinse. Add remaining ingredients. Cover and microwave on High for 30–35 minutes. For a thicker consistency, liquidize half the mixture. SERVES 6.

Vichyssoise (page 14), Chicken, Noodle and Vegetable Soup (page 22), and Cabbage, Apple and Tomato Soup (page 14) with Cheese Dumplings (page 22).

BARLEY AND VEGETABLE BROTH

50 g/1¾ oz pearl barley, soaked for 1 hour
1 large onion, chopped
1 clove garlic, crushed
2 sticks celery, thinly sliced
3 carrots, thinly sliced
1 turnip, chopped into small dice
50 g/1¾ oz green beans, cut into
   2.5 cm/1 inch lengths
bouquet garni (see page 80)
1.5 litres/2¾ pints Vegetable Stock (page 26)
15 ml/1 tablespoon soy sauce
4 tomatoes, peeled and chopped
salt and freshly ground black pepper to taste
30 ml/2 tablespoons chopped parsley to garnish

Rinse the pearl barley in cold water and drain well. Microwave the onion, garlic and celery on High for 4 minutes. Stir in the carrots and turnip, cover and microwave on High for 10 minutes. Stir in all remaining ingredients except seasoning. Cover and microwave on High for 20–25 minutes. Season and microwave, uncovered, on High for 10 minutes. Sprinkle with parsley and serve. SERVES 4–6.

TOMATO SOUP

Tofu is the bean curd produced from hot soy milk. It makes a valuable addition to soups, salads, desserts and stir-fries as it is a complete protein. Since it has a bland flavour, it needs to be dressed up to be appetizing.

1 large onion, finely chopped
410 g/14 oz canned tomatoes, chopped and
   liquid retained
375 ml/13 fl oz Vegetable Stock (page 26)
5 ml/1 teaspoon salt
2 cloves
5 ml/1 teaspoon dried dill
200 g/7 oz tofu
7.5 ml/1½ teaspoons oil

Using a medium-sized bowl, microwave the onion, tomatoes and their liquid, stock, salt, cloves and dill on High, covered, for 6 minutes. Stir and microwave on Medium for 8 minutes.

In a food processor blend tofu, oil and a little of the tomato mixture. Add the rest of the tomato mixture and blend thoroughly. Reheat on Medium for 3–5 minutes. SERVES 4.

Tomato Soup (this page) and Minestrone (page 17).

BEAN SOUP

500 g/1 lb 2 oz sugar beans or haricot beans,
    soaked overnight, then rinsed and drained
3 carrots, diced
2 leeks, diced
2 onions, diced
3 potatoes, diced
2 sticks celery, sliced
3 tomatoes, peeled and chopped (see Hint, below)
2 turnips, diced
30 ml/2 tablespoons olive oil
1.5 litres/2¾ pints hot Vegetable Stock
    (page 26)
salt and freshly ground black pepper to taste
30 ml/2 tablespoons red wine vinegar
30 ml/2 tablespoons chopped parsley to garnish

Place the beans in a large bowl. Add boiling water to
2.5 cm/1 inch above the top of the beans. Cover and
microwave on High for 30 minutes. Leave to stand for
15 minutes. Drain. Microwave vegetables and olive oil
on High for 8 minutes, stirring a few times. Add
500 ml/18 fl oz vegetable stock and microwave,
covered, on High for 10 minutes. Add beans and
remaining stock. Cover and microwave on High for
about 30 minutes, until tender. Add seasoning and
vinegar. Sprinkle parsley over the soup. SERVES 4–6.

HINT
To peel tomatoes easily, wash the tomatoes (but don't dry),
then microwave on High for 20–30 seconds per tomato.
Peel immediately.

PEA SOUP

30 ml/2 tablespoons butter
1 onion, chopped
2 cloves garlic, crushed
1 large carrot, grated
2 sticks celery, thinly sliced
1.25 litres/2¼ pints hot Vegetable Stock
    (page 26)
300 g/11 oz dried split peas
salt and freshly ground black pepper to taste
pinch of dried thyme

Microwave butter and vegetables on High for 4 minutes.
Add stock, split peas, seasoning and thyme. Cover and
microwave on High for 10 minutes, then on Medium
for 35–40 minutes, until peas are tender. Purée in a
food processor. Reheat for 3–5 minutes. SERVES 4.

MINESTRONE

30 ml/2 tablespoons olive oil
2 onions, chopped
2 leeks, sliced
2 potatoes, diced
1 turnip, diced
2 carrots, diced
2 sticks celery, sliced
2 cloves garlic, crushed
75 g/2½ oz shredded cabbage
90 g/3¼ oz canned kidney beans (drained)
90g/3¼ oz cooked chickpeas or lentils
    (see Cooking Chickpeas, page 86,
    or Cooking Beans and Lentils, page 86)
100 g/3½ oz frozen peas
4 tomatoes, peeled and chopped
    (see Hint, this page)
30 ml/2 tablespoons tomato paste
2.5 ml/½ teaspoon sugar
2.5 ml/½ teaspoon each dried thyme and basil
1.5 litres/2¾ pints Vegetable Stock (page 26)
salt and freshly ground black pepper to taste
30 ml/2 tablespoons grated Parmesan cheese and
30 ml/2 tablespoons chopped parsley to garnish

Microwave olive oil, onions, leeks, potatoes, turnip,
carrots, celery, garlic and cabbage on High for
10 minutes. Stir. Add beans, chickpeas or lentils, peas,
tomatoes, tomato paste, sugar, herbs and stock. Cover
and microwave on High for about 25 minutes, until
vegetables and beans are tender. Add salt and pepper to
taste. Top with cheese and parsley. SERVES 4–6.

HERB CROUTONS

45 ml/3 tablespoons butter, clarified
    (see Hint, below)
5 ml/1 teaspoon dried mixed herbs
2.5 ml/½ teaspoon paprika
2 thick slices crustless wholemeal bread, cubed

Preheat browning dish on High for 4 minutes. Add all
ingredients and toss to coat cubes. Microwave on High
for 3–4 minutes. Stir. Cubes become crisp as they cool.

HINT
To clarify butter, microwave it on High for 30–40 seconds,
until it begins to splutter. Leave to stand for a few seconds. Pour
off the clear golden liquid and discard the sediment. Always use
a little more butter than the amount required in a recipe.

CURRIED YELLOWTAIL SOUP

This is a wonderfully warming soup for a cold winter night. If you cannot find yellowtail, also known as albacore or amberjack, you could use any firm, white fish instead.

2 potatoes, cubed
100 ml/3½ fl oz water
30 ml/2 tablespoons butter
1 onion, chopped
1 carrot, coarsely grated
10–15 ml/2–3 teaspoons curry powder
5 ml/1 teaspoon coriander leaves
30 ml/2 tablespoons plain flour
1.5 litres/2¾ pints hot fish stock
7.5 ml/1½ teaspoons tomato paste
750 g/1¾ lb yellowtail, filleted and cubed
5 ml/1 teaspoon salt
100 ml/3½ fl oz single cream
fresh coriander leaves to garnish

Microwave the potatoes and water in a small bowl, covered, on High for 5 minutes.

Microwave butter and onion in a large glass bowl on High for 3 minutes. Stir in grated carrot, cover and microwave for 2 minutes on High. Stir in curry powder, coriander and flour. Blend in stock gradually. Add tomato paste and potatoes, cover and microwave on High for 12 minutes. Add fish, cover and microwave on High for 10 minutes. Add salt, stir in cream, and garnish with coriander leaves just before serving. SERVES 6.

CURRIED BUTTERNUT SQUASH SOUP

2 leeks, thinly sliced and washed
1 large onion, chopped
60 g/2 oz butter
2 butternut squash, peeled and diced
4 potatoes, peeled and diced
2 litres/3½ pints boiling water
2 vegetable stock cubes
salt and freshly ground black pepper to taste
2.5 ml/½ teaspoon ground cumin
2.5 ml/½ teaspoon ground cinnamon
pinch of ground cardamom
2.5 ml/½ teaspoon ground ginger
10 ml/2 teaspoons snipped garlic chives

Microwave leeks, onion and butter in a large glass bowl on High for 6 minutes. Add remaining ingredients and mix well. Cover and microwave on Medium for 30 minutes. Blend in a food processor to the desired texture, then add garlic chives. Reheat on Medium for 3–4 minutes. SERVES 8.

WATERBLOMMETJIE SOUP

Waterblommetjies, or water hawthorn, are sometimes available canned from delicatessens if you can't find fresh ones. Otherwise, substitute spinach and reduce cooking time to 12 minutes.

500 g/1 lb 2 oz waterblommetjies, washed well
100 ml/3½ fl oz water
1 onion, chopped
30 ml/2 tablespoons butter
1 clove garlic, crushed
30 ml/2 tablespoons plain flour
500 ml/18 fl oz hot Chicken Stock (page 21)
10 ml/2 teaspoons chopped fresh thyme or
    5 ml/1 teaspoon dried
5 ml/1 teaspoon grated lemon zest
10 ml/2 teaspoons lemon juice
a few sorrel or spinach leaves
salt and freshly ground black pepper to taste
500 ml/18 fl oz milk
100 ml/3½ fl oz soured cream or crème fraîche
30 ml/2 tablespoons chopped parsley to garnish

Microwave waterblommetjies and water, covered, on High for 6 minutes. Microwave onion and butter in a large glass bowl on High for 3 minutes. Stir in garlic and flour. Gradually blend in stock, thyme, lemon zest and juice, sorrel or spinach and waterblommetjies. Cover and microwave on High for 15–20 minutes, until tender. Cool slightly. Blend in a processor until smooth. Add seasoning and milk. Microwave on Medium for 8 minutes to heat through. Stir in soured cream or crème fraîche and sprinkle with parsley. SERVES 6.

COURGETTE AND TARRAGON SOUP

10 ml/2 teaspoons butter
10 ml/2 teaspoons oil
1 onion, chopped
6 medium courgettes, thickly sliced
1 medium potato, peeled and sliced
7.5 ml/1½ teaspoons chopped fresh tarragon or
    2.5 ml/½ teaspoon dried
750 ml/1¼ pints Chicken Stock (page 21)
salt and freshly ground black pepper to taste
60 ml/2 fl oz double cream (optional)
tarragon sprigs to garnish

Microwave butter, oil and onion for 3 minutes on High. Add courgettes, potatoes and tarragon, cover and microwave on High for 6–8 minutes. Add stock and seasoning. Microwave on High for 8–10 minutes. Cool, liquidize and reheat. Add a dollop of cream to each serving. Garnish with sprigs of tarragon. SERVES 4.

Curried Butternut Squash Soup (page 18), Courgette and Tarragon Soup (page 18) and Curried Yellowtail Soup (page 18).

Herb and Onion Bread (page 24), Sweet Potato and Carrot Soup (page 21) and Chilled Minted Pea Soup (page 21).

SWEET POTATO AND CARROT SOUP

Warm yourself on a cold winter night with this deliciously different soup.

30 ml/2 tablespoons butter
1 large onion, finely chopped
450 g/1 lb sweet potatoes, peeled
  and chopped
2 carrots, peeled and grated
750 ml/1¼ pints hot Vegetable Stock (page 26)
salt and freshly ground black pepper to taste
15 ml/1 tablespoon coriander leaves
10 ml/2 teaspoons lemon juice
5 ml/1 teaspoon grated lemon zest
carrots, cut in thin julienne strips, and fresh
  coriander leaves to garnish

Microwave butter and onion on High for 3 minutes. Add the sweet potatoes and carrots, then cover and microwave on High for 10 minutes until tender. Add the vegetable stock, seasoning, coriander leaves, lemon juice and zest. Cover and microwave on Medium-High for 15–20 minutes. Process slightly. Reheat for 5 minutes on Medium-High. Garnish with carrot matchsticks and fresh coriander. SERVES 4–6.

OKRA SOUP

250 g/9 oz okra, topped and tailed
3 sticks celery, sliced
1 green pepper, seeded and diced
1 onion, chopped
50 g/1¾ oz butter
2 tomatoes, peeled and chopped (see Hint,
  page 17)
5 ml/1 teaspoon brown sugar
1 litre/1¾ pints hot Vegetable Stock (page 26)
5 ml/1 teaspoon chopped fresh basil
salt and freshly ground black pepper to taste

Slice okra and microwave with celery, green pepper, onion and butter on High for 8 minutes, stirring twice. Add tomatoes, sugar and stock. Cover and microwave on High for 25–30 minutes, until vegetables are tender. Add basil about 10 minutes before the end of cooking time. Season to taste and serve. SERVES 4.

HINT
Delicately flavoured herbs should be added to soups towards the end, just long enough for the volatile oils to be released.

CHILLED MINTED PEA SOUP

450 g/1 lb frozen peas
5 ml/1 teaspoon chopped fresh mint
1 onion, chopped
30 ml/2 tablespoons butter
2 potatoes, peeled and cubed
800 ml/1 pint 8 fl oz milk
pinch of cayenne pepper
30 ml/2 tablespoons medium sherry
salt and freshly ground black pepper
  to taste
150 ml/¼ pint single cream
mint sprigs to garnish

Microwave the peas and mint in a medium-sized glass bowl, covered, on High for 6–8 minutes, until cooked.

Microwave onion and butter in a large bowl on High for 3 minutes. Stir in the potatoes, cover and microwave on High for 6 minutes. Add milk and cayenne pepper. Cover and microwave on High for 8 minutes. Add sherry. Allow to cool, then add peas and mint and liquidize. Season with salt and pepper. Chill, swirl in cream, and garnish with mint sprigs. SERVES 6.

CHICKEN STOCK

Chicken stock is an extremely useful basic item to keep in the freezer, as it not only forms the basis of many soups, but is also an ingredient in all manner of savoury dishes, from casseroles to rice dishes.

1.5 kg/3¼ lb chicken
2 leeks, sliced
2 large carrots, cut into chunks
2 onions, sliced
2 sticks celery, sliced
2 litres/3½ pints hot water
1 bouquet garni (see page 80)
6 white peppercorns
10 ml/2 teaspoons salt

Place all ingredients in a large glass bowl. Cover and microwave on High for 12 minutes. Microwave on Medium for 1 hour. Cool. Strain and refrigerate. Remove the layer of fat that forms on the surface. MAKES ABOUT 2 LITRES/3½ PINTS.

CHEESE DUMPLINGS

For a warming, filling meal on a cold winter's day, add these dumplings to a soup of your choice.

75 g/2½ oz butter
125 g/4½ oz wholemeal flour
50 g/1¾ oz plain flour
5 ml/1 teaspoon baking powder
2.5 ml/½ teaspoon powdered mustard
salt and freshly ground black pepper to taste
60 g/2 oz Cheddar cheese, grated
1 egg, beaten
125 ml/4½ fl oz low-fat milk

Sift dry ingredients together, then rub in butter until the mixture resembles fine breadcrumbs. Mix in cheese. Slowly add egg and milk until the mixture forms a soft dough. Drop spoonfuls of mixture into soup about 15 minutes before the end of cooking time. SERVES 4.

MINTY PEA SOUP

600 g/1¼ lb frozen peas
600 ml/1 pint 1 fl oz hot Chicken Stock (page 21)
5 ml/1 teaspoon sugar
30 ml/2 tablespoons chopped mint leaves
salt and freshly ground black pepper to taste
200 ml/7 fl oz low-fat milk
100 ml/3½ fl oz low-fat plain yoghurt
fresh mint sprigs to garnish

Microwave peas, stock, sugar and mint, covered, on High for 5 minutes and Medium-High for 12 minutes. Process until smooth. Add seasoning, milk and yoghurt. Heat through on Medium-High for 3–4 minutes. Garnish each serving with a sprig of mint. SERVES 4.

CARROT SOUP

500 g/1 lb 2 oz carrots, grated
1 stick celery, sliced
1 tomato, peeled and chopped (see Hint, page 17)
1 onion, chopped
1.25 litres/2¾ pints hot Vegetable Stock (page 26)
salt and freshly ground black pepper to taste
pinch of dried thyme
15 ml/1 tablespoon snipped chives to garnish

Microwave all ingredients in a large glass bowl, covered, on High for 25 minutes. Process until puréed. Sprinkle with chives. SERVES 6.

SPINACH AND LENTIL SOUP

This is a quick soup to make and is very versatile — add any seasonal vegetables and the soup always tastes different.

1 onion, chopped
1 leek, sliced
1 large potato, peeled and cubed
750 ml/1¼ pints hot Vegetable Stock (page 26)
500 g/1 lb 2 oz red lentils, washed and drained
250 g/9 oz spinach, washed and
    stalks removed
salt and freshly ground black pepper to taste

Microwave the onion, leek and potato in a large bowl with 30 ml/2 tablespoons of the stock, covered, on High for 5 minutes. Add lentils and remaining stock. Roll the spinach leaves into tight rolls and cut finely. Add to stock with seasoning. Cover and microwave on High for 15 minutes. SERVES 6.

CHICKEN, NOODLE & VEGETABLE SOUP

1 onion, chopped
1 stick celery, sliced
1 carrot, sliced
100 g/3½ oz broccoli florets
100 g/3½ oz baby corn, sliced
1.5 litres/2¾ pints hot Chicken Stock (page 21)
3 chicken breasts, skinned, boned and cubed
50 g/1¾ oz noodles
salt and freshly ground black pepper to taste

Place the onion, celery, carrot, broccoli and baby corn in a large glass bowl. Add 200 ml/7 fl oz of the hot stock. Cover and microwave on High for 5 minutes. Add all the remaining ingredients, then cover and microwave on High for 10–12 minutes. Serve as is for a clear soup; alternatively, thicken the soup by puréeing some of the mixture. SERVES 6.

GARLIC CROUTONS

45 ml/3 tablespoons butter
1 clove garlic, crushed
4–5 slices bread with crusts removed, cubed

Microwave the butter and garlic in a flat pie dish for 30 seconds. Add the bread cubes and stir until they are well coated with butter. Microwave for 6–8 minutes on High, stirring every minute. Croûtons become crisp during standing time. SERVES 6.

Spinach Dip (this page) and Aubergine Dip (this page).

SPINACH DIP

> 400 g/14 oz spinach
> pinch of nutmeg
> 200 ml/7 fl oz low-calorie mayonnaise
> 200 ml/7 fl oz low-fat plain yoghurt
> 5 spring onions, finely chopped
> 45 ml/3 tablespoons grated Parmesan cheese
> salt and freshly ground black pepper to taste
> nasturtiums to garnish

Remove the stems from the spinach, wash and place in a large dish. Cover and microwave for 3 minutes on High. Drain and process until smooth, then place in a sieve and allow excess liquid to drain off. Season with nutmeg, then combine with remaining ingredients. Place in a bowl, cover and chill. Serve on a bed of dark green spinach leaves, surrounded by savoury biscuits or potato crisps. If nasturtiums are in bloom, they provide a lovely contrast to the green. SERVES 6.

AUBERGINE DIP

Whole aubergines cook beautifully in the microwave, retaining their colour rather than turning an ugly brown as they tend to do when cooked conventionally.

> 1 large aubergine (approx. 500 g/1 lb 2 oz)
> 5 ml/1 teaspoon sunflower oil
> 2 cloves garlic, crushed
> 10 ml/2 teaspoons lemon juice
> 100 ml/3½ fl oz low-fat plain yoghurt

Rub the aubergine all over with oil and prick well with a cocktail stick. Place on a paper towel on the turntable and microwave on High for 8 minutes, until the flesh is tender, turning after 4 minutes. Leave to stand for 5 minutes, then scoop out the flesh and chop roughly. Purée the aubergine with the garlic, lemon juice and yoghurt until smooth. Serve with crudités and a variety of savoury biscuits. SERVES 4.

CUCUMBER VICHYSSOISE

A light, chilled soup for hot summer days.

2 medium potatoes, cut into cubes
100 ml/3½ fl oz water
1 small onion, chopped
1 cucumber, peeled, seeded and sliced
7.5 ml/1½ teaspoons chopped fresh dill or
    2.5 ml/½ teaspoon dried
750 ml/1¼ pints Chicken Stock (page 21)
125 ml/4½ fl oz plain yoghurt
30 ml/2 tablespoons fresh lemon juice
salt and freshly ground black pepper
    to taste
thin slices of cucumber and chopped
    fresh dill to garnish

Parboil the potatoes and water in a medium-sized glass bowl on High for 5 minutes.

Place the potatoes, onion, cucumber, dill and chicken stock in a large glass bowl. Cover and microwave on High for 8 minutes, then on Medium-High for 10 minutes, until vegetables are soft. Allow to cool, then purée.

Blend in the yoghurt, lemon juice, salt and pepper and chill for at least 4 hours. Serve in chilled bowls, garnished with cucumber and dill. SERVES 4.

CUCUMBER, LEEK AND SAGE SOUP

1 cucumber, peeled, seeded and diced
2 leeks, sliced
1 green pepper, seeded and diced
1 potato, coarsely grated
12 fresh sage leaves
5 ml/1 teaspoon mustard powder
salt and freshly ground black pepper to taste
pinch of sugar
1 bayleaf
1.25 litres/2¼ pints Chicken Stock (page 21)
250 ml/9 fl oz milk
15 ml/1 tablespoon double cream and
    a few sage sprigs to garnish

Place all ingredients except stock and milk in a large glass bowl. Add 500 ml/18 fl oz of the stock, cover and microwave on High for 8 minutes. Add remaining stock, then microwave soup on Medium-High for 20 minutes, until vegetables are soft. Remove bayleaf. Cool and purée until smooth, then add the milk.

Chill, or if serving hot, return to bowl and reheat gently (3–4 minutes on Medium-High). Garnish with a spoonful of cream and sprigs of sage. SERVES 6.

HERB AND ONION BREAD

500 g/1 lb 2 oz self-raising flour
50 g/1¾ oz packet white onion soup
10 ml/2 teaspoons chopped fresh mixed herbs
    or 5 ml/1 teaspoon dried
10 ml/2 teaspoons chopped parsley
2.5 ml/½ teaspoon freshly ground
    black pepper
500 ml/18 fl oz buttermilk
30 ml/2 tablespoons grated Cheddar cheese
pinch of paprika

Sift the flour. Mix in the soup powder, mixed herbs, parsley and pepper. Combine lightly with the buttermilk. Grease a 1 kg/2¼ lb loaf pan and line the base with waxed paper. Spoon in mixture and smooth the top. Sprinkle with cheese and paprika. Place on a low rack in the microwave and cook on Medium-High for 12–14 minutes, until a metal skewer inserted in the middle comes out clean.

COMBINATION OVEN: Bake at 220 °C and Medium-Low microwave power level for 18–20 minutes (25–30 minutes if your oven alternates convection and microwave energy).

SAVOURY BITES

1 egg
150 ml/¼ pint sunflower oil
30 ml/2 tablespoons sugar
45 ml/3 tablespoons cornflour
10 ml/2 teaspoons baking powder
2.5 ml/½ teaspoon salt
2.5 ml/½ teaspoon cayenne pepper
100 g/3½ oz plain flour
100 g/3½ oz wholemeal flour
15 ml/1 tablespoon butter
250 ml/9 fl oz milk
10 ml/2 teaspoons yeast extract
100 g/3½ oz butter
100 g/3½ oz Cheddar cheese, grated
30 ml/2 tablespoons snipped fresh chives

Beat together the egg, oil, sugar and cornflour. Add baking powder, salt, cayenne pepper, flours, butter and milk. Beat for 1 minute. Pour into a 17 x 28 cm/ 7 x 11 inch greased dish. Microwave on High for 7–8 minutes.

Melt yeast extract and butter in a jug on High for about 40 seconds. Pour this mixture over the hot cake. Sprinkle with grated cheese and chives, and cut into squares. SERVES 6.

AUBERGINE PATE

2 large aubergines, washed and pierced well
salt and freshly ground black pepper to taste
2.5 ml/½ teaspoon chopped fresh thyme or
    pinch of dried
30 ml/2 tablespoons lemon juice
45 ml/3 tablespoons oil
1 clove garlic, crushed
15 ml/1 tablespoon chopped parsley to garnish

Place aubergines on a paper towel on the turntable. Microwave on High for 8–12 minutes, until soft. Cool.

Cut the aubergines in half and scoop out the flesh. Place flesh in a food processor, add salt, pepper, thyme and lemon juice. Process until smooth. With machine running, add oil slowly until blended, then add garlic. Spoon into a container and refrigerate for at least 4–5 hours before serving. Garnish with parsley and serve with biscuits or brown bread. SERVES 6.

RADISH DIP

4 spring onions, finely sliced
10 ml/2 teaspoons water
1 bunch radishes, grated
15 ml/1 tablespoon garlic chives,
    finely snipped
60 ml/2 fl oz mayonnaise
60 g/2 oz chunky cottage cheese
5 ml/1 teaspoon lemon juice
salt and freshly ground black pepper
    to taste

Microwave spring onion and water in a ramekin dish, covered, for 20 seconds on High. Drain and refresh with cold water. Mix together thoroughly with remaining ingredients, spoon into a small serving bowl and smooth the surface. Surround with vegetable crudités, such as courgette, carrot and celery sticks, baby sweetcorn, broccoli florets, and so on. SERVES 4.

Savoury Bites (page 24) and Radish Dip (this page).

Cucumber Mousse (page 27).

VEGETABLE STOCK

A good vegetable stock is the basis of soups, sauces and many main courses. Make your own and freeze it for later use.

15 ml/1 tablespoon good olive oil
125 g/4½ oz onion, roughly chopped
2 sticks celery, chopped
125 g/4½ oz carrots, chopped
1 sprig parsley
10 ml/2 teaspoons white peppercorns
  or a dash of ground white pepper
1–2 whole cloves
1 bayleaf
1.25 litres/2¼ pints boiling water
5 ml/1 teaspoon salt

Microwave the oil, onion, celery, carrots and parsley in a large bowl on High for 4 minutes. Add the peppercorns or ground white pepper, cloves and bayleaf. Pour over the boiling water. Cover and microwave on High for 15 minutes, then add salt and microwave for a further 10 minutes, uncovered. Leave to cool, then strain through a sieve. MAKES ABOUT 1.5 LITRES/2¼ PINTS.

LENTIL AND RICE SOUP

1.25 litres/2¼ pints hot Vegetable Stock
  (this page)
185 g/6½ oz red lentils, soaked for 1 hour
200 g/7 oz brown rice, soaked overnight
875 g/1 lb 15 oz canned tomatoes, chopped
3 carrots, peeled and diced
1 onion, chopped
2 leeks, sliced
2 sticks celery, sliced
2 cloves garlic, crushed
2.5 ml/½ teaspoon each dried basil,
  oregano and thyme
1 bayleaf
30 ml/2 tablespoons red wine vinegar
salt and freshly ground black pepper to taste
60 ml/4 tablespoons chopped fresh parsley

Microwave all ingredients except vinegar, seasoning and parsley, covered, on High for 10 minutes and on Medium-High for 30–35 minutes, until rice and lentils are tender. Add vinegar and seasoning. Remove bayleaf. Add parsley and serve. (For a finer texture, process soup roughly.) SERVES 4.

POLENTA

125 g/4½ oz coarse yellow cornmeal
500 ml/18 fl oz water
5 ml/1 teaspoon salt
30 ml/2 tablespoons butter
pinch of pepper

Combine cornmeal, water and salt in a large, flat glass bowl. Stir well. Microwave on High for 6 minutes, stirring a few times. Cover and microwave on High for 4 minutes. Stir in butter and pepper and leave to stand for 4 minutes. Pour into a pie dish, pressing down firmly. Cut into wedges when cold. SERVES 4–6.

VARIATIONS:
♦ Top with a mixture of 100 g/3½ oz Cheddar or mozzarella cheese, grated, 30 ml/2 tablespoons seasoned dried breadcrumbs, and a pinch of paprika.
♦ For a pizza-style topping, layer with 20 ml/4 teaspoons tomato paste, 100 g/3½ oz cheese (such as mozzarella), grated, and 100 g/3½ oz mushrooms, sliced, or 30 g/1 oz pitted olives, halved.
♦ Dip in egg and breadcrumbs, then fry in 30 ml/2 tablespoons olive oil.

CUCUMBER MOUSSE

1 large cucumber, peeled and grated
salt
1 small onion, finely chopped
250 g/9 oz smooth cottage cheese (see page 7)
2.5 ml/½ teaspoon ground coriander
5 ml/1 teaspoon lemon pepper
20 ml/4 teaspoons gelatine
45 ml/3 tablespoons water
125 ml/4½ fl oz fish stock or chicken stock
15 ml/1 tablespoon white wine vinegar
10 ml/2 teaspoons caster sugar
250 ml/9 fl oz double cream
cucumber rings, watercress and
    alfalfa sprouts to garnish

Place cucumber in a colander and sprinkle with salt. Leave for 20 minutes, then drain, retaining liquid. Wash off salt. Combine onion, cottage cheese, coriander, lemon pepper and cucumber liquid. Sprinkle gelatine on to water. Leave to sponge (see Hint, this page) then microwave on High for 30 seconds until it starts to boil. Add to cheese mixture with stock. Pour vinegar and sugar over drained cucumber and add to cheese mixture. Whip cream until thick and fold into mixture. Pour into lightly greased ramekins. Refrigerate. When set, unmould and garnish as suggested. SERVES 6.

FELAFEL WITH SOURED CREAM AND CUCUMBER SAUCE

This is a deliciously spicy Middle Eastern appetizer.

250 g/9 oz chickpeas, cooked
    (see Cooking Chickpeas, page 86)
4 spring onions, chopped
1 clove garlic, crushed
45 ml/3 tablespoons water
1 sprig parsley
2.5 ml/½ teaspoon ground cumin
5 ml/1 teaspoon ground coriander
salt and freshly ground black pepper to taste
30 ml/2 tablespoons oil

SOURED CREAM AND CUCUMBER SAUCE
300 g/11 oz cucumber,
    seeded and grated
2.5 ml/½ teaspoon salt
175 ml/6¼ fl oz soured cream or
    Greek yoghurt
45 ml/3 tablespoons chopped
    spring onions
45 ml/3 tablespoons double cream or
    plain yoghurt
15 ml/1 tablespoon lemon juice
15 ml/1 tablespoon white wine vinegar
15 ml/1 tablespoon chopped dill

Drain the chickpeas and process to a purée, together with the spring onions, garlic, water and parsley. Add cumin, coriander, salt and pepper. Set aside for about an hour to thicken. Form the mixture into little balls the size of cocktail meatballs, then flatten slightly. Place in the refrigerator for at least 30 minutes.

Preheat a browning dish on High for 6 minutes. Add oil and felafel. Microwave on High for 1½ minutes. Turn balls over and microwave for a further 1 minute. Drain on paper towels.

Place cucumber in a colander, sprinkle with salt and leave to drain for 30 minutes. Squeeze out liquid thoroughly. Purée with all remaining sauce ingredients in a food processor. Taste for flavour. Chill for a few hours or, preferably, overnight. SERVES 6.

HINT

To sponge gelatine, sprinkle gelatine slowly on to water in a ramekin dish or teacup. Leave for a few minutes to thicken and become rubbery, then microwave on High for a few seconds, until mixture just starts to boil. (If it boils for too long it loses the gelatinous quality that sets food.) Pour gelatine in a thin stream into mixture, stirring with a fork.

PESTO

Top baked new potatoes with a little pesto to make a tasty appetizer.

50 g/1¾ oz shelled pine nuts
100 g/3½ oz grated Parmesan cheese
2 cloves garlic, crushed
50 g/1¾ oz basil leaves
45 ml/3 tablespoons extra virgin olive oil
salt and freshly ground black pepper to taste

Microwave pine nuts in a shallow dish for 6–8 minutes on High, stirring every minute until golden. Cool. Process or pulse nuts, cheese, garlic and basil until mixture resembles fine breadcrumbs. Slowly drizzle in olive oil until mixture is the desired consistency. Season, pour into a container, cover and refrigerate. SERVES 4.

SAVOURY CHEESE DIP

2.5 ml/½ teaspoon cumin seeds
125 g/4½ oz ricotta cheese
125 ml/4½ fl oz soured cream
10 ml/2 teaspoons lemon juice
30 ml/2 tablespoons chopped parsley
2.5 ml/½ teaspoon paprika
2.5 ml/½ teaspoon mustard powder
pinch of white pepper
pinch of cayenne pepper

Preheat a browning dish on High for 3 minutes. Add cumin seeds and microwave on High for 20–30 seconds until lightly browned. Cool and grind finely.

Blend or process ground, toasted cumin seeds with remaining ingredients. Spoon into a serving bowl. Cover and refrigerate for a few hours to allow flavours to develop. MAKES 250 G/9 OZ.

FISH PATE IN LEMON SHELLS

This simple and delicious pâté is ideal as a starter, or you can serve it as a light lunch with rye bread or savoury biscuits.

1 large lemon, halved
200 g/7 oz smoked or cooked fish (see Notes, page 54)
50–100 g/1¾–3½ oz smooth cottage cheese (see page 7)
salt and freshly ground black pepper to taste
10 ml/2 teaspoons chopped parsley
lettuce leaves and sprigs of dill or fennel to garnish

Squeeze the juice from the lemon (see Hint, page 123). Remove the flesh and pith with a spoon and discard. Slice off the rounded bottoms of the lemon halves with a knife so that they will stand firmly on a plate without toppling over.

To make the pâté, mix the fish with the cottage cheese (the amount you use depending on the size of the portions you want), a little of the reserved lemon juice, seasoning and parsley. Mound the pâté into two lemon shells and place them on side plates. Garnish with lettuce and sprigs of dill or fennel to serve. SERVES 4.

HUMMUS

150 g/5½ oz cooked chickpeas,
    liquid reserved (see Cooking Chickpeas, page 86)
45 ml/3 tablespoons tahini (sesame paste)
45 ml/3 tablespoons freshly squeezed
    lemon juice (see Hint, page 123)
15 ml/1 tablespoon olive oil
3 cloves garlic, crushed
15 ml/1 tablespoon chopped fresh parsley
salt to taste

Process the chickpeas with 150 ml/¼ pint of the reserved liquid. Add the tahini, lemon juice, olive oil, garlic, parsley and salt. Process until smooth, adding a little more liquid if too thick. Leave to stand for 1 hour to allow flavours to develop. SERVES 6.

MUSHROOM PATE

1 large onion, chopped
125 g/4½ oz butter
300 g/11 oz button mushrooms, roughly
    chopped
30 ml/2 tablespoons sweet sherry
salt and freshly ground black pepper to taste
60 g/2 oz Roquefort cheese, grated
15 ml/1 tablespoon chopped parsley and
    a few mushrooms, sliced, to garnish

Microwave onion and 30 ml/2 tablespoons butter in a glass bowl for 3 minutes on High. Add mushrooms and microwave on High for 4 minutes. Add sherry and microwave on High for 8–10 minutes to reduce liquid. Allow to cool. Season with salt and pepper. Place mixture in a blender with remaining butter and cheese. Blend until smooth. Adjust seasoning to taste and spoon into container. Refrigerate until set. Garnish with parsley and mushrooms. MAKES 250 G/9 OZ.

Felafel with Soured Cream and Cucumber Sauce (page 27), Mushroom Pâté (page 28) and Hummus (page 28).

CHAPTER THREE

LIGHT MEALS

EGG dishes are wonderfully versatile — hot or cold, they are great for breakfasts, light suppers and picnics alike. Most are easy to prepare, and savoury tarts in particular are good for using up leftovers. Also included here are ideas for sprucing up the humble baked potato.

NOTES
♦ Puff pastry requires circulating heat to crisp, so when cooked in a microwave it becomes soggy.
♦ Shortcrust pastry cooks very well in a microwave, although it does not brown.
♦ When making a quiche, tart or pie with a pastry crust, pre-bake the crust.
♦ Always place the pie, tart or quiche on a low rack in the microwave so that the centre will set.

CRUSTLESS SMOKED HADDOCK TART

250 g/9 oz smoked haddock, skinned,
  boned and flaked
30 ml/2 tablespoons plain flour
3 eggs, beaten
1 onion, chopped
5 ml/1 teaspoon mustard powder
15 ml/1 tablespoon chopped parsley
100 g/3½ oz Cheddar cheese, grated
250 ml/9 oz milk
paprika to taste

Mix the flaked haddock, flour, eggs, onion, mustard powder and parsley together. Stir in the cheese, then mix in the milk. Pour the mixture into a pie dish and sprinkle with paprika. Microwave on Medium for 12–14 minutes, until the tart sets in the middle. Leave to stand for about 5 minutes before serving. SERVES 4.

COMBINATION OVEN: Cook at 200 °C and Medium-Low microwave power level for 12–14 minutes (or for 20–25 minutes if your oven alternates convection and microwave energy).

VARIATIONS: Use smoked trout or mackerel or a mixture of seafood instead of the haddock.

SAVOURY VEGETABLE TART

A delicious and easy-to-make tart that forms its own base.

250 g/9 oz courgettes, grated or sliced
150 g/5½ oz tomatoes, peeled and
  chopped (see Hint, page 17)
1 medium onion, chopped
100 g/3½ oz mushrooms, sliced
30 ml/2 tablespoons chopped parsley
375 ml/13 fl oz milk
60 g/2 oz plain or wholemeal flour
5 ml/1 teaspoon salt
pinch of freshly ground black pepper
pinch of cayenne pepper
5 ml/1 teaspoon dried mixed herbs
3 eggs
100 g/3½ oz Cheddar cheese, grated
30 ml/2 tablespoons seasoned dried
  breadcrumbs
paprika to taste

Layer the courgettes, tomatoes, onion, mushroom and parsley in a deep, greased dish. Beat milk, flour, salt, black pepper, cayenne pepper, herbs and eggs together until smooth. Pour the mixture over the vegetables. Sprinkle with cheese, then scatter breadcrumbs on top. Dust with paprika. Microwave on Medium-High for 14–15 minutes, until the centre is set. Leave to stand for about 5 minutes before serving. SERVES 4.

COMBINATION OVEN: Cook at 200 °C and Medium-Low microwave power level for 12–14 minutes (or for 16–20 minutes if your oven alternates convection and microwave energy).

VARIATIONS: To turn this into a meaty dish, use 200 g/7 oz cooked and chopped chicken, diced ham, canned corned beef or canned tuna, drained and flaked, instead of the mushrooms and courgettes.

ASPARAGUS QUICHE

BASE
125 g/4½ oz self-raising flour
salt and freshly ground black pepper to taste
dried mixed herbs to taste
75 g/2½ oz butter
1 egg, beaten

FILLING
460 g/1 lb canned asparagus cuts, drained
3 eggs, beaten
200 ml/7 fl oz milk
5 ml/1 teaspoon plain flour
salt and freshly ground black pepper to taste
freshly grated nutmeg to taste
150 g/5½ oz hard cheese of your
　choice, grated
paprika to taste

To make the base, combine the flour, seasoning and herbs. Rub in the butter. Add the egg and mix well to obtain a smooth, pliable dough. Roll out the dough thinly and use to line a pie dish. Prick the dough with a fork, cover the dish with a paper towel and microwave on High for 2–3 minutes.

Spread the asparagus cuts over the cooked pastry base. Combine the remaining ingredients for the filling, except the cheese and paprika, and beat well. Pour the mixture over the asparagus. Sprinkle with cheese and paprika. Microwave on Medium-High for 14–15 minutes. Leave to stand for 5 minutes before serving.
SERVES 4.

VARIATIONS:
Instead of the asparagus cuts, use:
♦ 300 g/11 oz mushrooms, sliced, 4 rashers bacon, chopped, and 1 onion, finely chopped. Microwave in a bowl on High for 3–4 minutes.
♦ 200 g/7 oz canned tuna, drained, sliced tomato and chopped fresh herbs.
♦ 200 g/7 oz leftover chicken, cold meat or vegetables.

Instead of the 200 ml/7 fl oz milk, use:
♦ 100 ml/3½ fl oz milk mixed with 100 ml/3½ fl oz single cream.
♦ 200 ml/7 fl oz plain yoghurt.
♦ 170 g/6 oz canned evaporated milk.

Instead of the pastry base, use:
♦ 200 g/7 oz cheese-flavoured biscuits, crushed, combined with 75 g/2½ oz butter or margarine, melted.

Savoury Vegetable Tart (page 30).

SPINACH AND CHEESE QUICHE

WHOLEMEAL PASTRY
75 g/2½ oz cold butter, cubed
75 g/2½ oz wholemeal flour
75 g/2½ oz plain flour
30 ml/2 tablespoons grated Parmesan
  or Cheddar cheese
15 ml/1 tablespoon chopped parsley
2.5 ml/½ teaspoon salt
1 egg, beaten
10 ml/2 teaspoons soy sauce

FILLING
300 g/11 oz spinach
salt and freshly ground black pepper to taste
pinch of ground nutmeg
3 eggs, beaten
250 g/9 oz fromage frais or smooth cottage
  cheese (see page 7)
45 ml/3 tablespoons single cream

Rub butter into flours until mixture is crumbly. Mix in cheese, parsley and salt. Combine egg and soy sauce and add enough to form a firm dough. Wrap in cling film and chill for 30 minutes. Roll out dough and line a 20 cm/8 inch pie dish with it. Prick base with fork and cover with a paper towel. Microwave on High for 6 minutes. Pastry becomes crisp as it cools.

To make filling, wash spinach, remove stems and shred leaves. Microwave in a flat dish, covered, on High for 3 minutes. Allow to cool. Season with salt, pepper and nutmeg. Mix in eggs, fromage frais or cottage cheese and cream. Pour into pastry shell. Microwave on Medium-High for 14–16 minutes, until centre is set. SERVES 6.

COMBINATION OVEN: Bake at 200 °C and Medium-Low microwave power level for about 15 minutes (25–30 minutes if your oven alternates convection and microwave energy).

HINT
Don't place a fresh bunch of herbs in a jar of water on the window sill where they will soon wilt. Rather, to keep herbs fresh longer, rinse (if necessary) and shake dry. Place in a plastic bag and tie to make it airtight. This method should keep herbs fresh for a week in the refrigerator.

CHEESE DREAMS

4 slices white bread, buttered
2 slices cheese of your choice
2 eggs, beaten
15 ml/1 tablespoon butter
salt and freshly ground black pepper to taste

Cover two slices of bread with cheese. Microwave on a plate on High for 40–60 seconds, until the cheese bubbles. Top the melted cheese with remaining slices of bread. Soak sandwiches in egg for a few minutes on each side, until all the egg is absorbed. Meanwhile, preheat a browning dish on High for 4 minutes. Add butter, swirl around to coat the base and immediately place the sandwiches in the dish. Microwave on High for 30 seconds on one side, turn and microwave on High for 1 minute on the other side. Cut sandwiches into triangles, season, and serve immediately. SERVES 2.

SUMMER VEGETABLE QUICHE

WHOLEMEAL PASTRY
See Spinach and Cheese Quiche (this page)

FILLING
30 ml/2 tablespoons butter
1 leek, thinly sliced
50 g/1¾ oz button mushrooms, sliced
4 courgettes, thinly sliced
125 g/4½ oz cherry tomatoes, sliced
50 g/1¾ oz frozen peas
125 g/4½ oz smooth cottage cheese (see page 7)
150 ml/¼ pint skimmed milk
3 eggs
30 ml/2 tablespoons chopped fresh herbs
50 g/1¾ oz Cheddar cheese, grated
pinch of paprika

fresh chives and other herbs to garnish

Make pastry as for Spinach and Cheese Quiche. For the filling, microwave butter and leek on High for 3 minutes. Stir in mushrooms and courgettes; microwave for 3 minutes. Drain. Place mixture on pastry base. Spread tomatoes and peas over. Combine cottage cheese, milk, eggs and herbs; pour over vegetables. Top with cheese and paprika, and microwave on Medium for 14 minutes. Garnish as suggested. SERVES 6.

COMBINATION OVEN: Bake at 200 °C and Medium-Low microwave power level for 14–16 minutes until quiche is set in the middle (25–30 minutes if your oven alternates convection and microwave energy).

Vegetable Pie with Yoghurt Topping (page 96), Quiche Provençale (this page) and Spinach and Cheese Quiche (page 32).

QUICHE PROVENCALE

WHOLEMEAL PASTRY
125 g/4½ oz wholemeal flour
60 g/2 oz plain flour
pinch of salt
5 ml/1 teaspoon dried mixed herbs
100 g/3½ oz cold butter
30–45 ml/2–3 tablespoons iced water

FILLING
10 ml/2 teaspoons butter
1 onion, chopped
1 clove garlic, crushed
1 red pepper, seeded and sliced
200 g/7 oz courgettes, thinly sliced
3 tomatoes, peeled and chopped
   (see Hint, page 17)
10 ml/2 teaspoons chopped fresh basil
10 ml/2 teaspoons chopped fresh oregano or
   5 ml/1 teaspoon dried mixed herbs
salt and freshly ground black pepper to taste
3 eggs
200 ml/7 fl oz milk or single cream
50 g/1¾ oz Gruyère cheese, grated
15 ml/1 tablespoon chopped parsley

To make the pastry, combine dry ingredients and rub in butter (a food processor does the job beautifully in seconds). Gradually add iced water until a firm dough is formed. Cover and refrigerate for at least 30 minutes, then roll out the dough and line a 20 cm/8 inch pie dish. Prick base with a fork and microwave on High for 5 minutes. Allow to cool while preparing the filling.

To make the filling, microwave the butter and onion in a medium-sized glass bowl on High for 3 minutes. Add the garlic, red pepper, courgettes, tomatoes, herbs, salt and pepper. Cover and microwave on High for 5 minutes. Uncover and microwave a further 5 minutes. Pour mixture into cold pastry case.

Beat the eggs and milk together, adding a little seasoning. Pour over the filling. Sprinkle over the cheese, paprika and parsley. Place on a low rack and microwave on Medium-High for 14–16 minutes, until the centre is cooked. Serve warm or cold. SERVES 6

COMBINATION OVEN: Bake quiche at 200 °C and Medium-Low microwave power level for 18–20 minutes (25–30 minutes if your oven alternates convection and microwave energy).

NOTE: For a more colourful dish, sprinkle the top with paprika before cooking.

Piperade (page 35), Baked Potato with Herbs and Cheese (this page) and Pizza Bread Slices (page 35).

BAKED POTATO WITH BALSAMIC VINEGAR

This makes the basis of a wonderful meal when you're on your own and don't feel like cooking anything elaborate. Substitute balsamic vinegar for butter and you'll probably never eat a baked potato with butter again! The sweet, tart flavour of this syrupy Italian vinegar also makes it a superb ingredient in salad dressings and marinades, and it has very little trace of fat or calories. Serve potatoes with a salad and wholemeal bread and voilà — a healthy, satisfying meal!

1 large potato
5 ml/1 teaspoon balsamic vinegar

Scrub the potato clean. Dry with a paper towel and pierce all around with a sharp, pointed knife. Place on the turntable on a paper towel. Microwave on High for 2½ minutes. Turn potato over and microwave for a further 2½ minutes. Test to see when it is cooked by pressing with your fingers. If potato 'gives' under pressure, then it is cooked. Wrap in a paper towel or foil for 10 minutes. Cut a cross in the top and squeeze gently for potato to open up. Pour over the balsamic vinegar and enjoy eating! SERVES 1.

BAKED POTATOES WITH HERBS AND CHEESE

Fromage frais is a soft cheese made from skimmed milk. Light and creamy, it makes a wonderful addition to vegetables.

2 large potatoes
225 g/8 oz fromage frais
30 ml/2 tablespoons chopped fresh herbs
  (parsley, oregano, chervil, etc.)
salt and freshly ground black pepper to taste
10 ml/2 teaspoons grated Parmesan
  cheese (optional)
5 ml/1 teaspoon chopped fresh herbs

Scrub potatoes and pierce all over with a pointed knife. Place on a paper towel on the turntable and microwave on High for 6–8 minutes, until soft, turning halfway. Wrap in paper towels and leave to stand for 10 minutes. Halve potatoes lengthways and scoop out flesh, leaving the shell. Mash potato flesh with fromage frais, herbs and seasoning. Pile the mixture into the potato shells and arrange on the turntable. Microwave on High for 2 minutes to heat through. Sprinkle with Parmesan cheese, if using, and chopped herbs. SERVES 2.

PIZZA BREAD SLICES

Choose a heavy, wholemeal bread as a base for these tasty pizzas. Serve with a green salad.

4 slices wholemeal (granary) bread
4 tomatoes, peeled and chopped (see Hint, page 17)
15 ml/1 tablespoon tomato purée
1 clove garlic, crushed
pinch of sugar
5 ml/1 teaspoon dried oregano
50 g/1¾ oz button mushrooms, sliced
1 small onion, sliced in rings
1 green pepper, seeded and cut in rings
50 g/1¾ oz mozzarella cheese, grated

Take two dinner plates and place two slices of bread on each; set aside. Microwave tomatoes, tomato purée, garlic and sugar in a large pie dish for 8 minutes on High. Stir in oregano, allow to cool, then spoon tomato mixture on to bread slices. Arrange mushrooms, onion and green pepper on top. Sprinkle with cheese. Microwave one plate at a time for 2–3 minutes on High until cheese has melted. Serve immediately. SERVES 4.

CRUSTLESS SPINACH QUICHE

Serve these as individual quiches.

100 g/3½ oz spinach
30 g/1 oz spring onions, sliced
1 egg, beaten
45 ml/3 tablespoons low-fat milk
30 g/1 oz low-fat Edam cheese, grated
salt and freshly ground black pepper to taste

Wash the spinach thoroughly and remove tough stems. Place in a flat dish, cover and microwave on High for 2 minutes. Drain spinach, then chop or process it and combine with remaining ingredients. Pour mixture into a small, greased soufflé dish. Place on a flat rack on the turntable. Microwave on Medium-High for 4–5 minutes, until set in the middle. Two quiches take 6 minutes; four take 12 minutes. SERVES 1.

EGGS

Eggs are high in protein, vitamins, minerals and cholesterol. The body needs a certain amount of cholesterol, so they may be eaten in moderation by slimmers and the cholesterol conscious. Don't forget that boiled eggs must be cooked on the hob.

PIPERADE

1 large onion, thinly sliced
1 clove garlic, crushed
1 red pepper, seeded and cut in julienne strips
1 green pepper, seeded and cut in julienne strips
300 g/11 oz tomatoes, peeled and chopped (see Hint, page 17)
4 eggs
15 ml/1 tablespoon chopped parsley
salt and freshly ground black pepper to taste

Microwave onion, garlic, peppers and tomatoes in a large, shallow pie dish on High for 10–15 minutes, stirring occasionally, until vegetables are softened and all the liquid has evaporated. Beat the eggs lightly and stir into the vegetable mixture. Microwave on Medium-High for about 5 minutes, stirring frequently, until the eggs are very lightly set. Stir in the parsley and season with salt and pepper. Serve immediately with wholemeal bread. SERVES 4.

CURRIED EGGS

Although essentially a simple dish, you can turn this into an attractive presentation. I serve it on a dark green platter, piling up hot rice in the centre of the plate, surrounding this with egg halves, and pouring hot, curried sauce over the eggs; finally I garnish it with lemon sprigs. These make a charming and unusual garnish which is worth trying if you have a lemon tree in your garden or conservatory.

30 ml/2 tablespoons butter
1 onion, chopped
1 small Granny Smith apple, peeled, cored and coarsely grated
25 ml/5 teaspoons curry powder
30 ml/2 tablespoons plain flour
500 ml/18 fl oz Chicken Stock (page 21)
15 ml/1 tablespoon chutney
10 ml/2 teaspoons brown sugar
10 ml/2 teaspoons lemon juice
salt to taste
30 ml/2 tablespoons sultanas
8 hard-boiled eggs, halved
lemon sprigs to garnish

Microwave butter, onion and apple for 3 minutes on High. Stir in curry powder and microwave for a further minute, then stir in flour. Gradually blend in stock. Microwave on High for 4–5 minutes, stirring twice, until sauce thickens. Add chutney, sugar, lemon juice, salt and sultanas. Cover and microwave on Medium-High for 6 minutes. Serve as suggested. SERVES 8.

MUSHROOM QUICHE

SOURED CREAM PASTRY
175 g/6 oz plain flour
2.5 ml/½ teaspoon salt
125 g/4½ oz butter
125 ml/4½ fl oz soured cream

FILLING
30 ml/2 tablespoons butter
1 onion, chopped
300 g/11 oz mushrooms, sliced

TOPPING
200 ml/7 fl oz milk or single cream
3 eggs, beaten
pinch of ground nutmeg
pinch of mace
salt and freshly ground black pepper to taste
10 ml/2 teaspoons chopped fresh
  tarragon or 5 ml/1 teaspoon dried
15 ml/1 tablespoon sherry

Sift flour and salt together and rub in butter. Add soured cream and knead until a ball of dough forms. Allow to rest for 30 minutes. Roll out until pastry fits a 20 cm/8 inch flan dish.

Microwave butter, onion and mushrooms together in a small bowl on High for 4 minutes. Spread this mixture over pastry base.

In a jug, combine all topping ingredients and pour over filling. Microwave on a low rack (so that centre sets) on Medium-High for 14–16 minutes until quiche cooks through to the centre. SERVES 4–6.

COMBINATION OVEN: Bake at 200 °C and Medium-Low microwave power level for 18–20 minutes (25–30 minutes if your oven alternates convection and microwave energy).

CHERVIL

Chervil is one of the French fines herbes (see page 37), more delicate than parsley. Its green leaf is used to garnish chicken, veal, omelettes, green salad and spinach. Dried, it has hardly any flavour so is best used fresh.

SAVOURY BREAD TOMATO BAKE

2 tomatoes, sliced
50 g/1¾ oz butter
1 onion, grated and drained
salt and freshly ground black pepper to taste
8 slices of bread, crusts removed
100 g/3½ oz ham, diced
15 ml/1 tablespoon chopped parsley
200 ml/7 fl oz buttermilk
2 eggs, beaten
100 g/3½ oz Cheddar cheese, grated
pinch of paprika
chervil leaves to garnish

Put a layer of tomatoes in a casserole. Cream the butter, onion, salt and pepper, then spread on the slices of bread. Cut each slice into four triangles. Put a layer of bread triangles on top of the tomatoes. Sprinkle a layer of ham and parsley over the bread. Repeat layers.

Mix together the buttermilk and eggs. Season with salt and pepper. Pour the buttermilk mixture over the bread. Leave to stand for 20 minutes. Sprinkle with cheese and paprika. Microwave on Medium-High for 12–14 minutes until mixture is set. Garnish with chervil leaves. SERVES 4.

COMBINATION OVEN: Bake at 200 °C and Medium-Low microwave power level for 14–16 minutes until browned and set (25–30 minutes if your oven alternates convection and microwave energy).

STUFFED BAKED POTATO WITH APPLE

2 medium potatoes, scrubbed and pierced
15 ml/1 tablespoon butter
1 egg, separated
salt and freshly ground black pepper to taste
pinch of dried mixed herbs
1 small cooking apple, cored and grated
30 ml/2 tablespoons grated Cheddar cheese
pinch of paprika

Place the potatoes on a paper towel on the turntable. Microwave on High for 5–6 minutes (turning the potatoes after 3 minutes), until they yield slightly to finger pressure when squeezed. Leave to stand for 2 minutes, then cut the potatoes in half. Scoop out the soft centre without breaking the skin. Mash the flesh well, and add the butter, egg yolk, seasoning, herbs and apple. Whisk the egg white until stiff and fold in. Fill the potato shells with the mixture, sprinkle with cheese and paprika, then reheat on High for about 2 minutes. SERVES 2.

Omelette aux Fines Herbes (this page).

OMELETTE AUX FINES HERBES

3 eggs, separated
30 ml/2 tablespoons water
15 ml/1 tablespoon butter
salt and freshly ground black pepper or
   cayenne pepper to taste
15 ml/1 tablespoon finely chopped
   fines herbes (see below)

Preheat a large browning dish on High for 4 minutes. Beat the egg yolks lightly with a fork, adding the water. Beat egg whites with an electric mixer until just stiff, then fold into the beaten yolks. Add the butter to the browning dish, swirl it around to coat the base and immediately add prepared egg mixture, spreading it gently with a spatula to fill the dish. Microwave on High for 1½ minutes. Season with salt and pepper or cayenne pepper and sprinkle with the herbs. Fold over and slide on to a serving plate. SERVES 1–2.

FINES HERBES

Fines herbes is a traditional French blend of four subtle herbs — parsley, chives, tarragon and chervil. Finely chopped, they impart a wonderful flavour to egg dishes, salads, chicken and fish dishes. Add these herbs at the end of cooking time as heat diminishes their taste.

OMELETTE FU WONG

10 ml/2 teaspoons butter
½ or 1 small onion, finely chopped
50 g/1¾ oz button mushrooms, sliced
30 ml/2 tablespoons snipped fresh chives
30 ml/2 tablespoons bean sprouts
10 ml/2 teaspoons soy sauce
3 eggs, separated
30 ml/2 tablespoons water
salt and freshly ground black pepper to taste

Microwave butter and onion on High for 2 minutes. Stir in mushrooms and microwave for a further 2 minutes. Stir in chives, bean sprouts and soy sauce.

  Preheat a large browning dish on High for 4 minutes. Beat egg yolks lightly and stir in the mushroom mixture. Beat egg whites until stiff and fold in. Pour into the hot browning dish and spread out with a spatula. Microwave on High for 4–5 minutes, until cooked in the centre. Season, fold over omelette and slide on to a warmed serving plate. Serve immediately. SERVES 2.

HINT

Never take the browning dish out of the microwave when you want to add ingredients as the dish will lose heat rapidly and become less effective.

CHAPTER FOUR

SALADS

IN recent years salads have risen to the status of gourmet food, featuring a wide variety of vegetables in combination with cheese, fruit, meat, chicken and seafood, nuts and herbs, rice, pasta and grains. Whether served as a full meal or an accompaniment, the possibilities are endless.

THREE-RICE SALAD WITH BALSAMIC VINAIGRETTE

This makes an interesting accompaniment to meals that go best with rice, such as Vegetable Kebabs (page 125).

150 g/5½ oz brown rice
50 g/1¾ oz wild rice, soaked for 30 minutes
5 ml/1 teaspoon salt
625 ml/1 pint 2 fl oz boiling water
150 g/5½ oz basmati rice
5 ml/1 teaspoon salt
500 ml/18 fl oz boiling water
150 g/5½ oz dates, chopped
45 ml/3 tablespoons chopped chives or parsley

BALSAMIC VINAIGRETTE
125 ml/4½ fl oz olive oil
30 ml/2 tablespoons red wine vinegar
30 ml/2 tablespoons balsamic vinegar
pinch of salt
pinch of sugar
pinch of freshly ground black pepper
7.5 ml/1½ teaspoons Dijon mustard

Wash brown rice and wild rice separately. Place both in a deep, round casserole. Stir in salt. Add the 625 ml/1 pint 2 fl oz boiling water. Cover and microwave on High for 10 minutes and on Medium for 20 minutes. Leave to stand while cooking basmati rice.

Microwave the basmati rice, covered, with the 500 ml/18 fl oz boiling water and the salt on High for 8–10 minutes. Leave to stand, covered, for 15 minutes. Mix all three rices together and fluff with a fork, then fold in the dates and chives or parsley. Spoon this mixture into a serving bowl.

To make the vinaigrette, combine all ingredients in a screw-top jar and shake well. One hour before serving, pour dressing over the rice to moisten. Serve at room temperature. SERVES 6.

MARINATED SUMMER SALAD

A wonderful summer salad to serve as part of a buffet.

8 courgettes, sliced
15 ml/1 tablespoon water
12 baby sweetcorn
15 ml/1 tablespoon water
200 g/7 oz broccoli florets
15 ml/1 tablespoon water
200 g/7 oz button mushrooms, sliced
15 ml/1 tablespoon olive oil
salt and freshly ground black pepper to taste
5 ml/1 teaspoon mustard powder
1 clove garlic, crushed
5 ml/1 teaspoon chopped fresh tarragon or
   2.5 ml/½ teaspoon dried
12 cherry tomatoes, peeled (see Hint, page 17)

DRESSING
90 ml/3¼ fl oz olive oil
20 ml/4 teaspoons tarragon vinegar
20 ml/4 teaspoons lemon juice
salt and freshly ground black pepper to taste

Microwave courgettes with 15 ml/1 tablespoon water in a small bowl, covered, on High for 3 minutes. Refresh under cold water. Drain. Place sweetcorn in a small bowl with 15 ml/1 tablespoon water and microwave on High, covered, for 3 minutes. Refresh and drain. Microwave the broccoli, covered, in a small bowl with 15 ml/1 tablespoon water, on High for 2½ minutes. Refresh and drain. Place mushrooms in a small bowl with the olive oil, salt, pepper, mustard, garlic and tarragon. Cover and microwave on High for 2–3 minutes. Allow to cool. Mix all the vegetables together and place on a platter.

To make the dressing, whisk together all dressing ingredients until creamy. Pour over vegetables and serve. SERVES 6.

Marinated Summer Salad (page 38) and Spicy Couscous Salad (this page).

SPICY COUSCOUS SALAD

400 g/14 oz tomatoes, peeled and
  chopped (see Hint, page 17)
10 ml/2 teaspoons butter
4 spring onions, sliced
1 stick celery, finely sliced
2.5 ml/½ teaspoon ground cumin
2.5 ml/½ teaspoon turmeric
pinch of ground ginger
30 ml/2 tablespoons chopped parsley
200 ml/7 fl oz Vegetable Stock (page 26)
225 g/8 oz couscous
salt and freshly ground black pepper to taste

Drain tomatoes in a sieve. Microwave butter, spring
onions and celery for 2½ minutes on High. Stir in
spices, parsley, stock and tomatoes. Microwave on High
for 6 minutes. Stir in couscous and seasoning. Leave to
stand, covered, for 6 minutes, until liquid is absorbed.
Fluff with a fork. Serve when cool. SERVES 4–6.

CURRIED POTATO SALAD

A tangy, crunchy variation on the classic potato salad.

1 kg/2¼ lb potatoes, peeled
250 ml/9 fl oz water
salt and freshly ground black pepper to taste
50 g/1¾ oz celery, chopped
½ red pepper, seeded and diced
60 g/2 oz Granny Smith apple, chopped
125 ml/4½ fl oz mayonnaise
125 ml/4½ fl oz low-fat plain yoghurt
10 ml/2 teaspoons curry powder

Cut potatoes into chunks and microwave with the water,
covered, on High for 20 minutes, until tender. Leave to
stand for 10 minutes. Allow to cool and cut into cubes.
Season and mix with celery, red pepper and apple.

Combine mayonnaise, yoghurt and curry powder
and mix gently into potato mixture until potatoes are
well coated. SERVES 6–8.

LENTIL SALAD WITH A CRUNCH

500 g/1 lb 2 oz whole brown lentils
1 onion, quartered
1 carrot, cut into large chunks
2 sticks celery, cut into quarters
1 bayleaf
5 ml/1 teaspoon salt
2 spring onions, finely sliced
2 sticks celery, finely sliced
30 ml/2 tablespoons chopped fresh parsley

DRESSING
45 ml/3 tablespoons olive oil
15 ml/1 tablespoon lemon juice
5 ml/½ teaspoon chopped fresh herbs (such
    as oregano, rosemary and basil) or
    2.5 ml/½ teaspoon dried
freshly ground black pepper to taste

spring onions, curled, to garnish

Soak lentils in boiling water for 1 hour. Drain. Place with onion, carrot, celery and bayleaf in a large glass bowl. Add boiling water to cover the vegetables, and microwave, covered, on Medium-High for 25 minutes, until lentils are tender but not mushy. Add salt and leave to stand until cool. Drain and discard vegetables and bayleaf. Place lentils in a serving bowl.

Combine dressing ingredients in a screw-top jar. Shake well and pour over the lentils. Mix in remaining ingredients; chill. Garnish with spring onions. SERVES 6.

CUCUMBERS IN SOURED CREAM

¼ cucumber, halved, seeded and diced
½ small onion, chopped
2.5 ml/½ teaspoon salt
45 ml/3 tablespoons white vinegar
5 ml/1 teaspoon caster sugar
45 ml/3 tablespoons water
45 ml/3 tablespoons soured cream or yoghurt
pinch of dried dill
dash of Tabasco
freshly ground black pepper to taste

Combine the cucumber and onion in a bowl and sprinkle with salt. Combine the vinegar, sugar and water in a bowl and microwave on High for 1½ minutes. Cool and pour over the cucumber. Leave to stand for 1 hour, then drain.

Combine the soured cream or yoghurt, dill, Tabasco and pepper. Mix into the cucumber mixture. Cover and chill for 1 hour before serving. SERVES 2.

MEDITERRANEAN SALAD

Serve this on its own as a meal or as an accompaniment to steak. Use a bottled salad dressing (Italian is best), or make a vinaigrette dressing for the salad and to use as a marinade.

150 g/5½ oz baby beans, trimmed
100 ml/3½ fl oz water
1 aubergine, unpeeled, sliced and
    dégorged (see Hint, page 99)
oil for frying
salt and freshly ground black pepper
    to taste
1 red pepper, seeded and cut in
    julienne strips
1 yellow pepper, seeded and cut in
    julienne strips
30 ml/2 tablespoons water
100 g/3½ oz whole black mushrooms
100 ml/3½ fl oz Italian salad dressing
300 g/11 oz mixed salad leaves
100 g/3½ oz ham or beef shavings
100 g/3½ oz cherry tomatoes
1 clove garlic, crushed
100 ml/3½ fl oz mayonnaise
a few onion rings, soaked in cold water
    for 30 minutes
30 ml/2 tablespoons snipped fresh chives

Microwave the beans and the 100 ml/3½ fl oz water in a small bowl on High, covered, for 5 minutes. Drain and refresh under cold water.

Preheat a browning dish and fry aubergine slices in a little oil on High for 2 minutes, turning after 1 minute. Season. Microwave pepper strips in 30 ml/2 tablespoons water in a small bowl, covered, on High for 2½ minutes. Drain and refresh under cold water.

Marinate the beans and mushrooms in Italian dressing for 1 hour. Remove from dressing and arrange on a large platter with the salad leaves, aubergine, peppers, ham or beef shavings and tomatoes. Combine the garlic and mayonnaise and place a large dollop on the side of the salad. Scatter onion rings over the salad. Sprinkle with chives. SERVES 4.

HINT
It is best to use fresh herbs in salads to complement the flavours and textures of the other salad ingredients.

CALAMARI SALAD

A delicious, simple seafood salad that can be prepared a day in advance.

500 g/1 lb 2 oz calamari tubes
500 ml/18 fl oz boiling water
75 ml/2½ fl oz olive oil
75 ml/2½ fl oz sunflower oil
75 ml/2½ fl oz lemon juice
15 ml/1 tablespoon chopped fresh dill or
   5 ml/1 teaspoon dried
1 clove garlic, crushed
salt and freshly ground black pepper to taste
1 butterhead lettuce
sprigs of dill to garnish

Cut the calamari into thin rings. Place in a large pie dish and cover with boiling water. Microwave on High for 1–2 minutes, stirring halfway, until calamari is opaque and tender. Drain well.

Combine the olive oil, sunflower oil, lemon juice, dill, garlic and seasoning and mix into the calamari. Marinate salad for at least an hour at room temperature. Serve on a bed of lettuce leaves and garnish with sprigs of dill. SERVES 4.

FISH SALAD

500 g/1 lb 2 oz firm fish fillets, cubed
10 ml/2 teaspoons lemon juice
5 ml/1 teaspoon grated lemon zest
5 ml/1 teaspoon chopped fresh dill or
   2.5 ml/½ teaspoon dried
45 ml/3 tablespoons oil
45 ml/3 tablespoons soured cream
10 ml/2 teaspoons lemon juice
2.5 ml/½ teaspoon honey
salt and freshly ground black pepper to taste
300 g/11 oz mixed green salad leaves
50 g/1¾ oz diced cucumber
8 cherry tomatoes
1 small avocado, peeled and cut into wedges
15 ml/1 tablespoon snipped chives to garnish

Place fish in a pie dish. Sprinkle with lemon juice, zest and dill. Cover and microwave on High for 5 minutes. Cool and drain. Mix oil, soured cream, lemon juice, honey and seasoning. Place salad leaves on a platter and scatter fish pieces over. Arrange cucumber and tomatoes around the fish. Arrange avocado on top, then pour over dressing. Sprinkle with chives and serve immediately. SERVES 4 AS A STARTER OR 2 AS A MAIN DISH.

Calamari Salad (this page) and Mediterranean Salad (page 40).

TUNA, BEAN AND APPLE SALAD

This salad will help to keep your cholesterol level under control. Serve as a main course or as a starter.

185 g/6½ oz canned tuna chunks in
   brine, drained
220 g/8 oz canned pinto beans, drained
10 ml/2 teaspoons lemon juice
2 Golden Delicious apples, cored
   and cubed
1 onion, chopped
1 clove garlic, crushed
1 small lettuce, shredded
15 ml/1 tablespoon chopped parsley

Flake the tuna with a fork in a medium-sized glass bowl. Add the pinto beans. Sprinkle lemon juice over the apples and set aside. Place the onion and garlic in a small glass bowl. Cover and microwave on High for 2 minutes, then refresh under cold water and drain (this takes the strong taste out of the onion). Spread shredded lettuce on a serving platter. Combine all remaining ingredients and pile on top of the lettuce. SERVES 2 AS A MAIN COURSE, 4 AS A STARTER OR ACCOMPANIMENT.

VARIATION: To make this salad even tastier, a dressing could be poured over it. Drain the lemon juice from the apples and add enough extra lemon juice to make it up to 30 ml/2 tablespoons. Add 5 ml/1 teaspoon Dijon mustard, 45 ml/3 tablespoons olive oil, and salt and pepper to taste. Whisk well and pour over salad just before serving.

APPLE AND COURGETTE SALAD

500 g/1 lb 2 oz courgettes, sliced
45 ml/3 tablespoons water
3 red apples, cored and diced
1 onion, thinly sliced
1 green pepper, seeded and cut in julienne strips

DRESSING
75 ml/2½ fl oz oil
15 ml/1 tablespoon red wine vinegar
15 ml/1 tablespoon balsamic vinegar
5 ml/1 teaspoon chopped fresh basil
10 ml/2 teaspoons freshly squeezed lemon juice
   (see Hint, page 123)
30 ml/2 tablespoons chopped parsley
5 ml/1 teaspoon sugar
2.5 ml/½ teaspoon salt
pinch of freshly ground black pepper

Microwave courgettes with water in a medium-sized glass bowl, covered, on High for 3–4 minutes. Drain and refresh under cold running water.

Combine all dressing ingredients in a screw-top jar. Shake well and pour over apples, coating well. Mix in onion, green pepper and courgettes. Cover and chill before serving. SERVES 4–6.

MIXED PASTA SALAD

250 g/9 oz large shell noodles
1 litre/1¾ pints boiling water
5 ml/1 teaspoon salt
5 ml/1 teaspoon oil
1 small head of lettuce, shredded
a few mixed lettuce leaves
3 radishes, sliced thinly
125 g/4½ oz cucumber, sliced
1 tomato, diced
1 avocado, sliced
30 ml/2 tablespoons alfalfa sprouts
   or bean sprouts
1 stick celery, sliced
50 g/1¾ oz mangetouts, diagonally sliced
3 spring onions, sliced
sprigs of watercress to garnish

FRENCH DRESSING WITH HERBS
125 ml/4½ fl oz cold-pressed sunflower oil
100 ml/3½ fl oz dry white wine
100 ml/3½ fl oz buttermilk
5 ml/1 teaspoon clear honey
2.5 ml/½ teaspoon dried oregano
2.5 ml/½ teaspoon dried tarragon
1 clove garlic, crushed
pinch of celery salt

Microwave noodles, water, salt and oil in a large bowl on High for about 10 minutes, until cooked al dente. Leave to stand for 5 minutes, covered. Plunge into cold water and drain thoroughly. Place the shredded lettuce on a serving platter in the middle. Surround with the mixed lettuce leaves. Combine noodles with remaining ingredients and pile on top of the shredded lettuce.

Combine dressing ingredients in a bottle — dressing keeps for a few days in refrigerator. Shake well before pouring over salad. Garnish salad with watercress sprigs for a light, fresh look. SERVES 4.

Tuna, Bean and Apple Salad (page 42), Mixed Pasta Salad (page 42) and Couscous Salad (page 44).

43

Chinese Salad (page 45) and Orange and Bean Salad (page 45).

COUSCOUS SALAD

A delicious and simple salad to put together.

> 250 g/9 oz couscous
> 250 ml/9 fl oz boiling water
> pinch of salt
> 3 tomatoes, chopped and drained
> 100 g/3½ oz diced cucumber
> 1 avocado, diced
> 1 stick celery, sliced
> 20 ml/4 teaspoons chopped parsley
> freshly ground black pepper to taste

Place couscous in a serving bowl. Pour the boiling water over and add salt. Cover and microwave on High for 2 minutes. Leave to stand for 10 minutes, then fluff with a fork. When cold, gently fold in remaining ingredients. Serve as is or spoon into lettuce leaves for a decorative presentation. Spoon over 45 ml/3 table-spoons Low-fat Yoghurt Dressing (this page). SERVES 4.

LOW-FAT YOGHURT DRESSING

This dressing keeps for a few days in the refrigerator.

> 250 ml/9 fl oz low-fat plain yoghurt
> 30 ml/2 tablespoons lemon juice
> 2.5 ml/½ teaspoon onion salt
> pinch of garlic salt
> 1.25 ml/¼ teaspoon fresh tarragon
> 1.25 ml/¼ teaspoon fresh basil
> 1.25 ml/¼ teaspoon fresh lemon thyme

Mix all ingredients and leave for 15 minutes for the flavour to develop. MAKES 250 ML/9 FL OZ.

VARIATIONS:
♦ Blend 200 ml/7 fl oz low-fat smooth cottage cheese (see page 7) with 45 ml/3 tablespoons buttermilk and use in place of the yoghurt.
♦ If you do not have the herbs listed growing in your garden, substitute your own personal favourites.

CHINESE SALAD

1 Chinese cabbage, finely shredded
1 onion, chopped
15 ml/1 tablespoon water
150 g/5½ oz cucumber, diced
200 g/7 oz bean sprouts
10 radishes, sliced thinly
2 red apples, cored and diced
1 large carrot, coarsely grated
12 dates, stoned and chopped
1 stick celery, sliced
1 avocado, peeled and diced

DRESSING
100 ml/3½ fl oz white wine vinegar
30 ml/2 tablespoons soy sauce
45 ml/3 tablespoons clear honey
2.5 ml/½ teaspoon mustard powder
salt and freshly ground black pepper to taste

spring onion curls (see Hint, below) or
    toasted sesame seeds (see Hint, page 93)
    to garnish

Spread shredded cabbage on a serving platter. Micro-wave the onion and water for 1½ minutes on High, drain and refresh under cold running water. Mix the onion and remaining salad ingredients together gently.

Combine dressing ingredients in a screw-top jar and shake well. Pour over salad and toss well to coat. Pile on to the cabbage and garnish with spring onion curls or toasted sesame seeds. SERVES 6.

HINT

Trim spring onions so that about 10 cm/4 inches of green stem remains. Cut down through the green stem a few times with kitchen scissors. Drop into ice-cold water and leave until spring onion stems start to curl.

AUBERGINE SALAD

6 baby aubergines, diced
10 ml/2 teaspoons lemon juice
2.5 ml/½ teaspoon salt
30 ml/2 tablespoons water
15 ml/1 tablespoon grated onion
30 ml/2 tablespoons finely chopped celery
½ green pepper, seeded and diced
30 ml/2 tablespoons chopped parsley
30 ml/2 tablespoons low-calorie mayonnaise
30 ml/2 tablespoons low-fat plain yoghurt

Microwave aubergines, lemon juice, salt and water in a small bowl, covered, on High for 4–5 minutes. Drain and allow to cool. Mix in onion, celery, green pepper and parsley. Combine mayonnaise and yoghurt and pour over salad. Stir in gently. SERVES 4.

ORANGE AND BEAN SALAD

Canned red kidney beans make for a quick, easy and colourful salad.

4 oranges, peeled and pith removed
410 g/14 oz canned red kidney
    beans, drained
4 sticks celery, sliced
150 g/5½ oz cucumber, diced
100 g/3½ oz bean sprouts
1 small onion, chopped
15 ml/1 tablespoon water

DRESSING
60 ml/2 fl oz lemon juice
100 ml/3½ fl oz cold-pressed sunflower oil
pinch of freshly ground black pepper
2.5 ml/½ teaspoon vegetable salt
1 clove garlic, crushed
5 ml/1 teaspoon clear honey
pinch of mustard powder
5 ml/1 teaspoon chopped mixed herbs
    (such as mint, parsley, marjoram or oregano)

Remove all the pith from the oranges and cut into segments, between the membranes. Do this over a bowl to retain the juice. Add the well-drained beans to the oranges with the cucumber and bean sprouts. To blanch the onion, microwave with the water in a small bowl, covered, on High for 1½ minutes, then drain and refresh under cold running water. Add to other salad ingredients.

Place all dressing ingredients in a screw-top jar and shake well. Refrigerate until required. Mix and pour a little over salad. Toss. SERVES 6.

OIL

While oils cannot be considered healthy because of their high calorie count, some are less unhealthy than others. Cold-pressed oils, such as virgin olive oil, are extracted without the use of heat, so the nutrients (and flavour) are not destroyed. Oils are generally less unhealthy than fats like butter, lard and hard margarine, as the latter are saturated fats with a high cholesterol content.

CRUNCHY CAULIFLOWER AND LEEK SALAD

300 g/11 oz leeks, sliced and washed
150 g/5½ oz cauliflower florets
25 ml/5 teaspoons lemon juice
2 large carrots, diced
2 sticks celery, sliced
60 g/2 oz pecan nuts, chopped

DRESSING
1 clove garlic, crushed
5 ml/1 teaspoon salt
2.5 ml/½ teaspoon black pepper
60 ml/2 fl oz mayonnaise
60 ml/2 fl oz plain yoghurt
10 ml/2 teaspoons chopped fresh parsley

a few black olives and 15 ml/1 tablespoon
   chopped parsley to garnish

Microwave the wet leeks, cauliflower and lemon juice in a small bowl, covered, on High for 4 minutes. Leave to stand for 3 minutes, then drain and cool. Combine with carrots, celery and nuts. Combine all dressing ingredients in a jug and pour dressing over vegetables. Garnish with olives and parsley. SERVES 4–6.

VARIATION: Add sautéed mushrooms or courgettes.

HAWAIIAN RICE SALAD

450 g/1 lb brown rice
1.25 litres/2¼ pints boiling water
10 ml/2 teaspoons salt
15 ml/1 tablespoon curry powder
25 ml/5 teaspoons red wine vinegar
10 ml/2 teaspoons lemon juice
45 ml/3 tablespoons oil
5 ml/1 teaspoon prepared mustard
10 ml/2 teaspoons sugar
125 ml/4½ fl oz mayonnaise
440 g/1 lb canned pineapple chunks, drained
4 spring onions, chopped
50 g/1¾ oz almonds, toasted and
   chopped (see Hint, page 100)
3 sticks celery, chopped
125 ml/4½ oz coconut, toasted
6 radishes, finely chopped

Microwave the rice, boiling water and salt, covered, in a large glass bowl on High for 10 minutes and Medium-High for 40 minutes. Leave to stand for 20 minutes, then drain.

Combine curry powder, vinegar, lemon juice, oil, mustard and sugar. Whisk well. Pour over the warm rice and mix well with a fork. Allow to cool. Add remaining ingredients and toss carefully. Spoon into a serving bowl and refrigerate. SERVES 8.

CHICKEN AND AVOCADO SALAD

1 chicken (1.5 kg/3¼ lb)
chicken spice to taste
1 sprig rosemary
1 pineapple, cut into wedges
1 stick celery, sliced
45 ml/3 tablespoons roughly chopped pecan nuts
2 avocados, peeled and diced
75 ml/2½ fl oz mayonnaise
75 ml/2½ fl oz soured cream or plain yoghurt
salt and freshly ground black pepper to taste
few drops of Tabasco or lemon juice
30 ml/2 tablespoons snipped chives
30 ml/2 tablespoons sliced spring onions
1 lettuce, shredded
5 ml/1 teaspoon snipped chives to garnish

Season chicken and tuck a sprig of rosemary into cavity. Place in an oven roasting bag and microwave on High for 5 minutes, then on Medium-High for 25 minutes (10 minutes per 500 g/1 lb 2 oz chicken). Allow to cool. Skin and bone chicken and cut into small pieces. Mix into pineapple, celery, nuts and avocado.

In a jug, combine the mayonnaise, soured cream or yoghurt, seasoning, Tabasco or lemon juice, chives and spring onions. Mix into the chicken. Pile chicken on to a bed of lettuce and garnish with chives. SERVES 6.

MINTED APPLE AND DATE SALAD

3 Granny Smith apples, cored and cubed
100 g/3½ oz pitted dates, chopped
2 sticks celery, sliced
250 ml/9 fl oz plain yoghurt
30 ml/2 tablespoons honey
15 ml/1 tablespoon chopped fresh mint
30 ml/2 tablespoons flaked almonds

Combine the apples with the dates and celery. Microwave honey on High for a few seconds to soften, and mix with the yoghurt and mint. Combine with the apple mixture. Preheat a browning dish on High for 3 minutes, then microwave the almonds on High for 4–5 minutes to toast. Chop them roughly and sprinkle over the salad. SERVES 4.

Crunchy Cauliflower and Leek Salad (page 46) and Chicken and Avocado Salad (page 46).

LENTIL AND APPLE SALAD

250 g/9 oz brown lentils
1 litre/1¾ pints boiling water
1 green apple, diced and soaked in
   lemon juice
50 g/1¾ oz pecan nuts,
   roughly chopped

DRESSING
125 ml/4½ fl oz plain yoghurt
30 ml/2 tablespoons mayonnaise
1 clove garlic, crushed
30 ml/2 tablespoons chopped parsley

Soak the lentils overnight, then microwave with the boiling water in a deep glass bowl, covered, on High for 25–30 minutes. Leave to stand for 15 minutes before draining. Allow to cool.

Mix the lentils, apple and nuts in a serving bowl. Combine the dressing ingredients and pour dressing over the salad. SERVES 4.

CHICKPEA SALAD

150 g/5½ oz chickpeas
salt to taste
125 g/4½ oz shredded cabbage
1 onion (purple if possible), finely chopped
30 ml/2 tablespoons chopped pimiento
15 ml/1 tablespoon chopped fresh basil
100 ml/3½ fl oz apple cider vinegar
75 ml/2½ fl oz olive oil
15 ml/1 tablespoon honey
15 ml/1 tablespoon mayonnaise
1 lettuce, shredded

Soak chickpeas overnight, then rinse well. Cover with boiling water and microwave, covered, on High for 45 minutes. Add salt to taste and leave to stand, covered, for 20 minutes. Drain and allow to cool.

Combine chickpeas, cabbage, onion, pimiento and basil and add salt to taste. Combine vinegar, oil, honey and mayonnaise and mix into the chickpea mixture. Serve on a bed of shredded lettuce. SERVES 4.

Chicken and Peach Salad (page 49), Creamy Bean Salad (page 49) and Pineapple Chicken Salad (page 49).

FRUITY MUSHROOM PASTA SALAD

250 g/9 oz fusilli
1 litre/1¾ pints boiling water
5 ml/1 teaspoon salt
5 ml/1 teaspoon oil
10 ml/2 teaspoons butter
200 g/7 oz button mushrooms
5 ml/1 teaspoon honey
250 ml/9 fl oz pineapple and mango juice
10 ml/2 teaspoons red wine vinegar
5 ml/1 teaspoon cornflour
mango slices (optional) and 15 ml/1 tablespoon
    toasted sesame seeds to garnish

Microwave fusilli, water, salt and oil in a large bowl on High for about 10 minutes, stirring after 5 minutes, until cooked al dente. Leave to stand for 5 minutes, covered. Plunge into cold water and drain.

Preheat a browning dish for 3 minutes on High. Add butter and mushrooms. Microwave for 1½ minutes, stirring halfway. Remove from dish and set aside. Add honey, juice and vinegar to dish. Microwave on High for 3 minutes. Thicken with cornflour mixed to a paste with a little water. Microwave on High for 2 minutes until thickened. Add mushrooms.

If mangoes are available, garnish with slices of mango. Sprinkle over toasted sesame seeds for a crunchy topping. SERVES 4.

BROWN RICE AND PEACH SALAD WITH SWEET AND SOUR SAUCE

200 g/7 oz brown rice
625 ml/1 pint 2 fl oz boiling water
5 ml/1 teaspoon salt
4 yellow clingstone peaches, peeled
  and chopped
1 small red pepper, seeded and diced
3 sticks celery, sliced
5 spring onions, sliced
30 ml/2 tablespoons chopped parsley

DRESSING
100 ml/3½ fl oz cold-pressed sunflower oil
30 ml/2 tablespoons lemon juice
5 ml/1 teaspoon curry powder
5 ml/1 teaspoon soy sauce
5 ml/1 teaspoon clear honey

Microwave rice, boiling water and salt in a medium glass bowl, covered, on High for 30 minutes. Leave to stand for 15 minutes. Fluff with a fork and allow to cool. Add remaining salad ingredients.

Blend dressing ingredients together in a blender and mix into rice salad. Refrigerate until shortly before needed — best served at room temperature. SERVES 4.

PINEAPPLE CHICKEN SALAD

250 g/9 oz chicken breasts, skinned
  and boned
100 ml/3½ fl oz Chicken Stock (page 21)
200 g/7 oz warm, cooked rice
150 g/5½ oz pineapple, cut in wedges
100 g/3½ oz cucumber, diced
100 g/3½ oz spring onion, sliced
100 g/3½ oz celery, sliced
50 g/1¾ oz bean sprouts
45 ml/3 tablespoons low-calorie mayonnaise
5 ml/1 teaspoon low-fat plain yoghurt
20 ml/4 teaspoons lemon juice
1 lettuce, shredded
30 ml/2 tablespoons snipped chives to garnish

Place the chicken pieces in a flat-bottomed dish. Add chicken stock, cover and microwave on High for 3½ minutes. Allow to cool, then dice.

Mix chicken, rice, pineapple, cucumber, spring onion, celery and bean sprouts together lightly. Combine mayonnaise, yoghurt and lemon juice and fold into chicken salad. Pile up on a bed of shredded lettuce or into hollowed-out pineapple shells. Sprinkle with chives. SERVES 4.

CHICKEN AND PEACH SALAD

100 g/3½ oz brown rice, washed
300 ml/11 fl oz boiling water
2.5 ml/½ teaspoon salt
300 g/11 oz cooked chicken, cubed
  (see Notes, page 79)
410 g/14 oz canned peach slices in natural juice
2 bananas, sliced
50 g/1¾ oz spring onions, chopped
½ red pepper, seeded and diced
1 small lettuce, shredded
100 ml/3½ fl oz low-fat plain yoghurt
5 ml/1 teaspoon curry powder
salt and freshly ground black pepper to taste
15 ml/1 tablespoon snipped chives to garnish

Place rice, water and salt in a large bowl, cover and microwave on High for 15 minutes.

Place cubed chicken in a bowl. Drain peaches, reserving juice. Chop into pieces and add to chicken with bananas, rice, spring onions and red pepper. Pile on to shredded lettuce on a platter. Mix together 45 ml/3 tablespoons peach juice, yoghurt, curry powder and seasoning, and pour over the chicken salad. Sprinkle with chives. SERVES 4.

CREAMY BEAN SALAD

Beans are high in protein and fibre. For a dramatic presentation, serve this tasty salad chilled on a bed of glossy, dark green spinach leaves.

200 g/7 oz canned black-eyed beans
200 g/7 oz canned red kidney beans
200 g/7 oz canned butter beans
4 tomatoes, peeled and chopped (see Hint,
  page 17)
2 sticks celery, sliced
2.5 ml/½ teaspoon chopped basil
1 onion, chopped
15 ml/1 tablespoon water
10 ml/2 teaspoons tomato purée
60 ml/2 fl oz low-fat plain yoghurt
60 ml/2 fl oz low-calorie mayonnaise
salt and freshly ground black pepper to taste

Drain the beans thoroughly. Place in a large mixing bowl and pat dry with paper towels. Add the tomatoes, celery and basil. Blanch the onion by microwaving on High with the water for 1½ minutes, then refresh under cold running water. Combine with the tomato purée, yoghurt, mayonnaise and seasoning and stir into the beans. Serve chilled. SERVES 6.

Brown Rice Salad with Yoghurt Dressing (page 52) and Chickpea and Broccoli Salad (page 51).

MACARONI AND PEPPER SALAD

250 g/9 oz elbow macaroni
1 litre/1¾ pints boiling water
5 ml/1 teaspoon salt
5 ml/1 teaspoon oil
1 onion, chopped
½ green pepper, seeded and diced
½ red pepper, seeded and diced
10 ml/2 teaspoons oil
15 ml/1 tablespoon curry powder
1 pineapple, peeled and cubed
100 ml/3½ fl oz mayonnaise
45 ml/3 tablespoons plain yoghurt
30 ml/2 tablespoons chutney
5 ml/1 teaspoon coriander leaves and
   bunches of coriander leaves to garnish

Place macaroni, water, salt and the 5 ml/1 teaspoon oil in a large glass bowl. Microwave on High for about 10 minutes, stirring after 2 minutes. Leave to stand for 5 minutes, then drain.

Microwave the onion and peppers with the 10 ml/ 2 teaspoons oil in a medium-sized glass bowl on High for 3–4 minutes. Stir in the curry powder and microwave on High for 1 minute. Allow to cool, then add the pineapple.

Combine mayonnaise, yoghurt and chutney and mix into the macaroni, then refrigerate until ready to serve. Pile the salad up on a platter and sprinkle the top with coriander leaves. Surround the salad with bunches of coriander. SERVES 6–8.

HINT: Coriander (also known as danhia) is an acquired taste, and you may prefer to replace it with dill or basil.

LENTIL SALAD

185 g/6½ oz split red lentils
500 ml/18 fl oz boiling water
salt to taste
2 sticks celery, chopped
30 ml/2 tablespoons chopped green pepper
1 small onion, chopped
4 radishes, finely chopped
45 ml/3 tablespoons sunflower seeds
125 ml/4½ fl oz mayonnaise

DRESSING
30 ml/2 tablespoons white wine vinegar
45 ml/3 tablespoons olive oil
2.5 ml/½ teaspoon dried dill
pinch of curry powder

nasturtium leaves and flowers to garnish

Wash and pick over the lentils. Cover with boiling water and microwave, covered, on High for about 25 minutes, until cooked. Add salt. Leave to stand for 10 minutes, then drain. Mix in the celery, green pepper, onion, radish, sunflower seeds and mayonnaise.

To prepare the dressing, combine all the dressing ingredients in a screw top jar and shake well. Pour over the warm lentils. (The mixture can be stored like this overnight in the refrigerator.) Serve salad on a bed of nasturtium leaves and garnish with nasturtium flowers. SERVES 4.

VARIATION: Use whole brown lentils instead of split red lentils. Presoak them overnight, then cook according to the chart on page 86.

BUCKWHEAT AND LENTIL SALAD

250 g/9 oz buckwheat or bulgur wheat
250 g/9 oz split red lentils
850 ml/1½ pints boiling water
5 ml/1 teaspoon ground cinnamon
5 ml/1 teaspoon ground coriander
5 ml/1 teaspoon salt
1 onion, sliced
1 bunch spring onions, sliced
100 g/3½ oz button mushrooms, chopped
3 cloves garlic, crushed
15 ml/1 tablespoon sunflower oil
30 ml/2 tablespoons olive oil
30 ml/2 tablespoons chopped fresh parsley
150 ml/¼ pint plain yoghurt or soured cream
30 ml/2 tablespoons chopped coriander leaves
   and a pinch of ground cinnamon to garnish

Soak the buckwheat or bulgur wheat for 1 hour, then drain off water. Microwave lentils in a medium-sized bowl with the boiling water, spices and salt, covered, on High for 20 minutes, until the liquid has been absorbed and the lentils are tender. Cover the buckwheat or bulgur wheat with boiling water, cover and microwave on High for 12–15 minutes. Leave to stand for a few minutes, then drain and mix with the lentils.

Microwave onions, spring onions, mushrooms, garlic and sunflower oil in a medium-sized bowl on High for 4–5 minutes. Mix with buckwheat or bulgur wheat, lentils, olive oil and parsley. Pour yoghurt or soured cream on top. Sprinkle over cinnamon and garnish with coriander leaves. SERVES 4–6.

CHICKPEA AND BROCCOLI SALAD

An unusual and tasty salad which makes a wholesome meal in itself.

300 g/11 oz broccoli florets
1 onion, chopped
2 cloves garlic, crushed
15 ml/1 tablespoon olive oil
30 ml/2 tablespoons water
200 g/7 oz chickpeas, cooked
   (see Cooking Chickpeas, page 86)
2 tomatoes, peeled and chopped
   (see Hint, page 17)
salt and freshly ground black pepper
   to taste

DRESSING
45 ml/3 tablespoons sunflower oil
45 ml/3 tablespoons olive oil
45 ml/3 tablespoons lemon juice
salt and freshly ground black pepper
   to taste
10 ml/2 teaspoons Dijon mustard
5 ml/1 teaspoon brown sugar

crumbled feta cheese to garnish

Soak broccoli florets in water for 30 minutes. In a small bowl microwave onion, garlic and oil on High for 3 minutes. Drain the broccoli florets and microwave with the 30 ml/2 tablespoons water on High, covered, for 2½ minutes. Drain and refresh under cold water. Mix together the chickpeas, onion, broccoli, tomatoes and seasoning.

To make the dressing, combine all dressing ingredients in a screw-top jar and shake well. Leave for a few hours so that the flavours can develop, and pour over salad. Garnish with crumbled feta cheese. SERVES 6.

CRUNCHY RED LENTIL SALAD

200 g/7 oz red lentils
1 vegetable stock cube
600 ml/21 fl oz water
1 stick celery, sliced
1 red pepper, seeded and diced
60 ml/4 tablespoons chopped spring onions
10 ml/2 teaspoons snipped chives

DRESSING
30 ml/2 tablespoons olive oil
10 ml/2 teaspoons lemon juice
2.5 ml/½ teaspoon sugar
2.5 ml/½ teaspoon prepared mustard
salt and freshly ground black pepper to taste

Microwave the lentils, stock cube and water, covered, on High for about 20 minutes, until lentils are tender. Leave to stand for 15 minutes, then drain.

Mix the lentils with the celery, red pepper, spring onions and chives.

Blend the dressing ingredients together and pour over the lentil mixture. Pile on to a bed of lettuce leaves. SERVES 4.

VARIATION: Replace the red lentils with brown lentils and increase cooking time to 30 minutes — or use a mixture of the two, adding the red lentils 10 minutes after the brown lentils.

ROSY BEETROOT SALAD

4 large beetroot (about 500 g/1 lb 2 oz)
2 Granny Smith apples, peeled, cored and cubed

DRESSING
175 ml/6¼ fl oz plain yoghurt
15 ml/1 tablespoon caster sugar
45 ml/3 tablespoons mayonnaise
10 ml/2 teaspoons lemon juice
2.5 ml/½ teaspoon grated lemon zest

Place the beetroot in a large casserole and cover with boiling water. Cover the dish and microwave the beetroot on High for 18–20 minutes, until tender. Leave to stand for 10 minutes, then peel and cut into cubes. Toss apple cubes in lemon juice to prevent them from turning brown.

To make the dressing, combine the yoghurt and caster sugar, then add the mayonnaise, lemon juice and zest and combine thoroughly. Pour over the beetroot and apple and combine well. SERVES 6–8.

BROWN RICE SALAD WITH YOGHURT DRESSING

200 g/7 oz brown rice
700 ml/1¼ pints hot Vegetable Stock
    (page 26)
200 g/7 oz frozen peas
2 tomatoes, chopped
2 courgettes, grated
1 green pepper, seeded and chopped
2 carrots, peeled and grated
200 g/7 oz canned whole-kernel corn, drained

YOGHURT DRESSING
250 ml/9 fl oz plain yoghurt
45 ml/3 tablespoons lemon juice
10 ml/2 teaspoons grated lemon zest
30 ml/2 tablespoons olive oil
5 ml/1 teaspoon chopped basil or
    2.5 ml/½ teaspoon dried
1 clove garlic, crushed
salt and freshly ground black pepper to taste

Microwave the rice and stock in a deep casserole, covered, on High for 10 minutes and on Medium-High for 20 minutes. Leave to stand, covered, until cool. Microwave peas, covered, on High for 1 minute. Combine with remaining vegetables, then add the vegetables to the rice and mix together thoroughly.

Beat the dressing ingredients together. Pour over the salad and mix in lightly. SERVES 4–6.

POTATO SALAD

1 kg/2¼ lb potatoes, peeled
250 ml/9 oz water
salt and freshly ground black pepper to taste
1 small onion, finely chopped, or
    45 ml/3 tablespoons chopped spring onions
2 hard-boiled eggs, chopped
50 g/1¾ oz celery, chopped
125 ml/4½ fl oz mayonnaise
125 ml/4½ fl oz plain yoghurt
30 ml/2 tablespoons parsley

Cut potatoes into quarters. Place in a large glass bowl with the water, cover and microwave on High for about 20 minutes, until tender. Leave to stand for 10 minutes, then drain and allow to cool. Chop the potatoes into bite-sized pieces, season and mix in onion or spring onion, egg and celery.

Combine mayonnaise and yoghurt. Stir gently into the potato mixture until potatoes are evenly coated. Garnish with parsley. SERVES 6–8.

Potato Salad (page 52), Macaroni and Pepper Salad (page 50) and Rosy Beetroot Salad (page 52).

CHAPTER FIVE

SEAFOOD

DELICIOUS and nutritious, fish can be prepared in various ways, and is superb cooked in the microwave. It is a source of high-grade protein with very little fat, and should be an essential item on your weekly menu. Buy fresh fish whenever possible and cook it on the same day.

NOTES

♦ Fresh seafood is best for flavour; if you must use frozen, defrost completely before cooking.

♦ Cook seafood for 1 minute per 100 g/3½ oz, plus 3–4 minutes for the sauce. When fish is just cooked, it will be opaque, losing its pink colour, and it will flake easily at the thickest end. Shellfish is cooked when the flesh is opaque and just firm and the shell turns pink.

♦ Never prepare seafood ahead of time and then reheat it, as the result will be an overcooked, dried out and tasteless meal. In any case, seafood cooks so quickly in the microwave oven that there is no need to cook it in advance!

PAN-FRIED LINE FISH

750 g/1 lb 10 oz freshly caught fish
coarse sea salt
50 g/1¾ oz plain flour
freshly ground black pepper to taste
2 eggs, beaten
185 g/6½ oz dried breadcrumbs, seasoned
150 ml/¼ pint oil
15 ml/1 tablespoon butter

Sprinkle the fish generously with salt. Refrigerate for 30 minutes to firm the fish, then dust off the salt.

Mix the flour and pepper together. Dust the fish with the mixture, then dip it in the egg and coat with the breadcrumbs. Refrigerate for 30 minutes to set the crust.

Preheat a browning dish on High for 6–8 minutes, add the oil and butter, and microwave on High for 4 minutes. Add the crumbed fish fillets and microwave on High for about 7 minutes, turning after 3 minutes, until cooked. Drain and serve with Lemon Butter Sauce (page 57). SERVES 4.

GREEK PRAWNS AND RICE

It is absolutely essential to make this dish with fish stock for a wonderful seafood experience. Serve with crusty French bread, a tossed salad and some wine and you have a thoroughly enjoyable meal, prepared effortlessly. Don't forget the finger bowls!

30 ml/2 tablespoons olive oil
2 medium onions, chopped
2 cloves garlic, crushed
410 g/14 oz canned tomatoes, chopped,
   liquid reserved
200 g/7 oz rice
750 ml/1¼ pints hot fish stock
10 ml/2 teaspoons chopped fresh oregano
   or 5 ml/1 teaspoon dried
1 bayleaf
2.5 ml/½ teaspoon freshly ground
   black pepper
500 g/1 lb 2 oz peeled prawns
lemon sprigs and 30 ml/2 tablespoons
   chopped parsley to garnish
1 lemon, cut into wedges

Microwave oil, onions and garlic in a large glass bowl on High for 4½–5 minutes. Stir in the tomatoes and liquid. Mix in the rice. Microwave on Medium-High for 5 minutes, stirring every minute. Add the stock, herbs and pepper. Cover and microwave on High for 25 minutes if you are using white rice or 35–40 minutes for brown rice. In the meantime, devein the prawns (see Hint, page 62), then rinse them and leave to thaw.

When rice has cooked (not all the liquid will be absorbed), uncover, remove the bayleaf and place the prawns on the rice. Cover and microwave on High for 4–5 minutes until prawns turn pink. Leave to stand for about 10 minutes. Serve in the dish or turn out on to a serving platter. Garnish with lemon sprigs and parsley, and serve immediately with lemon wedges. SERVES 4.

Greek Prawns and Rice (page 54).

FISH IN TOMATO AND HERB SAUCE

1 onion, chopped
2 cloves garlic, crushed
30 ml/2 tablespoons chopped parsley
15 ml/1 tablespoon chopped basil
15 ml/1 tablespoon chopped dill
10 ml/2 teaspoons olive oil
4 tomatoes, peeled and chopped (see Hint,
  page 17)
100 ml/3½ fl oz dry white wine
10 ml/2 teaspoons lemon juice
salt and freshly ground black pepper to taste
500 g/1 lb 2 oz firm fish fillets, cubed

Microwave onion, garlic, herbs and oil in a large dish on High for 3 minutes. Mix in tomatoes, wine, lemon juice and seasoning; microwave on High for 8 minutes. (If sauce isn't thick enough, mix 12.5 ml/2½ teaspoons cornflour to a paste with a little water, stir into tomato mixture and microwave on High for 2 minutes.) Add fish and microwave on High for 6–8 minutes, until it turns opaque and is cooked. Serve on a bed of rice or pasta with a tossed green salad. SERVES 4.

FISH PROVENCAL

750 g/1 lb 10 oz fish fillets
1 large onion, chopped
15 ml/1 tablespoon olive oil
1 clove garlic, crushed
410 g/14 oz canned tomatoes, chopped
pinch of sugar
45 ml/3 tablespoons dry white wine
125 g/4½ oz button mushrooms, sliced
dash of lemon juice
salt and freshly ground black pepper to taste
10 ml/2 teaspoons chopped fresh dill

Place the fish fillets in a pie dish or casserole. Microwave the onion and oil in another pie dish on High for 3 minutes. Stir in garlic, tomatoes, sugar and wine. Microwave on High for 10 minutes. Add mushrooms, lemon juice and seasoning. Microwave on High for 4 minutes. Add dill.

Pour the sauce over the fish and microwave on High for 10½ minutes (1 minute per 100 g/3½ oz fish plus 3 minutes for the sauce). Flake the fish to check if it is done. SERVES 4.

Cheese and Mushroom Fish Bake (page 57) and Fish in Tomato and Herb Sauce (this page).

CHEESE AND MUSHROOM FISH BAKE

600 g/1 lb 5 oz firm white fish fillets
10 ml/2 teaspoons lemon juice
salt and freshly ground black pepper
   to taste
200 g/7 oz button mushrooms, sliced
4 spring onions, chopped
30 ml/2 tablespoons butter
30 ml/2 tablespoons plain flour
125 ml/4½ fl oz low-fat plain yoghurt

TOPPING
45 ml/3 tablespoons grated Cheddar cheese
45 ml/3 tablespoons dry wholemeal
   breadcrumbs
15 ml/1 tablespoon chopped parsley
5 ml/1 teaspoon paprika

Place the fish fillets in a large, shallow dish, sprinkle with lemon juice and seasoning, cover and microwave on High for 6 minutes (1 minute per 100g/3½ oz fish). Leave to stand until cool.

Drain off the liquid and reserve for the sauce. Flake the fish with a fork. Microwave the mushrooms, spring onions and butter in a medium glass bowl on High for 3 minutes. Stir in the flour and gradually blend in 125 ml/4½ fl oz of the fish stock (if the fish does not yield this amount of stock, top up the juices with low-fat milk). Stir in the yoghurt and seasoning. Microwave on High for about 3 minutes until mixture thickens, stirring after 1½ minutes. Add the flaked fish and check the seasoning.

Divide the mixture among four ramekin dishes (or place in a shallow dish). Mix the cheese, breadcrumbs and parsley together and sprinkle over the fish and mushroom mixture. Sprinkle paprika on top. Microwave on High for about 5 minutes and serve immediately. SERVES 4.

LEMON BUTTER SAUCE

Delicious and simple — this sauce is a classic.

30 ml/2 tablespoons butter
45 ml/3 tablespoons lemon juice
2.5 ml/½ teaspoon salt
10 ml/2 teaspoons caster sugar
freshly ground black pepper to taste
5 ml/1 teaspoon paprika

Mix all the ingredients together well, then microwave on High for 2 minutes. Pour the sauce over fried or grilled fish to serve. MAKES ABOUT 80 ML/2¾ FL OZ.

COLD BAKED FISH WITH THICK AVOCADO SAUCE

A lovely cold dish to serve in summer accompanied by a rice salad or a colourful salad of crisp lettuce leaves, tomato wedges, onion rings, cucumber slices and sliced hard-boiled eggs.

750 g/1 lb 10 oz firm fish fillets (such as cod,
   hake or salmon)
freshly ground black pepper to taste
pinch of dried dill
fish seasoning to taste
125 ml/4½ fl oz dry white wine

AVOCADO SAUCE
1 large, ripe avocado
salt and freshly ground black pepper to taste
100 ml/3½ fl oz pineapple yoghurt
2 slices fresh pineapple, grated
dash of lemon juice

fresh pineapple slices and snipped chives
   to garnish

Place the fish fillets in a flat-bottomed dish, season with pepper, dill and fish seasoning and pour the wine over. Microwave, covered, on High for 7–8 minutes, until the fish is cooked. Allow the fish to cool in the liquid, then remove it from the dish and place it on a bed of lettuce leaves on a serving plate.

To make the sauce, mash the avocado flesh, season, then mix in remaining ingredients. Spoon dollops of the avocado mixture on to the fish. Garnish with sliced pineapple and a sprinkling of snipped chives. SERVES 4.

VARIATION: Refrigerate the sauce until firm, then pipe it on the fish in an attractive pattern with a piping bag.

COLD SOURED CREAM SAUCE

This sauce also goes well with cold chicken.

250 ml/9 fl oz soured cream or thick plain
   yoghurt
25 ml/5 teaspoons lemon juice or vinegar
5 ml/1 teaspoon salt
5 ml/1 teaspoon Worcestershire sauce
2.5 ml/½ teaspoon mustard powder
15 ml/1 tablespoon grated onion
30 ml/2 tablespoons chopped parsley or chives
pinch of cayenne pepper

Combine the ingredients thoroughly and refrigerate until needed. MAKES ABOUT 325 ML/11 FL OZ

BAKED FISH IN SAFFRON SAUCE

6 firm fish fillets (about 750 g/1 lb 10 oz)
juice of 1 lemon (see Hint, page 123)
pinch of dried dill
salt and freshly ground black pepper to taste

SAUCE
30 ml/2 tablespoons butter
½ red pepper, seeded and cut into diamonds
1 clove garlic, crushed
pinch of saffron or 2.5 ml/½ teaspoon
   turmeric
dash of cayenne pepper
30 ml/2 tablespoons plain flour
200 ml/7 fl oz fish stock
200 ml/7 fl oz low-fat milk
pinch of dill
15 ml/1 tablespoon chopped fresh parsley

Place fish fillets in a flat, shallow dish. Sprinkle over the lemon juice, dill and seasoning. Microwave for 5 minutes on High. Drain off juices and use, topped up with milk, for the liquid in the sauce.

To make the sauce, microwave butter, red pepper, garlic, saffron or turmeric and cayenne pepper on High for 2 minutes in a medium-sized glass bowl. Stir in flour. Gradually stir in fish stock and milk, then microwave on High for 2 minutes. Stir well and microwave for another 2–3 minutes until sauce thickens. Pour over fish. Sprinkle with dill and parsley. Microwave on High for 4–5 minutes until fish flakes easily. Serve with new potatoes and a tossed salad. SERVES 4.

CHILLED SEAFOOD CURRY

400 g/14 oz firm fish fillets, cubed
10 ml/2 teaspoons lemon juice
pinch of dried dill
salt and freshly ground black pepper to taste
150 g/5½ oz prawns, cooked and peeled
   (see Notes, page 54)
1 red pepper, seeded and cut into long strips
1 avocado, peeled and cubed
juice of 1 lemon (see Hint, page 123)

CURRY SAUCE
60 ml/2 fl oz plain yoghurt
45 ml/3 tablespoons mayonnaise
10 ml/2 teaspoons curry powder
1 clove garlic, crushed
salt and freshly ground black pepper to taste

chopped fresh dill or coriander to garnish

Place the fish in a flat-bottomed dish and sprinkle with lemon juice, dill and seasoning. Microwave on High for 4 minutes, then drain and refrigerate until firm.

Mix the fish with the prawns. Add the pepper. Coat the avocado with lemon juice, then add to the fish, reserving the lemon juice. Cover the mixture and place it in the refrigerator to chill.

Combine all the ingredients for the sauce. Thin down with a little of the reserved lemon juice, then spoon the sauce over the chilled fish mixture. Garnish with chopped fresh herbs and serve. SERVES 4.

ANGELFISH WITH HERBS

Angelfish is a firm, dry white fish with very few bones. It cooks particularly well in the microwave oven. If you cannot find angelfish at the supermarket or a fishmonger's, use another firm, white fish.

750 g/1 lb 10 oz angelfish fillets, skinned
30 ml/2 tablespoons lemon juice
salt and freshly ground black pepper to taste
15 ml/1 tablespoon chopped mixed herbs
   (such as parsley, chives, marjoram, dill) or
   5 ml/1 teaspoon dried mixed herbs
15 ml/1 tablespoon butter (optional)

Cut fish into portions. Place flat in a large, shallow pie dish. Sprinkle with lemon juice, seasoning and herbs, and dot with butter. Cover and microwave on High for 7½–8 minutes (1 minute per 100g/3½ oz fish) or until fish flakes easily. Serve with new potatoes and a green salad. SERVES 4.

BAKED CREAMY FISH

A quick and easy fish dish with a mild but tangy flavour.

750 g/1 lb 10 oz firm white fish fillets
salt and freshly ground black pepper to taste
1 onion, grated
15 ml/1 tablespoon French mustard
20 ml/4 teaspoons grated Parmesan cheese
100 ml/3½ fl oz low-fat plain yoghurt
30 ml/2 tablespoons butter, softened

Place the fish fillets in a large, shallow dish and season. Combine all remaining ingredients and spread over the fish. Cover with greaseproof paper and microwave on High for about 10 minutes, until fish flakes when tested with a fork. Leave to stand for 3 minutes before serving with a tossed salad. SERVES 4.

Baked Fish in Saffron Sauce (page 58) and Angelfish with Herbs (page 58).

TUNA CASSEROLE

200g/7 oz canned tuna in brine, drained
150 g/5½ oz finely grated carrot
30 ml/2 tablespoons wheat germ
1 small onion, grated
3 eggs, lightly beaten
300 ml/11 fl oz low-fat milk
salt to taste
15 ml/1 tablespoon chopped parsley
pinch of paprika

Mix all ingredients except paprika lightly together, and pour into a round soufflé dish or casserole. Sprinkle top with paprika. Microwave on Medium-High for about 12 minutes until a metal skewer inserted in the centre comes out clean. SERVES 4.

COMBINATION OVEN: Bake at 200 °C and on Medium-Low power for 12–14 minutes (25 minutes if your oven alternates convection and microwave energy).

HINT
If fish is fresh, it should be springy to the touch, the eye should be clear and rounded, and the scales shiny and firm.

BAKED FISH WITH MUSTARD SAUCE

750 g/1 lb 10 oz firm white fish fillets
15 ml/1 tablespoon lemon juice
5 ml/1 teaspoon dried dill
salt and freshly ground black pepper

MUSTARD SAUCE
15 ml/1 tablespoon butter
15 ml/1 tablespoon flour
2.5 ml/½ teaspoon mustard powder
20 ml/4 teaspoons lemon juice
2.5 ml/½ teaspoon prepared mustard
10 ml/2 teaspoons brown sugar

Place the fish fillets in a large, shallow pie dish. Sprinkle with lemon juice, dill and seasoning. Cover and microwave on High for 7½ minutes (1 minute for every 100 g/3½ oz of fish). Drain off the liquid to use in sauce. Keep fish warm.

To prepare the sauce, microwave the butter in a 1 litre/1¾ pint jug for 20 seconds until melted. Stir in the flour and mustard powder. Gradually blend in 250 ml/9 fl oz of fish stock (use the juices from cooking the fish). Microwave on High for 2 minutes. Stir well, adding lemon juice, mustard powder and brown sugar. Microwave for a further 2 minutes, then serve hot with the hot fish. SERVES 4.

Fish in Fruity Spiced Sauce (page 61) and Calamari in Tomato Fennel Sauce (this page).

FISH PORTUGUESE

An adaptation of a traditional Portuguese dish.

1 kg/2¼ lb white fish or salmon fillets
5 ml/1 teaspoon salt
2 onions, chopped
2 cloves garlic, crushed
freshly ground black pepper to taste
3 tomatoes, peeled and chopped (see Hint,
   page 17)
30 ml/2 tablespoons chopped parsley
1 green pepper, seeded and thinly sliced
pinch of rosemary
5 ml/1 teaspoon chopped basil
100 ml/3½ fl oz fish or chicken stock
30 ml/2 tablespoons lemon juice

Place fish flat in a large pie dish, sprinkle with salt and set aside. Microwave onions and garlic, covered, on High for 4 minutes. Stir in remaining ingredients and microwave on High for 8–10 minutes. (Sauce should thicken; if not, mix 12.5 ml/2½ teaspoons cornflour with a little water and add.) Pour sauce over fish and microwave on High for 13 minutes (1 minute per 100 g/3½ oz fish plus 3 minutes for the sauce). SERVES 4.

CALAMARI IN TOMATO FENNEL SAUCE

2 onions, chopped
2 cloves garlic, crushed
1 green pepper, seeded and diced
30 ml/2 tablespoons butter
3 tomatoes, peeled and chopped (see Hint,
   page 17)
45 ml/3 tablespoons tomato paste
5 ml/1 teaspoon paprika
2.5 ml/½ teaspoon peri-peri
salt and freshly ground black pepper to taste
10 ml/2 teaspoons chopped fresh fennel
1 bayleaf
5 ml/1 teaspoon sugar
100 ml/3½ fl oz fish or chicken stock
750 g/1 lb 10 oz calamari, cut into rings
   5 mm/¼ inch thick

Microwave onion, garlic, green pepper and butter on High for 5 minutes, stirring after 3 minutes. Add all remaining ingredients except calamari, and microwave on High for 8 minutes. Add calamari and microwave on High for a further 2–3 minutes, stirring once, until it is opaque. (Don't overcook, or the calamari will become tough.) Serve with rice. SERVES 6.

FISH IN FRUITY SPICED SAUCE

This is a very simple fish curry with a Malaysian feel, adding an interesting blend of flavours to fish.

750 g/1 lb 10 oz firm fish fillets, cubed
juice of 1 large lemon (see Hint, page 123)
2 stalks lemon grass, cut into pieces
salt and freshly ground black pepper to taste
pinch of ground nutmeg
2½ cm/1 inch piece of root ginger, peeled
   and grated
2 cloves garlic, crushed
1 large onion, finely chopped
30 ml/2 tablespoons butter
300 ml/11 fl oz dry white wine
pinch of saffron
2 bananas, mashed
60 g/2 oz salted cashew nuts, roughly chopped
sprigs of coriander and lime or lemon
   wedges to garnish

Place fish in a shallow dish. Sprinkle with the lemon juice and lemon grass. Add salt, pepper, nutmeg, ginger and garlic. Cover and marinate for at least 4 hours — preferably overnight — turning fish twice.

Microwave the onion and butter on High for 3 minutes. Add the wine and saffron. Microwave on High for 7 minutes. Blend in the banana and microwave on High for 3 minutes. Mix in the fish with its marinade and the cashew nuts. Microwave on High for 8–10 minutes until fish is cooked, stirring gently after 4–5 minutes. Garnish with sprigs of coriander and lime or lemon wedges. Serve with wild rice. SERVES 4.

PILCHARD THERMIDOR

This is a quick, easy supper dish if you have leftover rice, and is one of my family's favourites. The cheese and onion sauce complements the fish beautifully.

350 g/12 oz cooked rice (see Cooking Rice,
   page 118)
410 g/14 oz canned pilchards in tomato sauce
1 large onion, chopped
30 ml/2 tablespoons butter
30 ml/2 tablespoons plain flour
250 ml/9 fl oz milk
salt and freshly ground black pepper to taste
60 g/2 oz Gruyère cheese, grated
60 g/2 oz Cheddar cheese, grated
30 g/1 oz Parmesan cheese, grated
30 ml/2 tablespoons chopped parsley
pinch of paprika

Layer the rice and pilchards in a casserole. Microwave the onion and butter in a medium-sized glass bowl on High for 3 minutes. Stir in the flour, then gradually blend in the milk. Microwave on High for 3–4 minutes until the sauce has thickened. Stir in seasoning, Gruyère and Cheddar cheeses. Pour the sauce over the fish, and sprinkle with Parmesan cheese, parsley and paprika. Microwave on Medium-High for 10–12 minutes, until heated through. SERVES 4.

VARIATION: Sauté 300 g/11 oz button mushrooms in 15 ml/1 tablespoon butter for 3 minutes, and layer on top of the fish.

COMBINATION OVEN: Cook at 200 °C and Medium-Low microwave power level for 12 minutes (or 20–25 minutes if your oven alternates convection and microwave energy).

CREAMY TROUT

These days trout is easily available from fishmongers or supermarkets. Always defrost it completely before cooking in the microwave oven.

4 trout, cleaned (about 750 g/1 lb 10 oz)
juice of 1 lemon (see Hint, page 123)
zest of 1 lemon, grated
15 ml/1 tablespoon chopped fresh herbs
   (such as parsley, chives, chervil or dill)
200 ml/7 fl oz double cream
salt and freshly ground black pepper to taste
lemon wedges and sprigs of fresh herbs
   to garnish

Place the fish in a large pie dish. Sprinkle with lemon juice, zest and herbs. Cover with cling film, pierced, and microwave on High for 7½ minutes (1 minute per 100 g/3½ oz fish). Test if fish is cooked by flaking with a fork. Remove fish and keep warm.

Stir cream, salt and pepper into the juices in the pie dish. Microwave on Medium-High for 2–3 minutes until heated through. Pour sauce over the trout, garnish with lemon wedges and sprigs of herbs, and serve immediately. SERVES 4.

HINT
To get rid of the smell of fish in your microwave, place a couple of slices of lemon in a jug of water, or add a teaspoon of lemon juice or a few drops of vanilla essence to a jug of water, and microwave on High for 2–3 minutes.

BAKED FISH WITH SPICY YOGHURT SAUCE

750 g/1lb 10 oz fish fillets
15 ml/1 tablespoon lemon juice or
  30 ml/2 tablespoons dry white wine
5 ml/1 teaspoon grated lemon zest
15 ml/1 tablespoon chopped fresh dill
salt and freshly ground black pepper to taste

SPICY YOGHURT SAUCE
10 ml/2 teaspoons oil
5 ml/1 teaspoon ground cumin
2.5 ml/½ teaspoon paprika
pinch of turmeric
200 ml/7 fl oz plain yoghurt
5 ml/1 teaspoon lemon juice
15 ml/1 tablespoon whole coriander leaves
salt and freshly ground black pepper to taste

Place fish fillets in a shallow dish, top to tail. Sprinkle lemon juice or wine over fish. Scatter over the lemon zest and dill. Season. Cover and microwave on High for 7½ minutes (1 minute per 100 g/3½ oz fish).

To make the sauce, microwave oil, cumin, paprika and turmeric on High for 30 seconds. Mix in yoghurt, lemon juice, coriander leaves and seasoning. Pour over fish and serve with a tossed salad. SERVES 4.

LEMON BAKED FISH

750 g/1 lb 10 oz fish fillets
5 stalks lemon grass, chopped
juice of 1 lemon (see Hint, page 123)
5 ml/1 teaspoon grated lemon zest
15 ml/1 tablespoon butter
salt and lemon pepper to taste

Place the fish in a flat dish, thicker parts to the outside. Sprinkle the lemon grass, lemon juice and zest over the fish. Microwave the butter for 20 seconds on High and pour over the fish. Season with a little salt and lemon pepper. Cover and microwave on High for 8 minutes. Leave to stand for 2 minutes, then serve. SERVES 4.

NOTE: Do not reheat the fish – it will spoil.

HINT

It is easiest to devein prawns when they are just beginning to thaw. Cut the prawn down the centre of the back with a sharp knife and scrape out the dark red vein.

SALMON MOUSSE WITH DILL AND CUCUMBER CREAM SAUCE

This easy-to-make salmon mousse is great for entertaining, or it can be served as a lunch with salads. The creamy sauce adds a contrast of flavour and colour.

SALMON MOUSSE
400 g/14 oz firm white fish fillets (such as hake)
30 ml/2 tablespoons butter
30 ml/2 tablespoons plain flour
300 ml/11 fl oz milk
225 g/8 oz canned salmon
100 ml/3½ fl oz tomato sauce
100 ml/3½ fl oz mayonnaise
1 small onion, grated
10 ml/2 teaspoons chopped fresh dill
15 ml/1 tablespoon chopped parsley
30 ml/2 tablespoons powdered gelatine
45 ml/3 tablespoons water
salt and freshly ground black pepper to taste
a few drops of Tabasco
2 egg whites

DILL AND CUCUMBER CREAM SAUCE
500 g/1 lb 2 oz cucumber, peeled, seeded
  and grated
5 ml/1 teaspoon salt
250 ml/9 fl oz soured cream
60 ml/4 tablespoons chopped spring onion
60 ml/2 fl oz double cream or plain yoghurt
20 ml/4 teaspoons lemon juice
20 ml/4 teaspoons white wine vinegar
30 ml/2 tablespoons chopped fresh dill

Microwave fish fillets in a pie dish, covered, on High for 4 minutes (1 minute per 100 g/3½ oz fish), then flake.

Microwave butter on High for 30 seconds, until melted. Stir in flour. Gradually blend in milk. Microwave on High for 3–4 minutes, until thickened, stirring halfway. Allow to cool. Add cooked fish, salmon, tomato sauce and mayonnaise. Mix in onion, dill and parsley.

Sprinkle gelatine on to water in a small bowl. Leave to sponge. Microwave on High for about 30 seconds, until just boiling. Pour gelatine in a thin trickle into the fish mixture, stirring. Add salt, pepper and Tabasco. Beat egg whites stiffly and fold in. Pour into wet moulds or ramekin dishes. Refrigerate. When set, dip moulds in hot water and turn upside down on a serving platter.

To make the sauce, put cucumber in a colander, sprinkle with salt and leave to drain for 30 minutes. Rinse, squeeze out liquid, and pat dry with paper towels. Purée with remaining sauce ingredients in a food processor. Taste for flavouring and chill overnight. Pour a little of the sauce over the mousse and serve the rest separately in a jug. SERVES 6–8.

Creamy Trout (page 61) and Salmon Mousse with Dill and Cucumber Cream Sauce (page 62).

CHAPTER SIX

MEAT

RED meat is a rich source of protein, iron, and vitamin B, and the microwave provides a quick, economical way of preparing a wide range of dishes, from meatballs and stews to the Sunday roast. Follow the instructions, and the results should be tasty and succulent!

BEEF STEW WITH WINE

A spicy, nourishing dish for a cold winter's night.

750 g/1 lb 10 oz stewing beef, cubed
15 ml/1 tablespoon sunflower oil
1 onion, chopped
1 clove garlic, crushed
1 stick celery, sliced
1 bayleaf
2.5 ml/½ teaspoon freshly ground
   black pepper
2 sprigs parsley
2 sprigs thyme
1 small piece ginger, peeled and sliced
250 ml/9 fl oz dry red wine
250 ml/9 fl oz beef stock
15 ml/1 tablespoon cornflour
30 ml/2 tablespoons chopped parsley
   to garnish

Preheat a large browning dish on High for 8 minutes. Pat the meat dry with paper towels. Add with the oil to the hot dish and microwave on High for 4 minutes, stirring after 2 minutes. Remove meat to a plate.

Add onion, garlic and celery to the dish. Microwave on High for 3 minutes. Add bayleaf, pepper, herbs, ginger, wine and stock. Add the meat to the dish, cover and microwave on Medium-Low for 1–1½ hours, until meat is tender, stirring occasionally.

Mix the cornflour into a paste with a little water and stir into the meat juices. Microwave for a further 5 minutes until the sauce has thickened. Garnish with parsley and serve with rice. SERVES 4.

COMBINATION OVEN: Prepare as above until meat has been added. Cover dish and cook at 180 °C and on Medium-Low microwave power level for about 1 hour (1½ hours if your oven alternates convection and microwave energy), then thicken and proceed as above.

LAMB AND GINGER CASSEROLE

Ask your butcher to bone the lamb. To save yourself the bother of crushing garlic and grating ginger, use garlic-and-ginger paste, available from Indian spice shops and some supermarkets.

750 g/1lb 10 oz leg of lamb, boned
   and cubed
5 ml/1 teaspoon ground coriander
15 ml/1 tablespoon sunflower oil
1 onion, chopped
1 clove garlic, crushed
1 bayleaf
freshly ground black pepper to taste
5 ml/1 teaspoon freshly grated ginger
5 ml/1 teaspoon turmeric
30 ml/2 tablespoons lemon juice
300 ml/11 fl oz hot beef stock
15 ml/1 tablespoon cornflour
125 ml/4½ fl oz low-fat plain yoghurt

Preheat a large browning dish on High for 8 minutes. Pat meat dry with paper towels and dust with coriander. Add oil and meat to the hot dish. Microwave on High for 4 minutes, stirring after 2 minutes. Add onion and microwave on High for 3 minutes. Stir in garlic, bayleaf, pepper, ginger, turmeric, lemon juice, and beef stock. Cover and microwave on Medium-Low for about 35 minutes, stirring after about 20 minutes. Thicken with cornflour mixed to a paste with a little water, then stir in yoghurt and microwave on Medium-Low for 5 minutes to thicken further. Serve with brown rice. SERVES 4.

COMBINATION OVEN: Prepare as described above until stock has been added. Cover and cook at 160 °C and on Medium-Low microwave power level for 50 minutes (90 minutes if your oven alternates convection and microwave energy). Thicken with cornflour, then continue as above.

Veal Niçoise (page 66) and Lamb and Ginger Casserole (page 64).

VEAL OLIVES

A lean variation on the classic beef olives.

1 onion, chopped
30 ml/2 tablespoons butter
100 g/3½ oz brown mushrooms, finely chopped
2 tomatoes, peeled and chopped (see Hint, page 17)
45 ml/3 tablespoons wholemeal breadcrumbs
15 ml/1 tablespoon chopped parsley
5 ml/1 teaspoon grated lemon zest
salt and freshly ground black pepper to taste
4 thin veal escalopes
45 ml/3 tablespoons hot Chicken Stock (page 21)
30 ml/2 tablespoons dry white wine
12.5 ml/2½ teaspoons cornflour (optional)
15 ml/1 tablespoon tomato paste
100 ml/3½ fl oz low-fat plain yoghurt
dash of paprika and 15 ml/1 tablespoon chopped parsley to garnish

Microwave onion and half the butter for 3 minutes on High. Add mushrooms, microwave for 2 minutes, then add tomatoes and microwave for a further 2 minutes. Stir in breadcrumbs, parsley, lemon zest and seasoning. Moisten if necessary to make a stuffing mixture. Divide into four sausage shapes.

Flatten escalopes with a rolling pin. Place stuffing on each and roll up, securing with a cocktail stick. Preheat a browning dish on High for 8 minutes. Pat rolls dry with paper towels, and place with remaining butter in the dish. Microwave on High for 4 minutes, turning every minute to brown all over. Pour over stock and wine. Microwave, covered, on Medium-Low for 15 minutes. Remove veal rolls and thicken meat juices, if necessary, with cornflour mixed with a little water. Add tomato paste and yoghurt; microwave for 3 minutes and spoon over the rolls. Garnish as suggested. SERVES 4.

VEAL NICOISE

750 g/1 lb 10 oz veal, cubed
30 ml/2 tablespoons butter
2 onions, chopped
1 clove garlic, crushed
10 ml/2 teaspoons paprika
3 tomatoes, peeled and chopped (see Hint, page 17)
1 green pepper, seeded and diced
salt and freshly ground black pepper to taste
12.5 ml/2½ teaspoons cornflour
30 ml/2 tablespoons soured cream, a dash of paprika and about 12 black olives to garnish

Pat meat dry with a paper towel. Preheat a browning dish on High for 8 minutes, add butter and swirl around. Immediately add veal and microwave on High for 4 minutes, stirring after 2 minutes to brown meat on both sides. Remove meat to a plate and set aside.

Add onion and garlic to the dish and microwave on High for 5 minutes, stirring once. Stir in paprika and mix thoroughly. Add tomato, green pepper and veal, cover and microwave on Medium-Low for 25 minutes, until veal is tender. Season and thicken with cornflour mixed to a paste with a little water, if needed. Microwave for a further 5 minutes. Swirl in soured cream, sprinkle with paprika and dot with olives. SERVES 4.

COMBINATION OVEN: Brown meat and onions as above (or fry on the hob if you don't have a browning dish). Place in a casserole, cover and cook at 160 °C and on Medium-Low microwave power level for 30 minutes (45 minutes if your oven alternates convection and microwave energy), then proceed as above.

MEATLOAF WITH APPLE TOPPING

A versatile dish that can be served hot with vegetables or cold with salads for a picnic; you can even use leftover slices in sandwiches!

60 g/2 oz fresh wholemeal breadcrumbs
2 egg whites
1 small onion, roughly chopped
125 ml/4½ fl oz low-fat milk
5 ml/1 teaspoon dried mixed herbs
salt and freshly ground black pepper to taste
600 g/1 lb 5 oz lean minced beef

TOPPING
15 ml/1 tablespoon Worcestershire sauce
5 ml/1 teaspoon soft brown sugar
15 ml/1 tablespoon Dijon mustard
1 Granny Smith apple, peeled, cored and grated

Process breadcrumbs, egg whites, onion, milk, herbs and seasoning to a purée. Mix into the minced beef. Press into a greased 1 kg/2¼ lb loaf pan. Microwave on High for 8–10 minutes. Combine Worcestershire sauce, sugar and mustard and spread on top of the meatloaf. Top with grated apple. Microwave on High for 4–5 minutes (or pop under a hot grill for a quick brown finish). SERVES 6.

COMBINATION OVEN: Cook at 200 °C and on Medium microwave power level for about 12 minutes (or 20 minutes if your oven alternates convection and microwave energy).

CHEESY SPINACH MEATBALLS

750 g/1 lb 10 oz lean minced beef
170 g/6 oz low-fat smooth cottage cheese
  (see page 7)
30 g/1 oz mozzarella cheese, grated
1 onion, grated
1 egg, beaten
250 g/9 oz frozen spinach, thawed and drained
50 g/1¾ oz rolled oats
salt and freshly ground black pepper to taste
pinch of garlic salt
300 ml/11 fl oz beef stock
100 ml/3½ fl oz tomato purée (passata)
45 ml/3 tablespoons sherry
20 ml/4 teaspoons cornflour

Combine minced beef, cheeses, onion, egg, spinach, oats and seasoning. Form into balls and place in a large casserole. Microwave on High for 8–10 minutes. Drain off fat. Combine stock, tomato purée, sherry and cornflour in a jug. Microwave on High for 3–4 minutes, until thickened. Stir and pour over meatballs. Microwave on Medium-High for 6–8 minutes. SERVES 4–6.

ROAST BEEF FILLET

Using this method, much of the meat's goodness is retained, making it one of the healthiest ways to prepare roast beef.

1 kg/2¼ lb fillet of beef
10 ml/2 teaspoons prepared wholegrain mustard
salt and freshly ground black pepper to taste

Preheat a large browning dish on High for 8 minutes. Remove excess fat and sinew from the meat, then pat dry with a paper towel and rub mustard all over. Place the fillet in the hot browning dish and microwave on High for 4 minutes, turning every minute. Microwave on Medium-High for a further 4 minutes for rare, 6 minutes for medium, and 8–10 minutes for well done. Season meat, then leave to stand, covered, for 10 minutes before slicing. SERVES 4.

COMBINATION OVEN: Brown fillet. Place on a rack or in a large pie dish and roast at 200 °C and on Medium microwave power level for the same times as indicated above (add 2 minutes to the cooking times if your oven alternates convection and microwave energy).

Cheesy Spinach Meatballs (this page) and Veal Olives (page 66).

LAMB CASSEROLE

When buying stewing lamb, check with your butcher that the meat is not in fact mutton — microwave cooking does not tenderize tough meat in the same way as conventional cooking.

750 g/1 lb 10 oz stewing lamb, cubed
15 ml/1 tablespoon oil
1 large onion, chopped
2 sticks celery, chopped
30 ml/2 tablespoons plain flour
10 ml/2 teaspoons curry powder
25 ml/5 teaspoons vinegar
45 ml/3 tablespoons tomato sauce
10 ml/2 teaspoons light brown sugar
15 ml/1 tablespoon Worcestershire sauce
300 ml/11 fl oz beef stock
freshly ground black pepper to taste
1 bouquet garni (see page 80)

Pat meat dry with paper towels. Preheat a browning dish on High for 8 minutes. Add oil, lamb and onion. Microwave on High for 4 minutes, stirring after 2 minutes. Add celery. Stir in flour and curry powder, mixing well. Mix in remaining ingredients. Cover and microwave on Medium-Low for 45–60 minutes until lamb is tender. Remove bouquet garni. SERVES 4.

VARIATION: Use mushrooms instead of celery, adding halfway through cooking time.

KASSELER CHOPS WITH PEACHES

2 medium kasseler chops (smoked
    pork chops)
5 ml/1 teaspoon oil
5 ml/1 teaspoon butter
30 ml/2 tablespoons soft brown sugar
200 g/7 oz canned peach slices,
    juice retained
30 ml/2 tablespoons wine vinegar
5 ml/1 teaspoon mustard powder
10 ml/2 teaspoons cornflour (optional)

Pat the meat dry with a paper towel. Preheat a browning dish on High for 8 minutes, then add the oil and butter and microwave on High for 20 seconds. Add the sugar and the chops, and microwave on High for 2–3 minutes.

Add the peaches and their juice, vinegar and mustard and microwave on High for 2 minutes. If necessary, thicken the liquid by stirring in the cornflour, mixed to a paste with a little water, and microwave on High for 1½ minutes. Serve. SERVES 2.

ROAST LEG OF LAMB WITH HERB SAUCE

An unusual medley of flavours make this moist roast a wonderful treat for family and friends.

1.5 kg/3¼ lb leg of lamb
500 ml/18 fl oz buttermilk
5 ml/1 teaspoon ground ginger
2.5 ml/½ teaspoon freshly ground black pepper
10 ml/2 teaspoons chopped fresh mixed
    herbs or 5 ml/1 teaspoon dried
2 cloves garlic, crushed
5 ml/1 teaspoon mustard
2.5 ml/½ teaspoon paprika
30 ml/2 tablespoons oil for roasting

HERB SAUCE
30 ml/2 tablespoons butter
300 g/11 oz button mushrooms, sliced
2 cloves garlic, crushed
freshly ground black pepper to taste
10 ml/2 teaspoons chopped fresh mixed herbs
    (such as rosemary and oregano)
15 ml/1 tablespoon chopped parsley
10 ml/2 teaspoons plain flour
5 ml/1 teaspoon mustard powder
30 ml/2 tablespoons sherry
15 ml/1 tablespoon brandy
250 ml/9 fl oz soured cream

Marinate lamb in buttermilk in a glass casserole for 24–36 hours. Pat the meat dry with paper towels. Combine ginger, pepper, herbs, garlic, mustard and paprika, and rub into the meat.

Preheat a large browning dish on High for 8 minutes. Add the oil. Add the lamb and brown for 1 minute on each side. Microwave for 30–36 minutes (10–12 minutes per 500 g/1 lb 2 oz) on High, turning twice during the cooking. Salt, remove from dish and leave to rest for 12–15 minutes before carving.

To make the sauce, add butter and mushrooms to the browning dish. Microwave on High for 3 minutes. Stir in garlic, pepper and herbs. Blend flour, mustard, sherry and brandy together. Stir into mushrooms. Microwave on High for 3–4 minutes until thickened. Mix in soured cream and microwave on Medium-Low for 2 minutes to heat through. SERVES 4–6.

HINT

Cook the food that takes the longest time first as it has the longest standing time; cover it to keep it warm. When preparing a roast dinner, cook the rice first. Par-cook potatoes, then roast with the meat. Make gravy and cook vegetables while the meat is standing.

Roast Leg of Lamb with Herb Sauce (page 68) and Potatoes Provençals (page 104).

SPRING LAMB RAGOUT

750 g/1 lb 10 oz leg of lamb, boned and cubed
30 ml/2 tablespoons oil
1 large onion, chopped
2 cloves garlic, crushed
freshly ground black pepper to taste
30 ml/2 tablespoons plain flour
300 ml/11 fl oz hot beef or chicken stock
100 ml/3½ fl oz dry white wine
12.5 ml/2½ teaspoons Worcestershire sauce
15 ml/1 tablespoon chopped fresh rosemary
   or 5 ml/1 teaspoon dried
1 bayleaf
15 ml/1 tablespoon tomato paste
2 large tomatoes, peeled and chopped (see Hint,
   page 17)
200 g/7 oz brown mushrooms, sliced
3 courgettes, cut in julienne strips
75 g/2½ oz Calamata olives
30 ml/2 tablespoons chopped parsley

Preheat a browning dish on High for 8 minutes. Microwave oil on High for 1 minute. Pat meat dry with paper towels. Add to dish with onion and garlic. Microwave on High for 4 minutes, stirring halfway. Stir in pepper and flour. Slowly add the stock. Mix in well, then add wine, Worcestershire sauce, rosemary, bayleaf, tomato paste and tomatoes. Mix well. Cover and microwave on Medium-Low for 45 minutes, stirring halfway. Add mushrooms and courgettes 12 minutes before end of cooking time. Stir in olives and parsley. Check seasoning. Leave to stand for 10 minutes, then remove bayleaf and serve with buttered noodles, couscous or rice. SERVES 6.

HINT: If you don't have a browning dish, brown the meat on the hob.

COMBINATION OVEN: Cover dish and cook at 160 °C and Medium-Low microwave power level for about 45 minutes (60 minutes if your oven alternates convection and microwave energy).

Lamb with Aubergine and Tomato (page 71) and Lamb Hotpot (page 72).

MARINATED BEEF FILLET

*Make this a day in advance for a wonderful buffet or picnic.
Fillet is expensive, but it goes a long way.*

1 kg/2¼ lb beef fillet
15 ml/1 tablespoon oil
150 g/5½ oz button mushrooms, sliced

MARINADE
250 ml/9 fl oz oil
250 ml/9 fl oz dry white wine
4 cloves garlic, crushed
10 ml/2 teaspoons seasoned salt
2.5 ml/½ teaspoon freshly ground black pepper
10 ml/2 teaspoons sugar
5 ml/1 teaspoon chopped fresh thyme
10 ml/2 teaspoons prepared Dijon mustard
30 ml/2 tablespoons chopped parsley

Preheat a large browning dish on High for 8 minutes.
Pat the meat dry with paper towels. Add the oil and
fillet to the hot dish, and microwave on High for
4 minutes, turning after 2 minutes. Microwave on
Medium-High for 8 minutes, turning after 4 minutes.
(Cooking time for fillet = 6–8 minutes per 500 g/
1 lb 2 oz.) Allow the fillet to cool, then cut into
5 mm/¼ inch slices and arrange in a large, shallow dish
with the sliced mushrooms.

Blend all the marinade ingredients until they are
thoroughly combined. Pour marinade over meat and
mushrooms, cover and refrigerate overnight, turning
meat once during the marinating.

Remove meat from the marinade and place on a
serving platter with the mushrooms. SERVES 6.

VARIATION: For a buffet lunch spread, serve on a bed
of fresh, dark green spinach leaves. Garnish with
asparagus spears, black olives and cherry tomatoes.

LAMB WITH AUBERGINE AND TOMATO

1 large aubergine (400 g/14 oz), unpeeled,
    cubed and dégorged (see Hint, page 99)
450 g/1 lb boneless lamb (such as leg
    or shoulder), cubed
30 ml/2 tablespoons oil
1 onion, chopped
1 clove garlic, crushed
4 tomatoes, peeled and chopped (see Hint,
    page 17), or 410 g/14 oz canned tomatoes,
    drained and chopped
5 ml/1 teaspoon chopped fresh basil
salt and freshly ground black pepper
    to taste
5 ml/1 teaspoon shredded basil

Pat the aubergine cubes and meat dry. Preheat a
browning dish on High for 8 minutes, add the oil and
meat and microwave on High for 4 minutes, stirring
after 2 minutes. Stir in the onion and garlic, and
microwave for a further 3 minutes. Add the aubergine
and microwave on High for 4 minutes. Add the
tomatoes, basil and pepper.

Cover and microwave on Medium-High for about
20 minutes until meat is tender. Add salt and sprinkle
with shredded basil. Serve with brown or wild rice,
garnished with a sprig of basil. SERVES 4.

ROAST BEEF WITH MUSTARD TOPPING

*Cooking a roast in a microwave oven is quick enough to do
during the week — a rare roast of 1.5 kg/3¼ lb will take
only half an hour!*

1.5 kg/3¼ lb boned forerib of beef
30 ml/2 tablespoons oil
30 ml/2 tablespoons mustard powder
10 ml/2 teaspoons chopped fresh thyme or
    5 ml/1 teaspoon dried
10 ml/2 teaspoons lemon pepper
15 ml/1 tablespoon oil

GRAVY
30 ml/2 tablespoons gravy powder
200 ml/7 fl oz beef stock

Brush meat with the 30 ml/2 tablespoons oil. Sprinkle
with mustard powder, thyme and lemon pepper. Allow
to stand at room temperature for 1 hour.

Preheat a large browning dish on High for 8 minutes.
Add the 15 ml/1 tablespoon oil and the meat. Microwave on High for 3 minutes, turning every minute until
browned all over. Continue cooking at the following
rate per 500 g/1 lb 2 oz: 9–10 minutes for rare beef,
10–12 minutes for medium and 12–14 minutes for well
done. Turn roast every 10 minutes. Remove from dish
and leave to stand for 12–15 minutes before serving.

To make the gravy, stir gravy powder and beef stock
into the juices in the browning dish. Microwave on
High for 2–3 minutes, until thickened, stirring after
1–2 minutes. SERVES 4–6.

SATURDAY PIE

This meat pie has an unusual cheesy topping.

1 onion, chopped
15 ml/1 tablespoon oil
500 g/1 lb 2 oz minced topside beef
salt and freshly ground black pepper to taste
5 ml/1 teaspoon Worcestershire sauce
10 ml/2 teaspoons chopped fresh mixed
    herbs or 5 ml/1 teaspoon dried
3 slices wholemeal bread, crumbed
150 g/5½ oz Cheddar cheese, grated
125 g/4½ oz smooth cottage cheese (see page 7)
2 eggs, beaten
125 ml/4½ fl oz plain yoghurt
pinch of ground nutmeg
salt and freshly ground black pepper to taste
10 ml/2 teaspoons chopped fresh thyme or
    5 ml/1 teaspoon dried
pinch of paprika

Microwave onion and oil in a large glass bowl on High
for 3 minutes. Stir in minced beef, seasoning,
Worcestershire sauce and herbs. Microwave on High
for 4 minutes, breaking up minced beef with a fork as
it cooks. Stir in the breadcrumbs. Spread into a deep
pie dish. Sprinkle half the Cheddar over the meat.

Blend together cottage cheese, eggs, yoghurt, nutmeg,
seasoning and thyme. Pour this mixture into the pie
dish. Sprinkle remaining Cheddar on top. Dust with
paprika. Microwave on Medium-High for about
15 minutes. SERVES 4.

COMBINATION OVEN: Bake at 200 °C and Medium-
Low microwave power level for 16–18 minutes
(25–30 minutes if your oven alternates convection and
microwave energy).

MEATBALLS WITH SOURED CREAM SAUCE

The soured cream sauce makes for a deliciously moist variation on classic family fare.

2 thick slices white bread
200 ml/7 fl oz milk
750 g/1 lb 10 oz lean minced beef
5 ml/1 teaspoon salt
pinch of freshly ground black pepper
5 ml/1 teaspoon chopped fresh basil or
   2.5 ml/½ teaspoon dried
1 apple, peeled, cored and grated
1 clove garlic, crushed
15 ml/1 tablespoon chopped fresh parsley
25 ml/5 teaspoons oil

SAUCE
1 onion, chopped
10 ml/2 teaspoons butter
salt and freshly ground black pepper to taste
180 ml/6¼ fl oz dry white wine, heated
200 ml/7 fl oz soured cream

Soak the bread in the milk for a few minutes, then break into small pieces. Combine with all remaining meatball ingredients except the oil, and form into balls. Preheat a large browning dish on High for 8 minutes. Add oil and immediately arrange the meatballs in the dish. Microwave on High for 2 minutes. Turn and microwave for another 2–3 minutes, until cooked.

To make the sauce, microwave the onion and butter on High for 3 minutes in a pie dish. Add salt, pepper and wine. Microwave on High for 5–6 minutes, until liquid has reduced. Stir in soured cream and serve sauce separately. SERVES 6.

GROUND BEEF BAKE WITH PIZZA-STYLE TOPPING

Serve wedges of this colourful ground beef bake to your family — they'll love it!

1 onion, chopped
1 clove garlic, crushed
1 stick celery, chopped
30 ml/2 tablespoons chopped parsley
5 ml/1 teaspoon chopped fresh basil
5 ml/1 teaspoon chopped fresh oregano
600 g/1 lb 5 oz lean minced beef
5 ml/1 teaspoon Worcestershire sauce
100 g/3½ oz wholemeal breadcrumbs
1 egg, lightly beaten
salt and freshly ground black pepper to taste

PIZZA-STYLE TOPPING
100 ml/3½ fl oz tomato sauce
200 g/7 oz mozzarella cheese cut into
   thick rounds
1 tomato, sliced into rounds
1 green pepper, seeded and sliced into rings
a few black olives, pitted and halved

Combine all ingredients for the base and press mixture down firmly into a greased 20 cm/8 inch soufflé dish. Microwave on Medium-High for about 20 minutes until the centre is cooked through. Leave to stand for a few minutes. Turn out on to a round serving platter and top with the pizza topping.

Arrange the topping ingredients decoratively on the meat base and return it to the microwave on Medium-High for 6 minutes until cheese melts and runs down the side of the meat. SERVES 6.

HINT: To make this dish even simpler, use a food processor to chop the vegetables and herbs finely.

LAMB HOTPOT

450 g/1 lb potatoes, scrubbed
1 large onion, sliced into rings
2 sticks celery, sliced
10 ml/2 teaspoons oil
2 carrots, peeled and sliced
6 lamb chops
5 ml/1 teaspoon chopped fresh rosemary
12.5 ml/2½ teaspoons cornflour or
   gravy powder
275 ml/½ pint hot beef stock
salt and freshly ground black pepper to taste

Pierce potatoes and microwave on High for 6 minutes. Peel and slice thinly. Microwave onion, celery and oil in a small bowl on High for 3 minutes. Add carrots and microwave for a further 2 minutes.

Preheat a browning dish on High for 8 minutes. Add chops and microwave on High for 4 minutes, turning after 2 minutes. Layer vegetables and chops in the dish. Sprinkle with the rosemary.

Mix cornflour or gravy powder into a paste with a little water and add to the stock. Pour the stock over the meat and vegetables, cover and microwave on Medium-Low for about 30 minutes. Season and leave to stand for 10 minutes. SERVES 4.

COMBINATION OVEN: Cover and cook at 160 °C and Medium-Low microwave power level for about 25 minutes (35 minutes if your oven alternates convection and microwave energy).

HEARTY COUNTRY STEW

    1 kg/2¼ lb shoulder of lamb, cubed
    15 ml/1 tablespoon oil
    1 onion, chopped
    15 ml/1 tablespoon plain flour
    1 clove garlic, crushed
    2 rashers rindless bacon, chopped
    2 carrots, thinly sliced
    200 g// oz button mushrooms, sliced
    250 ml/9 fl oz hot beef stock
    125 ml/4½ fl oz dry red wine
    10 ml/2 teaspoons chopped fresh marjoram
    2.5 ml/½ teaspoon freshly ground black pepper

Preheat a browning dish on High for 8 minutes. Pat meat dry with paper towels. Add with oil and onion to the hot dish. Microwave on High for 4 minutes, stirring after 2 minutes. Stir in flour. Add garlic, bacon, carrots and mushrooms. Stir in stock, wine, marjoram and pepper. Cover and microwave on Medium-Low for 50 minutes, until meat is tender, stirring after 25 minutes. Check seasoning and add salt if necessary. Leave to stand for 10 minutes. SERVES 4.

COMBINATION OVEN: Cover and cook at 160 °C and Medium-Low microwave power level for about 50 minutes (or 70 minutes if your oven alternates convection and microwave energy).

ORIENTAL PORK

Use pork steaks or boned shoulder of pork for this simply prepared dish.

    750 g/1 lb 10 oz pork
    15 ml/1 tablespoon oil
    45 ml/3 tablespoons peanut butter
    10 ml/2 teaspoons soy sauce
    1 clove garlic, crushed
    5 ml/1 teaspoon prepared mustard
    5 ml/1 teaspoon chopped fresh sage
    7.5 ml/1½ teaspoons brown sugar
    2.5 ml/½ teaspoon ground ginger
    30 ml/2 tablespoons apricot juice

Pat meat dry with paper towels. Preheat a large browning dish on High for 8 minutes. Add oil and pork steaks, and microwave on High for 3 minutes, turning after 1 minute.

Combine remaining ingredients in a plastic jug. Microwave on High for 40 seconds. Mix well and pour the sauce over the pork. Cover and microwave on Medium-High for about 15 minutes. SERVES 4.

COMBINATION OVEN: Cook at 180 °C and Medium-Low microwave power level for 15–18 minutes (25–30 minutes if your oven alternates convection and microwave energy).

Oriental Pork (this page) and Meatballs with Soured Cream Sauce (page 72).

STIR-FRIED PORK

450 g/1 lb pork fillet
10 ml/2 teaspoons sunflower oil
1 onion, sliced
1 clove garlic, crushed
5 ml/1 teaspoon freshly grated ginger
2 sticks celery, diagonally sliced
200 g/7 oz button mushrooms, sliced
2 carrots, peeled and cut in julienne strips
½ green pepper, seeded and cut in strips
½ red pepper, seeded and cut in strips
75 ml/2½ fl oz soy sauce
200 ml/7 fl oz hot beef stock
salt and freshly ground black pepper to taste

Preheat a large browning dish on High for 8 minutes. Cut pork into thin strips and pat dry with paper towels. Add with oil to dish. Microwave on High for 3 minutes, stirring halfway. Add vegetables, ginger, soy sauce and stock. Cover and microwave on High for 7–8 minutes, until vegetables are just cooked. Season. SERVES 4.

VEAL BOLOGNAISE

1 onion, chopped
2 cloves garlic, crushed
10 ml/2 teaspoons olive oil
500 g/1lb 2 oz minced veal
410 g/14 oz canned tomatoes, chopped
100 ml/3½ fl oz tomato purée (passata)
5 ml/1 teaspoon dried oregano
5 ml/1 teaspoon dried basil
salt and freshly ground black pepper to taste
5 ml/1 teaspoon lemon juice
250 g/9 oz spaghetti
1 litre/1¾ pints boiling water
5 ml/1 teaspoon salt
5 ml/1 teaspoon oil
30 ml/2 tablespoons freshly grated
    Parmesan cheese
15 ml/1 tablespoon chopped parsley to garnish

Microwave onion, garlic and oil on High for 3 minutes. Add minced veal and mix in with a fork. Microwave on High for 4 minutes, stirring to break up mince, until it loses its pink colour. Add tomatoes with their liquid, tomato purée, herbs, sugar, seasoning and lemon juice. Microwave on High for 15–20 minutes, stirring twice.

Place spaghetti, water, salt and oil in a large bowl. Microwave on High for 8–10 minutes, stirring halfway. Drain, then spoon the sauce over the spaghetti. Heat through for a few minutes, sprinkle with Parmesan cheese and parsley and serve. SERVES 4.

CHINESE-STYLE PORK

450 g/1 lb pork fillet, cut into strips
15 ml/1 tablespoon sunflower oil
1 onion, sliced
5 ml/1 teaspoon freshly grated ginger
1 clove garlic, crushed
½ green pepper, seeded and cut in thin strips
½ red pepper, seeded and cut in thin strips
12.5 ml/2½ teaspoons cornflour
30 ml/2 tablespoons red wine vinegar
15 ml/1 tablespoon clear honey
15 ml/1 tablespoon tomato purée (passata)
45 ml/3 tablespoons mango juice
15 ml/1 tablespoon soy sauce

Preheat a browning dish on High for 8 minutes. Pat meat dry with paper towels and microwave in the dish with oil, onion, ginger and garlic on High for 4 minutes, stirring halfway. Add peppers and microwave on High for 6 minutes. Mix cornflour into remaining ingredients and stir into pork. Microwave on High for 4–5 minutes, until sauce thickens. Serve with brown rice. SERVES 4.

STEAK WITH HORSERADISH SAUCE

HORSERADISH SAUCE
150 ml/¼ pint low-calorie mayonnaise
75 ml/2½ fl oz prepared white horseradish sauce
30 ml/2 tablespoons Dijon mustard
2.5 ml/½ teaspoon coarsely ground black pepper
pinch of salt

4 thick fillet steaks
freshly ground black pepper to taste
5 ml/1 teaspoon garlic-and-herb seasoning
5 ml/1 teaspoon oil
10 ml/2 teaspoons butter

Blend sauce ingredients in a bowl and set aside. Preheat a large browning dish on High for 8 minutes. Pat steaks dry with paper towels, then season. Add oil and butter to the dish, then add steaks immediately. Microwave on High for 2½–3½ minutes on each side, depending on how well done you like your steak. Serve with the horseradish sauce separately. SERVES 4.

HINT
Make sure that the turntable in your microwave oven is clean and dry before heating a browning dish, otherwise the dish will not heat up properly.

Stir-fried Pork (page 74), Chinese-style Pork (page 74) and Steak with Horseradish Sauce (page 74).

CHAPTER SEVEN

CHICKEN

CHICKEN is healthy and very versatile, as it goes well with a wide range of flavours and can be prepared in many ways. When cooked in the microwave, it turns out wonderfully tender and full of flavour; with the help of a browning dish, you can even have delicious 'fried' chicken!

CRISPY CHICKEN WITH MUSTARD AND TARRAGON SAUCE

75 g/2½ oz fresh breadcrumbs
5 ml/1 teaspoon finely chopped fresh tarragon
10 ml/2 teaspoons finely chopped parsley
5 ml/1 teaspoon paprika
7.5 ml/1½ teaspoons coarse-grained Dijon mustard
5 ml/1 teaspoon melted butter (see Hint, page 13)
1 clove garlic, crushed
4 chicken breasts, skinned and boned
15 ml/1 tablespoon oil

SAUCE
60 ml/2 fl oz dry white wine
100 ml/3½ fl oz hot Chicken Stock (page 21)
2.5 ml/½ teaspoon Dijon mustard
5 ml/1 teaspoon chopped fresh tarragon
salt and freshly ground black pepper to taste
45 ml/3 tablespoons double cream or plain yoghurt

Mix breadcrumbs, tarragon, parsley and paprika in a pie dish. Combine mustard, butter and garlic. Coat the chicken breasts with this mixture, then roll them in the breadcrumb mixture, pressing the crumbs down firmly.

Preheat a large browning dish on High for 8 minutes. Microwave oil and chicken on High for 6–8 minutes, turning halfway, until chicken is cooked. Drain off the oil. Add wine, stock, mustard and tarragon to the dish. Microwave on High for 6 minutes.

Add seasoning and stir in the cream or yoghurt. Microwave on Medium for 1 minute, pour over the chicken and serve. SERVES 4.

HINT
To peel onions easily, pour boiling water over to cover, leave for 5 minutes, then drain, rinse and peel.

CHICKEN NORMANDY

This dish originated from a region in the north of France where apples grow. It is delicious served with sweet potatoes and a mixed salad.

1 kg/2¼ lb chicken pieces
chicken spice to taste
30 ml/2 tablespoons butter
1 onion, chopped
1 clove garlic, crushed
3 Granny Smith apples, peeled, cored and sliced
30 ml/2 tablespoons plain flour
300 ml/11 fl oz pint cider
5 ml/1 teaspoon chicken stock powder or
   1 chicken stock cube
10 ml/2 teaspoons chopped fresh thyme
salt and freshly ground black pepper to taste
15 ml/1 tablespoon chopped parsley to garnish

Pat chicken dry with a paper towel. Rub in chicken spice. Preheat a browning dish on High for 8 minutes. Add butter and swirl to coat base of dish. Immediately add chicken and microwave on High for 5 minutes, turning after 3 minutes. Remove chicken to a plate.

Add onion, garlic and apples to the browning dish. Microwave on High for 5 minutes, stirring after 3 minutes. Blend in flour and gradually stir in the cider. Mix in stock powder or crumbled stock cube, thyme and seasoning. Add chicken pieces and coat with sauce. Cover and microwave on Medium-High for about 25 minutes. Garnish with parsley. SERVES 4.

HINT: If you don't have cider, substitute apple juice plus 12.5 ml/2½ teaspoons apple cider vinegar.

COMBINATION OVEN: Cover and cook chicken in sauce at 180 °C and Medium-Low microwave power level for 25 minutes (30–35 minutes if your oven alternates convection and microwave energy).

Chicken Normandy (page 76), Chilli Chicken with Rosemary (page 78) and Crispy Chicken with Mustard and Tarragon Sauce (page 76).

Chicken Cassoulet (page 79).

CHILLI CHICKEN WITH ROSEMARY

750 g/1 lb 10 oz chicken pieces
chicken spice to taste
2 cloves garlic, crushed
2 red chillis, seeded and finely sliced
15 ml/1 tablespoon chopped fresh rosemary or
  7.5 ml/1½ teaspoons dried
45 ml/3 tablespoons dry white wine
salt and freshly ground black pepper to taste

Pat chicken pieces dry with paper towels, then rub chicken spice into the skin.

Preheat a large browning dish for 8 minutes on High. Add chicken pieces, skin-side down, and microwave on High for 6 minutes, turning after 3 minutes. Mix in the garlic, chillis and rosemary. Microwave for a further 3 minutes.

Pour the wine over the chicken. Cover and microwave on Medium-Low for 20–25 minutes until chicken is tender. Season. Serve with rice or potatoes and a mixed green salad. SERVES 4.

TANGY CHICKEN

This is a quick dish to prepare with a minimum of fuss and maximum of flavour.

750 g/1 lb 10 oz chicken pieces
250 ml/9 fl oz orange juice
250 ml/9 fl oz chutney
250 ml/9 fl oz mayonnaise
5 ml/1 teaspoon chopped fresh thyme

Place chicken pieces in an oven roasting bag. Combine all remaining ingredients and pour over the chicken in the bag. Tie a loose knot and place the bag in a large pie dish. Spread the chicken pieces flat so that they are not overlapping. Microwave on Medium–High for 25–30 minutes. SERVES 4.

COMBINATION OVEN: Cook at 200 °C and on Medium microwave power level for about 20 minutes (or 30–35 minutes if your oven alternates convection and microwave energy).

CHICKEN CASSOULET

This is a quick and easy version of a traditional French dish that takes nearly all day to put together!

750 g/1 lb 10 oz chicken pieces
chicken spice to taste
1 large onion, chopped
2 rashers rindless streaky bacon, chopped
1 clove garlic, crushed
100 ml/3½ fl oz dry white wine
250 ml/9 fl oz hot Chicken Stock (page 21)
15 ml/1 tablespoon tomato paste
100 g/3½ oz garlic sausage, diced
15 ml/1 tablespoon chopped fresh thyme
1 bayleaf
410 g/14 oz canned baked beans in
    tomato sauce
25 ml/5 teaspoons cornflour
salt and freshly ground black pepper
    to taste

Pat the chicken pieces dry with a paper towel and dust with chicken spice. Preheat a large browning dish on High for 8 minutes. Add chicken, skin-side down. Microwave on High for 6 minutes, turning after 3 minutes. Remove chicken.

Add onion and bacon to dish and microwave on High for 3 minutes. Stir in garlic, wine, stock and tomato paste. Add garlic sausage, thyme, bayleaf and baked beans. Mix well. Add chicken and mix together. Cover and microwave on Medium-Low for about 40 minutes until chicken is tender. Remove bayleaf.

Mix cornflour and a little water into a paste and add with seasoning. Microwave on Medium-Low for 4–5 minutes until thickened. SERVES 4.

NOTES

♦ To cook a chicken, season and place in a roasting bag or pie dish. Microwave on High for the first 5 minutes, then Medium-High. Microwave for 10 minutes per 500 g/1 lb 2 oz, i.e. 30 minutes for a 1.5 kg/3¼ lb chicken, and 25 minutes for a 1.3 kg/2¾ lb chicken.
♦ To defrost, remove wrapping, place chicken on a plate, cover with a bowl and microwave on 'defrost' setting. Separate portions halfway through. A whole chicken takes about 12 minutes per 500 g/1 lb 2 oz; portions take about 5 minutes per 500 g/1 lb 2 oz to defrost. Allow poultry to stand for a while to complete the defrosting.

CHICKEN MANGO CURRY

30 ml/2 tablespoons butter
1 large onion, chopped
15–25 ml/3–5 teaspoons curry powder
30 ml/2 tablespoons plain flour
300 g/11 oz canned mangoes, drained,
    liquid reserved
hot Chicken Stock (page 21) to make mango
    liquid up to 425 ml/¾ pint
30 ml/2 tablespoons sultanas
20 ml/4 teaspoons desiccated coconut
salt and freshly ground black pepper to taste
1 cooked chicken, skinned, boned and diced
    (see Notes, this page)
15 ml/1 tablespoon coriander leaves
    to garnish

Microwave butter and onion on High for 3 minutes. Stir in curry powder. Microwave for a further minute. Stir in flour and mix well.

Slowly stir the mango liquid and hot chicken stock into the onion mixture. Microwave on High for 5 minutes, stirring after 3 minutes. Add sultanas, coconut, seasoning, chicken and chopped mangoes. Microwave on High for 6–8 minutes, until heated through. Garnish with coriander leaves. Serve with rice, poppadums, sliced bananas, chopped onion and tomato, and so on. SERVES 4.

TARRAGON CHICKEN

4 sprigs tarragon
45 ml/3 tablespoons butter
4 chicken breasts, boned
chicken spice to taste
10 ml/2 teaspoons butter
10 ml/2 teaspoons oil
150 ml/¼ pint double cream
salt and freshly ground black pepper
    to taste

Strip leaves from tarragon sprigs and chop finely. Cream butter and tarragon. Lift skin gently from chicken breasts to create a pocket. Stuff with tarragon butter. Pull skin over and tuck under each side of the chicken breast to form a parcel. Season with chicken spice.

Preheat a large browning dish on High for 8 minutes. Add butter and oil. Add chicken breasts, skin-side down. Microwave on High for 6–8 minutes, turning after 3–4 minutes, until cooked. Remove chicken and drain off oil in the dish. Stir in cream, salt and pepper. Microwave on Medium for 2 minutes. Pour sauce over chicken breasts and serve. SERVES 4.

CHICKEN CRUMBLE

Make this tasty dish with leftover chicken or start from scratch as described in the recipe. Serve with baked potatoes and a mixed salad.

CRUMBLE TOPPING
75 g/2½ oz wholemeal flour
75 g/2½ oz plain flour
salt and freshly ground black pepper to taste
75 g/2½ oz cold butter
50 g/1¾ oz cashew nuts, roughly chopped

CHICKEN MIXTURE
4 chicken breasts, skinned, boned and diced
chicken spice to taste
45 ml/3 tablespoons butter
1 onion, chopped
200 g/7 oz button mushrooms, sliced
45 ml/3 tablespoons plain flour
150 ml/¼ pint milk
150 ml/¼ pint hot Chicken Stock (page 21)
30 ml/2 tablespoons chopped mixed herbs (such as thyme, parsley, oregano and marjoram)
pinch of paprika

Combine the flours, salt and pepper. Add pieces of cold butter and rub into the flour until the mixture resembles fine breadcrumbs (or use a food processor — it's much easier!). Mix in the cashew nuts. Set aside.

Preheat a browning dish on High for 8 minutes. Pat chicken dry with paper towels. Dust with chicken spice. Add butter to the hot dish, then the chicken. Microwave on High for 4–5 minutes, stirring after 2–3 minutes, until cooked. Remove chicken. Add onion and microwave on High for 3 minutes. Add mushrooms and microwave for a further 3 minutes. Stir in the flour. Gradually blend in milk and stock. Add the herbs and microwave on High for 3 minutes until sauce thickens. Add chicken. Place chicken mixture in a pie dish, sprinkle with the crumble topping, dust with paprika and microwave on High for 8 minutes. SERVES 4.

COMBINATION OVEN: Bake at 200 °C and Medium microwave power level for 12 minutes (20–25 minutes if your oven alternates convection and microwave energy).

BOUQUET GARNI
Bouquet garni is traditionally a bunch of herbs tied together with string. The classic combination is three sprigs of parsley, a bayleaf and a sprig of thyme. The herbs may be varied to complement the food: instead of thyme use rosemary with lamb, sage with pork, basil with tomatoes and dill with fish.

CURRIED CHICKEN AND HAM PIE

WHOLEMEAL SHORTCRUST PASTRY
150 g/5½ oz butter
125 g/4½ oz wholemeal flour
125 g/4½ oz plain flour
pinch of salt
1 egg yolk
25 ml/5 teaspoons water

FILLING
30 ml/2 tablespoons butter
1 large onion, chopped
5 ml/1 teaspoon curry powder
2.5 ml/½ teaspoon turmeric
50 g/1¾ oz plain flour
300 ml/11 fl oz Chicken Stock (page 21)
125 ml/4½ fl oz milk
15 ml/1 tablespoon chopped parsley
5 ml/1 teaspoon chopped fresh mint
2.5 ml/½ teaspoon English mustard powder
pinch of crushed cardamom
10 ml/2 teaspoons lemon juice
salt and freshly ground black pepper to taste
2 hard-boiled eggs, chopped
125 g/4½ oz ham, diced
1 chicken, cooked and cut into chunks (see Notes, page 79)
pinch of paprika (optional)

Using a food processor, rub butter into the flours and salt until mixture is the consistency of fine breadcrumbs. Combine egg yolk with water and, with processor running, pour slowly through feed tube until pastry forms a ball. It should not be too damp. Cover with waxed paper and refrigerate for 30 minutes.

To make the filling, microwave butter and onion in a glass bowl for 3 minutes on High. Stir in curry powder, turmeric and flour; microwave for another minute. Add stock and milk; stir well. Microwave for 5 minutes, until mixture thickens. Add parsley, mint, mustard, cardamom, lemon juice and seasoning. Microwave for 2 minutes on High. Allow mixture to cool. Mix in chopped eggs, ham and chicken. Pour into a pie dish.

Roll out the pastry and place on top of the filling. Decorate with pastry leaves. Brush with beaten egg and dust with paprika, if desired. Microwave on Medium-High for 12–15 minutes. SERVES 6.

COMBINATION OVEN: Omitting the paprika, bake at 220 °C and Medium-Low microwave power level for 12–15 minutes (25–30 minutes if your oven alternates convection and microwave energy).

VARIATION: Replace the ham with about 200 g/7 oz chopped mushrooms.

CHICKEN AND HAM CROQUETTES WITH LEMON AND BASIL SAUCE

30 ml/2 tablespoons butter
30 ml/2 tablespoons plain flour
300 ml/11 fl oz milk
350 g/12 oz cooked chicken, finely chopped
  (see Notes, page 79)
100 g/3½ oz ham, finely chopped
5 ml/1 teaspoon Dijon mustard
45 ml/3 tablespoons grated Cheddar cheese
2 egg yolks, lightly beaten
salt and freshly ground black pepper to taste
10 ml/2 teaspoons chopped fresh mixed
  herbs or 5 ml/1 teaspoon dried
1 egg, lightly beaten
100 g/3½ oz seasoned dried breadcrumbs
30 ml/2 tablespoons oil

LEMON AND BASIL SAUCE
45 ml/3 tablespoons lemon juice
5 ml/1 teaspoon grated lemon zest
150 ml/¼ pint hot Chicken Stock (page 21)
10 ml/2 teaspoons cornflour
30 ml/2 tablespoons dry white wine
10 ml/2 teaspoons chopped fresh basil

Microwave butter for 30–40 seconds on High until melted. Stir in flour until well blended. Gradually stir in milk. Microwave on High for 4–5 minutes, until sauce thickens, stirring after 2 minutes.

Mix in the chicken, ham, mustard, cheese, egg yolks, salt, pepper and herbs. Spread the mixture in a large, shallow dish and refrigerate until cold — if possible overnight.

When cold and set, divide the mixture into eight equal portions. Roll into sausage shapes. Dip in egg and roll in breadcrumbs. Repeat.

Preheat a large browning dish on High for 8 minutes. Add the oil and the croquettes, and microwave on High for 4–5 minutes until cooked, turning after 2–3 minutes. Set aside.

To make the sauce, drain off the oil from the browning dish. Add the lemon juice and zest to the dish and scrape the base of the dish. Microwave on High for 1 minute. Add the stock. Mix the cornflour and wine into a paste and add, stirring well. Microwave on High for 2 minutes. Stir in the basil and microwave on High for a further 2 minutes. Pour over the croquettes and serve. SERVES 4.

VARIATION: Replace the ham with an equal quantity of finely chopped mushrooms.

Curried Chicken and Ham Pie (page 80) and Chicken Crumble (page 80).

CHICKEN ASPARAGUS

4 chicken breasts, skinned and boned
30 ml/2 tablespoons plain flour
30 ml/2 tablespoons butter
1 onion, finely chopped
410 g/14 oz canned green asparagus spears
75 ml/2½ fl oz dry white wine
45 ml/3 tablespoons low-fat milk
10 ml/2 teaspoons cornflour
20 ml/4 teaspoons grated Parmesan cheese
salt and freshly ground black pepper to taste

Preheat a browning dish on High for 8 minutes. Dust chicken with flour. Add butter to hot dish and swirl around. Add chicken breasts immediately and microwave on High for 3 minutes, turning halfway. Remove chicken and add onion to dish. Microwave on High for 3 minutes. Add asparagus (reserving a few spears for garnish), asparagus liquid and wine to onions, mix in chicken, cover and microwave on Medium-High for 12 minutes, until chicken is tender. Remove chicken and process sauce until smooth. Return to dish. Mix milk and cornflour to a paste and add to the purée to thicken it. Stir in cheese and seasoning. Place chicken in the sauce and microwave on Medium-High for 3–4 minutes until sauce is thick and heated through. Garnish with reserved asparagus spears. SERVES 4.

CHINESE ORANGE CHICKEN

4 chicken breasts, skinned and boned
15 ml/1 tablespoon dry sherry
15 ml/1 tablespoon thick, dark soy sauce
5 ml/1 teaspoon freshly grated ginger
15 ml/1 tablespoon sunflower oil
2 cloves garlic, crushed
100 g/3½ oz mangetout, trimmed
4 spring onions, sliced diagonally
1 red pepper, seeded and cut in julienne strips
60 g/2 oz salted peanuts, chopped
1 orange, cut into segments
5 ml/1 teaspoon grated orange zest
100 ml/3½ fl oz orange juice
12.5 ml/2½ teaspoons cornflour

Slice chicken breasts diagonally into thin strips, then halve. Marinate chicken in sherry, soy sauce and ginger for 2 hours. Preheat a large browning dish on High for 5 minutes. Add sunflower oil and chicken with the marinade. Microwave on High for 2 minutes, stirring after a minute. Add garlic, mangetout, spring onions, red pepper and peanuts. Microwave on High for 2 minutes. Add orange segments, zest and juice. Mix cornflour into a paste with a little water, add to the chicken mixture and microwave on High for 2 minutes until the sauce thickens. Serve with rice. SERVES 4.

Chinese Orange Chicken (this page) and Sweet and Sour Chicken (page 83).

SWEET AND SOUR CHICKEN

300 g/11 oz chicken breast fillets,
    skinned and cubed
10 ml/2 teaspoons butter
1 onion, chopped
100 ml/3½ fl oz tomato purée
125 ml/4½ fl oz orange juice
pinch of peri-peri powder
10 ml/2 teaspoons brown sugar
30 ml/2 tablespoons Worcestershire sauce
200 g/7 oz pineapple, chopped
salt and freshly ground black pepper to taste

Preheat a large browning dish on High for 8 minutes. Pat chicken pieces dry with paper towels and place with the butter in the hot dish. Microwave on High for 2 minutes, stirring after a minute. Add onion and microwave for a further 2 minutes. Stir in remaining ingredients, cover and microwave on Medium-High for about 8 minutes, until chicken is cooked. Serve on a bed of rice. SERVES 4.

CHICKEN AND VEGETABLE CASSEROLE

1 large onion, chopped
1 clove garlic, crushed
1 leek, sliced
2 carrots, peeled and sliced
2 sticks celery, sliced
3 tomatoes, peeled and chopped (see Hint,
    page 17)
5 ml/1 teaspoon dried mixed herbs
150 ml/¼ pint Chicken Stock (page 21)
750 g/1 lb 10 oz chicken thighs, skinned
200 g/7 oz button mushrooms, quartered
15 ml/1 tablespoon cornflour
salt and freshly ground black pepper to taste
20 ml/4 teaspoons chopped parsley

Microwave onion, garlic, leek, carrots, celery, tomatoes, herbs and stock in a deep casserole, covered, on High for 8 minutes. Add chicken and mushrooms, cover and microwave on Medium-Low for 30–35 minutes, until chicken is tender. To thicken the liquid, mix cornflour to a paste with a little water and stir into the casserole. Season with salt and pepper and microwave for a further 5 minutes to thicken. Sprinkle with parsley. SERVES 4.

COMBINATION OVEN: Prepare as above, until you have added the chicken and mushrooms to the vegetables, then cover and cook at 180 °C and Medium-Low microwave power level for 30 minutes (45 minutes if your oven alternates convection and microwave energy).

CHICKEN A LA KING

300 g/11 oz button mushrooms, sliced
45 ml/3 tablespoons butter
45 ml/3 tablespoons plain flour
500 ml/18 fl oz Chicken Stock (page 21)
250 ml/9 fl oz low-fat milk
salt and freshly ground black pepper to taste
1 cooked chicken, boned, skinned and diced
    (see Notes, page 79)
½ green pepper, seeded and diced
45 ml/3 tablespoons diced pimento or
    1 small red pepper, seeded and diced
45 ml/3 tablespoons sherry
15 ml/1 tablespoon chopped parsley to garnish

Microwave mushrooms and butter for 3 minutes on High. Stir in flour. Gradually blend in stock and milk. Microwave on High for 4–5 minutes until thickened, stirring halfway. Season, add chicken, green pepper, pimento or red pepper and sherry, and Heat through on High for 5 minutes. Sprinkle over parsley. SERVES 4.

CHICKEN RISOTTO

Risotto is a rice-based dish from northern Italy, and is usually served on its own with grated Parmesan on the side.

15 ml/1 tablespoon butter
1 bunch spring onions, sliced
1 stick celery, thinly sliced
200 g/7 oz button mushrooms, sliced
450 g/1 lb chicken breasts, skinned, boned
    and cubed
100 g/3½ oz rice
2 tomatoes, peeled and chopped (see Hint,
    page 17)
1 litre/1¾ pints hot Chicken Stock (page 21)
freshly ground black pepper to taste
100 g/3½ oz frozen peas
30 ml/2 tablespoons chopped parsley

Microwave butter, spring onions and celery in a large bowl on High for 3 minutes. Add mushrooms and microwave on High for 1½ minutes. Stir in chicken and rice and microwave on High for 2 minutes, stirring every 30 seconds. Add tomatoes, stock and pepper, cover and microwave on High for 20 minutes. Stir in peas and microwave for a further 5 minutes. Leave to stand, covered, for about 12 minutes, until the liquid is absorbed. Add parsley and fluff with a fork. SERVES 4.

VARIATION: Substitute 125 ml/4½ fl oz stock with the same quantity of dry white wine.

CHICKEN MARENGO

This dish, made famous by Napoleon, benefits from being made a day in advance — ideal to prepare ahead of time for guests.

> 200 g/7 oz rice
> 625 ml/1 pint 2 fl oz boiling water
> 5 ml/1 teaspoon salt
> 1 kg/2¼ lb chicken portions
> 5 ml/1 teaspoon chicken seasoning
> 15 ml/1 tablespoon sunflower oil
> 1 onion, sliced
> 125 ml/4½ fl oz dry white wine
> 2 cloves garlic, crushed
> 2.5 ml/½ teaspoon dried thyme
> 1 bayleaf
> 2 sprigs parsley
> 250 ml/9 oz hot Chicken Stock (page 21)
> 5 medium tomatoes, peeled and chopped (see Hint, page 17), or 410 g/14 oz canned tomatoes, chopped
> 10 pickling onions, peeled (see Hint, page 76)
> 300 g/11 oz brown mushrooms, sliced
> 15 ml/1 tablespoon butter
> 10 ml/2 teaspoons lemon juice
> 30 ml/2 tablespoons brandy
> 100 g/3½ oz black olives, stoned
> 30 ml/2 tablespoons chopped parsley

Place rice in a bowl with boiling water and salt, cover and microwave on High for 12 minutes. Leave to stand while you prepare the rest of the dish.

Preheat a large browning dish on High for 8 minutes. Pat chicken portions dry with a paper towel, season and place in the hot dish with oil. Microwave on High for 4 minutes, turning chicken after 2 minutes. Remove to a plate. Add onion to the dish and microwave on High for 3 minutes. Add wine, garlic, herbs, stock, tomatoes and chicken, cover and microwave on Medium-High for about 25 minutes. Set aside, covered.

Microwave the pickling onions, mushrooms and butter in a pie dish on High for 4–5 minutes. Stir in the lemon juice. Remove the chicken portions from the sauce. Fluff up rice and reheat, covered, on High for 5 minutes. Place chicken on top of rice. Add the pickling onions and mushrooms to the sauce with the brandy and microwave on High for 3–4 minutes, until piping hot. Pour over the chicken. Scatter over the olives and sprinkle with parsley. SERVES 4.

COMBINATION OVEN: Brown the chicken portions, then onions as above. Add the wine, garlic, herbs, stock, tomatoes and chicken, cover and cook at 200 °C and Medium microwave power level for 25 minutes (35–40 minutes if your oven alternates convection and microwave energy). Finish off dish as described above.

MUSTARD CHICKEN FRICASSEE

Mustard spices up many dishes from salads to stews. Grainy mustards add a savoury, crunchy bite, while creamy ones add smoothness and a tangy flavour. Some are flavoured with herbs such as tarragon or mixed herbs. Experiment with mustards — they are all fat-free!

> 1 onion, sliced
> 1 leek, sliced
> 30 ml/2 tablespoons butter
> 100 g/3½ oz button mushrooms, thickly sliced
> 1 kg/2¼ lb chicken pieces
> 30 ml/2 tablespoons plain flour
> 30 ml/2 tablespoons oil
> 150 ml/¼ pint Chicken Stock (page 21)
> 100 ml/3½ fl oz dry white wine
> 15 ml/1 tablespoon Dijon mustard
> 5 ml/1 teaspoon cornflour
> 75 ml/2½ fl oz low-fat plain yoghurt
> salt and freshly ground black pepper to taste
> 10 ml/2 teaspoons chopped tarragon

Microwave onion, leek and butter in a small bowl on High for 2 minutes. Stir in mushrooms and continue microwaving for another 2 minutes. Set aside.

Preheat a large browning dish for 8 minutes on High. Pat the chicken pieces dry with paper towels and dust with flour. As soon as the browning dish is ready, put oil and chicken in the dish. Microwave on High for 4 minutes, turning chicken after 2 minutes. Add the vegetable mixture, stock and wine to the chicken and mix well. Cover and microwave on Medium-High for about 25 minutes, then remove chicken pieces to a plate and keep warm.

Blend the mustard, cornflour and yoghurt together. Add to the vegetable mixture in the browning dish. Mix in seasoning and tarragon. Microwave on Medium-High for 4 minutes. Pour over the chicken and serve with brown rice and a salad. SERVES 4.

COMBINATION OVEN: Brown the chicken pieces as suggested above or in a frying pan on the hob. Proceed as above until vegetables, stock and wine are added to the chicken. Cook at 200 °C and Medium microwave power level for about 25 minutes (35–40 minutes if your oven alternates convection and microwave energy).

HINT
If you wish to double the quantities, double the time and deduct one third of the total time.

SHERRY CHICKEN AND MUSHROOMS

10 ml/2 teaspoons oil
10 ml/2 teaspoons butter
1 kg/2¼ lb chicken portions
1 onion, chopped
1 clove garlic, crushed
300 g/11 oz button mushrooms, sliced
15 ml/1 tablespoon chopped rosemary
    or 5 ml/1 teaspoon dried
125 ml/4½ fl oz Chicken Stock (page 21)
125 ml/4½ fl oz medium sherry
10 ml/2 teaspoons lemon juice
salt and freshly ground black pepper to taste
15 ml/1 tablespoon cornflour
100 ml/3½ fl oz low-fat plain yoghurt
30 ml/2 tablespoons chopped parsley

Preheat a large browning dish on High for 8 minutes. Add oil and butter to dish. Pat chicken dry with paper towels and place in the dish, skin-side down. Microwave on High for 4 minutes, turning after 2 minutes.

Remove chicken portions, add onion, garlic and mushrooms to the dish and microwave on High for 4 minutes. Stir in the rosemary, stock, sherry and lemon juice. Add chicken pieces and spoon the sauce over until pieces are well coated.

Cover dish and microwave on Medium-High for 25–30 minutes, stirring after 15 minutes. Season and thicken with cornflour mixed to a paste with a little water. Stir in the yoghurt. Microwave on Medium-Low for 4–5 minutes, until sauce thickens. Sprinkle over parsley. SERVES 4.

COMBINATION OVEN: Cook at 200 °C and Medium microwave power level for about 25 minutes (35–40 minutes if your oven alternates convection and microwave energy).

HINT: If you make this dish the day before, omit the cornflour, cool and refrigerate. When cold, skim off the fatty layer which forms on the surface. Reheat and then thicken with cornflour if necessary. Add yoghurt and sprinkle with parsley.

Sherry Chicken and Mushrooms (this page) and Chicken Marengo (page 84).

CHAPTER EIGHT

VEGETARIAN

VEGETARIAN food gives your body what is often a much-needed break from fatty animal proteins. In addition, many vegetable proteins are much cheaper than meat, don't require tedious chopping, and keep for months in the cupboard, so meals require less careful forethought.

NOTES

♦ Certain pulses cook very successfully in a microwave, saving much time, and these are included in the chart below. Pulses with very tough skins, such as red kidney beans, black beans, butter beans, cannelini beans and haricot beans are, however, better cooked conventionally.

♦ Cooking in large quantities is best done conventionally.

♦ Pulses weigh a little over double after cooking, so if a recipe requires 225 g/8 oz cooked beans, start off with 100 g/3½ oz dried beans.

♦ To speed up the presoaking, add 1 litre/1¾ pints boiling water to 225 g/8 oz dried beans, peas or lentils. Cover and microwave for 12–15 minutes on High. Soak for 2 hours. Drain. Rinse very well — this is believed to reduce flatulence!

♦ To save time use canned peas or beans, drained and rinsed.

COOKING BEANS AND LENTILS

Presoak the beans or lentils, then rinse and drain. Add boiling water and for 225 g/8 oz dry weight cook as follows:

TYPE	TIME (ON HIGH)	STANDING TIME*
Flageolet beans	40–45 minutes	15 minutes
Mung beans	30–35 minutes	10 minutes
Aduki beans	30–35 minutes	10 minutes
Black-eyed beans	25–30 minutes	10 minutes
Whole lentils	30–35 minutes	10 minutes
Split lentils**	25–30 minutes	10 minutes

*Add salt to beans or lentils before standing time.
**No presoaking needed.

COOKING CHICKPEAS

Pour 1 litre/1¾ pints boiling water over 200 g/7 oz dried chickpeas, picked over (grit removed). Cover and leave to soak for 30 minutes. Drain. Add 1 litre/1¾ pints boiling water. Cover and microwave on High for 45 minutes. Leave to stand until cool. Drain.

VEGETARIAN BOBOTIE

30 ml/2 tablespoons butter
2 onions, chopped
225 g/8 oz brown lentils, cooked (see Cooking Beans and Lentils, this page)
15 ml/1 tablespoon curry powder
10 ml/2 teaspoons garam masala
2 medium carrots, peeled and grated
15 ml/1 tablespoon yeast extract, dissolved in 30 ml/2 tablespoons warm water
1 egg, beaten
15 ml/1 tablespoon desiccated coconut
60 g/2 oz wholemeal breadcrumbs
15 ml/1 tablespoon apricot jam
5 ml/1 teaspoon turmeric
30 ml/2 tablespoons raisins
15 ml/1 tablespoon chutney
10 ml/2 teaspoons vinegar or lemon juice
salt and freshly ground black pepper to taste

TOPPING
2 eggs
125 ml/4½ fl oz buttermilk
salt and freshly ground black pepper to taste
4 bayleaves

Microwave butter and onions on High for 4 minutes. Add remaining ingredients, and mix in a little water if too dry. Place in a greased casserole and microwave on High for 8 minutes. Combine eggs, buttermilk and seasoning; pour over. Insert bayleaves and microwave on Medium-High for about 20 minutes. SERVES 4.

COMBINATION OVEN: Bake at 200 °C and Medium-Low microwave power level for 8 minutes. Add the topping and continue at the same settings for another 12–14 minutes, until topping is browned and set (12 minutes plus 20 minutes if your oven alternates convection and microwave energy).

LENTIL AND VEGETABLE PATTIES

125 g/4½ oz split red lentils
1 litre/1¾ pints boiling water
5 ml/1 teaspoon salt
6 wheat-flake breakfast bars, crushed
1 onion, finely chopped
1 stick celery, finely chopped
2 carrots, grated
60 g/2 oz almonds, toasted then ground
  (see Hint, page 100)
3 eggs
7.5 ml/1½ teaspoons salt
pinch of freshly ground black pepper
5 ml/1 teaspoon dried mixed herbs
30 ml/2 tablespoons oil

Place lentils in a large bowl and cover with boiling water. Cover and microwave on High for 25 minutes until the lentils are tender but not mushy. Add salt. Leave to stand for 10 minutes, then drain. Mix lentils with two thirds of the crushed cereal bars, the onion, celery, carrots, almonds, two of the eggs, salt, pepper and herbs, until thoroughly combined. Place remaining crushed cereal bars on a plate. Beat the third egg in a small, shallow dish. Form the lentil mixture into 8–10 balls with lightly floured hands, and flatten into patties. Dip in egg, then in cereal. Refrigerate for 30–60 minutes before cooking.

Preheat a browning dish on High for 8 minutes. Add oil and place patties in the dish. Microwave on High for 2 minutes. Turn over and microwave for 3–4 minutes, until browned and cooked. Repeat in batches. SERVES 4.

Lentil and Vegetable Patties (this page) and Sweet and Sour Courgettes (page 124).

Creamy Split Peas with Shredded Spinach (page 89), Black-eyed Beans with Tomato (page 89) and Bean and Vegetable Goulash (page 89).

BEAN AND VEGETABLE GOULASH

Serve with brown rice for a complete, balanced meal.

300 g/11 oz pumpkin, cubed
1 onion, chopped
1 clove garlic, crushed
10 ml/2 teaspoons oil
15 ml/1 tablespoon paprika
5 ml/1 teaspoon dried mixed herbs
4–5 tomatoes, peeled, seeded and chopped
   (see Hint, page 17)
200 g/7 oz black mushrooms, sliced
150 g/5½ oz black-eyed beans, cooked
   (see Cooking Beans and Lentils, page 86)
410 g/14 oz canned baked beans
440 g/1 lb canned pinto beans
45 ml/3 tablespoons plain yoghurt
salt and freshly ground black pepper to taste
15 ml/1 tablespoon chopped parsley to garnish

Place pumpkin in a pie dish. Cover and microwave on High for 8 minutes. Set aside.

In a large glass bowl, microwave the onion, garlic, oil and paprika on High for 3 minutes. Add the herbs, tomatoes and mushrooms to the onions and microwave on High for 4 minutes. Add the beans to the tomato mixture, with the pumpkin. Cover and microwave on High for about 8 minutes.

Stir in half of the yoghurt and season to taste. Drizzle over the remaining yoghurt. Sprinkle with parsley. Serve hot with brown rice (see Cooking Rice, page 118). SERVES 4–6.

BLACK-EYED BEANS WITH TOMATO

225 g/8 oz black-eyed beans,
   soaked overnight
1 large onion, chopped
2 cloves garlic, crushed
10 ml/2 teaspoons oil
2.5 ml/½ teaspoon dried thyme
5 ml/1 teaspoon dried oregano
100 ml/3½ fl oz Vegetable Stock (page 26)
3 tomatoes, peeled and chopped
   (see Hint, page 17)
30 ml/2 tablespoons tomato paste
10 ml/2 teaspoons soy sauce
salt and freshly ground black pepper to taste
250 g/9 oz pasta, cooked (see Cooking
   Pasta, page 108)
30 ml/2 tablespoons finely grated Parmesan
   cheese and 15 ml/1 tablespoon chopped
   fresh coriander leaves or parsley to garnish

Drain the beans and rinse them in a colander.

Microwave onion, garlic and oil in a large bowl on High for 3 minutes. Stir in the herbs, vegetable stock, tomatoes, tomato paste, soy sauce and black-eyed beans. Mix together thoroughly. Cover and microwave on High for 25 minutes. Leave to stand for about 10 minutes. Add salt and pepper, then spoon over pasta and sprinkle with cheese and parsley. SERVES 4.

CREAMY SPLIT PEAS WITH SHREDDED SPINACH

A tasty, economical dish that cooks up quickly.

200 g/7 oz split peas, rinsed
750 ml/1¼ pints hot Vegetable Stock (page 26)
5 ml/1 teaspoon turmeric
5 ml/1 teaspoon ground coriander
7.5 ml/1½ teaspoons salt
200 g/7 oz spinach, shredded
30 ml/2 tablespoons clarified butter (see Hint,
   page 17)
5 ml/1 teaspoon cumin seeds
pinch of asafoetida (see below) or
   garam masala
pinch of cayenne pepper
2.5 ml/½ teaspoon freshly squeezed
   lemon juice (see Hint, page 123)

Microwave split peas, stock, turmeric and coriander, covered, on High for 10 minutes, and on Medium for 20 minutes, until cooked. Add salt, then beat with an electric mixer until smooth and creamy.

Mix in the spinach and butter, and microwave for 6 minutes on High. Keep warm.

Preheat a browning dish on High for a few seconds. Add the cumin seeds, asafoetida or garam masala and cayenne pepper, and microwave on High for a further 20–30 seconds. Stir into the pea mixture with the lemon juice and serve. SERVES 4.

ASAFOETIDA

Asafoetida is a resinous substance which is obtained from the giant fennel plant. Widely used in vegetarian dishes from many parts of Asia, it is popularly believed to reduce flatulence. Asafoetida is generally used in its ground form; as it has a strong flavour, it is used sparingly. In its raw state, it has a repulsive smell because of its sulphur content, but this smell disappears during the cooking process. It can be bought at Indian spice shops.

RED KIDNEY BEANS WITH RICE

Brown rice and red kidney beans are both rich in fibre. The vegetables add flavour and a range of nutrients, while the nuts, beans and cheese provide protein.

1 onion, chopped
1 clove garlic, crushed
10 ml/2 teaspoons butter
300 g/11 oz courgettes, sliced
300 g/11 oz button mushrooms, sliced
250 g/9 oz tomatoes, peeled and
  chopped (see Hint, page 17)
200 g/7 oz brown rice
700 ml/1¼ pints hot Vegetable Stock
  (page 26)
410 g/14 oz canned red kidney beans,
  drained
50 g/1¾ oz cheese (such as
  Edam or mozzarella), grated, and
  75 g/2½ oz cashew nuts, toasted,
  to garnish (see Hint, page 100)

Microwave the onion, garlic and butter in a large glass bowl on High for 3 minutes. Stir in the courgettes and mushrooms and microwave on High for 3 minutes. Stir in the tomatoes, rice and stock, then cover and microwave on High for 30 minutes. Leave to stand for about 10 minutes.

Fluff rice with a fork and add the kidney beans. Cover and microwave on High for 3–4 minutes to heat through. Sprinkle cheese and nuts on top and serve with a green salad. SERVES 4.

CHICKPEA STEW

Chickpeas, also known as garbanzo beans, have a deliciously nutty flavour and a crunchy texture which makes them the feature of this tomato-based stew.

1 onion, chopped
1 clove garlic, crushed
1 stick celery, sliced
10 ml/2 teaspoons oil
2 potatoes, peeled and diced
1 carrot, peeled and diced
410 g/14 oz canned tomatoes,
  chopped, liquid reserved
10 ml/2 teaspoons chopped
  fresh basil or 5 ml/1 teaspoon dried
salt and freshly ground black pepper
  to taste
350 g/12 oz cooked chickpeas
  (see Cooking Chickpeas, page 86)

Microwave the onion, garlic, celery and oil in a large pie dish on High for 4 minutes. Add potatoes, carrot, tomatoes and their liquid, basil and pepper. Cover and microwave on High for 15–20 minutes, until the vegetables are soft. Add salt.

Stir in the chickpeas and microwave on High for 8 minutes to heat through. SERVES 4.

HINT: Fresh chickpeas are best (even though preparation takes longer), but to save time, use canned ones.

FETTUCINI WITH SPRING VEGETABLES

1 large leek, washed thoroughly and sliced
2 cloves garlic, crushed
1 bunch spring onions, sliced
200 g/7 oz button mushrooms, sliced
10 ml/2 teaspoons oil
pinch of cayenne pepper
100 g/3½ oz canned asparagus spears,
  diagonally sliced
100 g/3½ oz cauliflower florets
100 g/3½ oz broccoli florets
1 carrot, peeled and diced in small cubes
1 red pepper, seeded and sliced
60 g/2 oz yellow patty-pan squash, sliced
2 tomatoes, peeled and chopped (see Hint,
  page 17)
50 g/1¾ oz frozen peas
salt and freshly ground black pepper to taste
250 g/9 oz fettucini, cooked (see Cooking
  Pasta, page 108)
30 ml/2 tablespoons grated Parmesan cheese
30 ml/2 tablespoons chopped parsley to garnish

Microwave leek, garlic, spring onions, mushrooms, oil and cayenne pepper on High for 3 minutes. Stir in asparagus, cauliflower, broccoli, carrot, red pepper and squash. Cover and microwave on High for 5 minutes, stirring halfway. Add tomatoes, peas, salt and pepper. Cover and microwave for 5 minutes, until vegetables are tender-crisp. Spoon over hot fettucini, sprinkle with Parmesan cheese and garnish with parsley. SERVES 4.

HINT
For the best results, try to use vegetables that are in season, as these will be the freshest (and in some cases the cheapest!). Often vegetables can be substituted for each other — experiment to find out what works best for your palate and adapt accordingly. Variety is essential in a vegetarian diet, so this is a healthy way to eat too.

Red Kidney Beans with Rice (page 90) and Lentil and Vegetable Lasagne (page 113).

BUTTER BEAN BAKE

45 ml/3 tablespoons butter
50 g/1¾ oz plain or wholemeal flour
5 ml/1 teaspoon French mustard
salt and freshly ground black pepper to taste
875 g/2 lb canned butter beans, drained,
   liquid reserved
milk to make up liquid from butter beans
   to 400 ml/14 fl oz
125 g/4½ oz Cheddar cheese, grated
5 ml/1 teaspoon dried mixed herbs
50 g/1¾ oz wholemeal breadcrumbs
pinch of paprika

Microwave the butter on High for 1 minute. Stir in the flour, mustard, salt and pepper. Add the reserved liquid and milk gradually and mix well. Microwave on High for 5 minutes, stirring after 2 minutes, until sauce thickens. Add half the cheese, the herbs and butter beans. Check seasoning.

Pour into a greased casserole. Sprinkle with remaining cheese, breadcrumbs and paprika. Microwave on Medium-High for 10–12 minutes. SERVES 6.

COMBINATION OVEN: Cook at 200 °C and Medium-Low microwave power level for 12–14 minutes (20–25 minutes if your oven alternates convection and microwave energy).

Stuffed Peppers (page 93) and Cauliflower Loaf with Tomato Sauce (this page).

CAULIFLOWER LOAF WITH TOMATO SAUCE

1 medium cauliflower, broken into florets
30 ml/2 tablespoons water
salt to taste
250 ml/9 fl oz Cheese Sauce (page 93)
45 ml/3 tablespoons soured cream or plain yoghurt
3 eggs, separated
15 ml/1 tablespoon tomato paste
5 ml/1 teaspoon paprika
30 ml/2 tablespoons chopped parsley
5 ml/1 teaspoon salt

TOMATO SAUCE
3 tomatoes, peeled and chopped (see Hint, page 17)
30 ml/2 tablespoons butter or oil
salt and freshly ground black pepper to taste
15 ml/1 tablespoon chopped parsley
pinch of sugar
45 ml/3 tablespoons dry white wine

Microwave the cauliflower and water in a medium-sized bowl, covered, on High for 8–10 minutes, until cauliflower is tender-crisp. Add salt, leave to stand for 5 minutes then drain, reserving liquid. Mash or process cauliflower roughly.

Make up the cheese sauce, replacing some of the milk with reserved cauliflower liquid, then mix in cauliflower with the soured cream or yoghurt, egg yolks, tomato paste, paprika and parsley. Season.

Beat egg whites stiffly and fold gently into cauliflower mixture. Pour into a greased loaf pan. Microwave on a low rack on Medium-High for 10–12 minutes, until the centre is cooked (test with a skewer).

To make the tomato sauce, place all sauce ingredients in a pie dish and microwave on High for 8 minutes, until the sauce thickens slightly. Pour over slices of cauliflower loaf and serve. SERVES 4.

COMBINATION OVEN: Cook at 200 °C and Medium-Low microwave power level for 16–18 minutes (25–30 minutes if your oven alternates convection and microwave power).

CURRIED LENTIL AND ALMOND BAKE

200 g/7 oz brown lentils, soaked overnight
1 litre/1¾ pints boiling water
200 g/7 oz rice
100 g/3½ oz currants or raisins
grated zest of 1 lemon
15 ml/1 tablespoon butter
1 onion, chopped
10 ml/2 teaspoons curry powder
750 ml/1¼ pints hot Vegetable Stock (page 26)
75 g/2½ oz slivered almonds
salt to taste
50 g/1¾ oz finely shredded spinach leaves
250 ml/9 fl oz low-fat plain yoghurt

Microwave lentils and boiling water, covered, on High for 30 minutes. Drain well, mix in rice, currants or raisins and lemon zest and place in a casserole.

Microwave butter and onion on High for 3 minutes. Add curry powder and cook for another minute. Stir in stock, almonds and salt. Pour over rice mixture, cover and bake on Medium-High for 25–30 minutes. Microwave, uncovered, for another 10 minutes. Cool slightly. Stir in spinach. Top with yoghurt. SERVES 6.

COMBINATION OVEN: Cover and bake at 180 °C and Medium microwave power level for 25 minutes (35–40 minutes if your oven alternates convection and microwave energy).

CHEESE SAUCE

30 ml/2 tablespoons butter
30 g/1 oz plain flour
250 ml/9 fl oz milk
50 g/1¾ oz Cheddar cheese, grated
pinch of freshly grated nutmeg
salt and freshly ground black pepper to taste
2.5 ml/½ teaspoon prepared mustard

Microwave the butter on High for 50 seconds to melt it. Stir in the flour, then gradually add the milk. Microwave on High for 5–6 minutes, stirring twice. Stir in the cheese, then nutmeg, seasoning and mustard. MAKES ABOUT 250 ML/9 FL OZ.

HINT
To toast sesame seeds, preheat a browning dish on High for 2 minutes. Spread sesame seeds in the dish, then microwave on High for 2 minutes, stirring twice, until golden brown.

STUFFED PEPPERS

1 large onion, chopped
1 clove garlic, crushed
30 ml/2 tablespoons butter
150 g/5½ oz cooked rice (see Cooking Rice, page 118)
100 g/3½ oz pecan nuts, finely chopped
100 g/3½ oz chunky cottage cheese
salt and freshly ground black pepper to taste
2 small eggs, beaten
50 g/1¾ oz Cheddar cheese, grated
1 red pepper, halved and seeded
1 green pepper, halved and seeded
1 yellow pepper, halved and seeded
30 ml/2 tablespoons water
toasted sesame seeds (optional; see Hint, this page)

Microwave the onion, garlic and butter on High for 3 minutes. Mix in the rice, pecan nuts, cottage cheese, seasoning, eggs and Cheddar cheese. Spoon this mixture into the pepper halves.

Place stuffed peppers in a large pie dish. Pour water around the peppers. Microwave on Medium-High for 12–15 minutes. For a crunchy topping, sprinkle with toasted sesame seeds before serving. SERVES 6.

COMBINATION OVEN: Cook on 180 °C and Medium-Low microwave power level for 14–16 minutes (20–25 minutes if your oven alternates convection and microwave energy).

OKRA CURRY

450 g/1 lb okra
1 onion, chopped
1 clove garlic, crushed
15 ml/1 tablespoon oil
15 ml/1 tablespoon grated fresh ginger
5 ml/1 teaspoon chilli powder
5 ml/1 teaspoon turmeric
5 ml/1 teaspoon ground coriander
5 ml/1 teaspoon cumin
2 tomatoes, peeled and chopped (see Hint, page 17)
5 ml/1 teaspoon salt

Wash okra and dry with paper towels. Cut into rounds 1 cm/⅜ inch thick.

Microwave onion, garlic and oil in a medium-sized bowl on High for 3 minutes. Add okra and microwave for 3 minutes. Add spices and tomatoes. Microwave on Medium-High for 8–10 minutes. Add salt. Serve hot on a bed of rice. SERVES 4.

VEGETARIAN COTTAGE PIE

1 leek, finely sliced
15 ml/1 tablespoon olive oil
125 g/4½ oz carrot, grated
150 g/5½ oz courgettes, grated
75 g/2½ oz brown mushrooms,
  finely chopped
3 sticks celery, finely sliced
4 medium tomatoes, peeled and
  chopped (see Hint, page 17)
150 g/5½ oz cooked brown rice
  (see Cooking Rice, page 118)
10 ml/2 teaspoons chopped fresh basil
10 ml/2 teaspoons chopped fresh oregano
10 ml/2 teaspoons vegetable stock powder
salt and freshly ground black pepper
  to taste
1 kg/2¼ lb potatoes, peeled
250 ml/9 fl oz water
15 ml/1 tablespoon butter
125–250 ml/4½–9 fl oz milk

In a large glass bowl microwave the leek and olive oil on High for 2 minutes. Stir in the carrots, courgettes, mushrooms, and celery and microwave for a further 5 minutes on High. Add the tomatoes, cover and microwave on High for 6 minutes.

Add the rice, basil, oregano, stock powder and seasoning, and microwave on High for 4 minutes. Pour mixture into a casserole.

Cut the potatoes into quarters. Place in a large glass dish with the water, cover and microwave on High for 20 minutes, until tender. Leave to stand for 5 minutes, then drain. Mash with butter, salt to taste, and enough milk so that the desired consistency is reached. Spread mashed potato over vegetable mixture and microwave for 8 minutes on High. SERVES 6.

VARIATIONS:
♦ Sprinkle 100 g/3½ oz grated Cheddar cheese on top of the mashed potato.
♦ Replace some or all of the rice with cooked brown or red lentils (see Cooking Beans and Lentils, page 86).

HINT
If you are unsure whether or not a dish can be used in the microwave oven, fill it with water and microwave for a couple of minutes on High, until the water is hot. If the dish remains relatively cool, it is suitable for microwaving. If it heats up, this means that the material it is made of contains moisture that will interfere with the cooking time of the food, and it should not be used when timing is important.

BROCCOLI WITH SPICY BLACK-EYED BEAN SAUCE

A delightfully unusual dish that can be served either on its own or, for a more filling meal, as a main course accompanied by rice or pasta.

300 g/11 oz broccoli florets
4 spring onions, sliced
2 cloves garlic, crushed
5 ml/1 teaspoon grated fresh ginger
10 ml/2 teaspoons oil
100 g/3½ oz Black-eyed Beans with
  Tomato (page 89; sauce only)

Cover the broccoli florets with water and soak for 30 minutes. Microwave the spring onions, garlic, ginger and oil in a medium-sized bowl, covered, on High for 2 minutes.

Drain the broccoli and stir in the spring onion mixture. Cover and microwave on High for 5 minutes, until broccoli is tender-crisp. Stir in the bean sauce and microwave for a further 2 minutes. SERVES 4.

SWEETCORN CASSEROLE

This dish is simplicity itself — perfect for a cook in a hurry!

410 g/14 oz canned cream-style sweetcorn
30 ml/2 tablespoons plain flour, sifted
250 g/9 oz smooth cottage cheese (see page 7)
30 ml/2 tablespoons chopped parsley
2 eggs, beaten
pinch of freshly ground black pepper
2.5 ml/½ teaspoon dried thyme

Mix all ingredients together. Pour into a greased casserole, smooth the top and microwave on Medium-High for 12–14 minutes. SERVES 4–6.

COMBINATION OVEN: Bake at 200 °C and Medium-Low microwave power level for 20 minutes until the centre is cooked (30–35 minutes if your oven alternates convection and microwave energy).

RATATOUILLE BAKE

20 ml/4 teaspoons olive oil
2 onions, chopped
2 cloves garlic, crushed
4 courgettes, sliced
1 aubergine, cubed and dégorged
  (see Hint, page 99)
1 green pepper, seeded and chopped
50 g/1¾ oz black olives, pitted
1 bayleaf
5 ml/1 teaspoon chopped fresh oregano
15 ml/1 tablespoon chopped fresh basil or
  5 ml/1 teaspoon dried
2 large tomatoes, peeled and chopped
  (see Hint, page 17)
salt and freshly ground black pepper to taste
30 ml/2 tablespoons chopped parsley

TOPPING
225 g/8 oz yellow cornmeal
5 ml/1 teaspoon salt
500 ml/18 fl oz boiling water
2 eggs, separated

Microwave olive oil and onions on High for 5 minutes. Add all remaining ingredients except seasoning and parsley. Microwave, covered, on High for 5 minutes and on Medium for 15 minutes, until the vegetables are tender. Season, add parsley, and pour into a casserole.

To make the topping, add cornmeal and salt to the boiling water. Stir well, then microwave on High for 6 minutes, stirring a few times. Cover and microwave on High for 4 minutes. Beat egg yolks until pale lemon in colour. Stir into cornmeal. Beat egg whites until stiff, and fold in. Pour mixture over vegetables and microwave on Medium-High for 8 minutes. SERVES 4.

COMBINATION OVEN: Bake at 200 °C and Medium microwave power level for 12 minutes (20–25 minutes if your oven alternates convection and microwave energy).

STANDING TIME

Microwaved food continues to cook after you have removed it from the microwave oven. The denser the food, the longer it needs to stand.

Vegetarian Delight (page 111) and Ratatouille Bake (this page).

VEGETABLE PAELLA

15 ml/1 tablespoon sunflower oil
15 ml/1 tablespoon olive oil
1 onion, chopped
2 cloves garlic, crushed
3 sticks celery, sliced diagonally
200 g/7 oz brown rice
200 g/7 oz courgettes, sliced
100 g/3½ oz broccoli florets
200 g/7 oz button mushrooms
1 aubergine, dégorged and cubed
  (see Hint, page 99)
5 ml/1 teaspoon turmeric
5 ml/1 teaspoon chopped fresh basil
3 tomatoes, peeled and chopped
  (see Hint, page 17)
100 g/3½ oz frozen peas
625 ml/1 pint 2 fl oz Vegetable Stock (page 26)
salt and freshly ground black pepper to taste
30 ml/2 tablespoons chopped parsley, and
  any of the following to garnish:
  100 g/3½ oz cashew nuts, chopped; 100 g/
  3½ oz feta cheese, crumbled; 2 hard-boiled
  eggs, chopped; 50 g/1¾ oz olives

In a glass bowl microwave oils, onion, garlic and celery on High for 4 minutes. Stir in rice, courgettes, broccoli, mushrooms, aubergine, turmeric and basil. Microwave on High for 4 minutes. Add tomatoes, peas, stock and seasoning; mix well. Cover and microwave on High for 10 minutes and on Medium-High for 35–40 minutes, until liquid is absorbed. Garnish as suggested. SERVES 4.

VEGETABLE PIE WITH YOGHURT TOPPING

CRUST
75 g/2½ oz butter
30 ml/2 tablespoons chopped parsley
2 cloves garlic, crushed
125 g/4½ oz wholemeal breadcrumbs
50 g/1¾ oz toasted cashew nuts, finely chopped
  (see Hint, page 100)

FILLING
30 ml/2 tablespoons butter
3 leeks, sliced into rings
2 sticks celery, finely sliced
4 carrots, coarsely grated
200 g/7 oz button mushrooms, sliced
3 tomatoes, peeled and chopped
  (see Hint, page 17)
salt and freshly ground black pepper to taste
5 ml/1 teaspoon dried mixed herbs

TOPPING
5 ml/1 teaspoon custard powder
200 ml/7 fl oz plain yoghurt
1 egg, beaten
60 g/2 oz Cheddar cheese, grated
salt and freshly ground black pepper to taste
pinch of paprika

To make the crust, microwave butter, parsley and garlic in a medium-sized bowl on High for 1½ minutes. Stir in the breadcrumbs and nuts. Line a 23 cm/9 inch pie dish with the mixture, pressing down firmly. Refrigerate while you make the filling.

For the filling, microwave butter, leeks and celery on High for 4 minutes. Stir in carrots and mushrooms and microwave on High for 2 minutes. Stir in tomatoes, salt, pepper and herbs and microwave on High for 6 minutes. If necessary, thicken with 10 ml/ 2 teaspoons cornflour mixed to a paste with a little water. Pour filling into pie crust and smooth the top.

To make the topping, stir custard powder into yoghurt, and mix in egg, cheese, salt and pepper. Pour over the filling. Sprinkle paprika on top, and microwave on Medium for about 12 minutes. SERVES 4–6.

COMBINATION OVEN: Bake at 200 °C and Medium-Low microwave power level for 12–14 minutes, until firm (18–20 minutes if your oven alternates convection and microwave energy).

CARROT AND CASHEW LOAF

1 onion, finely chopped
1 stick celery, finely chopped
10 ml/2 teaspoons sunflower oil
185 g/6½ oz cooked brown rice
  (see Cooking Rice, page 118)
200 g/7 oz grated carrot
45 ml/3 tablespoons chopped fresh parsley
45 ml/3 tablespoons rice flour or soya flour
60 g/2 oz cashew nuts, chopped
2 eggs, beaten
salt and freshly ground black pepper to taste
10 ml/2 teaspoons olive oil

Microwave onion, celery and oil in a large glass bowl on High for 3 minutes. Mix in remaining ingredients and press into a greased loaf pan. Microwave on Medium-High for 12–14 minutes. SERVES 4.

COMBINATION OVEN: Bake at 200 °C and Medium-Low microwave power level for 12–14 minutes (20–25 minutes if your oven alternates convection and microwave energy).

Vegetable Paella (page 96).

STUFFED AUBERGINES

*Aubergines are very low in calories if they are not fried.
They cook extremely well in a microwave.*

3 medium aubergines
salt
10 ml/2 teaspoons sunflower oil
10 ml/2 teaspoons butter or olive oil
1 large onion, chopped
100 g/3½ oz button mushrooms, sliced
2.5 ml/½ teaspoon dried thyme
2.5 ml/½ teaspoon dried oregano
185 g/6½ oz brown rice (see Cooking Rice,
    page 118)
250 g/9 oz smooth cottage cheese (see page 7)
30 ml/2 tablespoons snipped fresh chives
    or chopped parsley
100 g/3½ oz Cheddar cheese, grated
freshly ground black pepper to taste
pinch of paprika

Halve aubergines and scoop out flesh, leaving a thick shell. Chop flesh roughly. Dégorge by sprinkling shells and flesh with salt and leaving for 30 minutes. Rinse off the bitter juices, drain, and pat dry with paper towels.

Microwave the sunflower oil, butter or olive oil and onion on High for 2 minutes. Stir in mushrooms and herbs and microwave for a further 2 minutes. Mix in the aubergine flesh and microwave, covered, on High for 4–5 minutes, until tender.

Mix rice, cottage cheese, chives or parsley, half the Cheddar cheese and the black pepper into the aubergine and mushroom mixture. Pile into the aubergine shells. Sprinkle over remaining cheese and paprika. Place the stuffed aubergines in a large pie dish. Cover lightly with cling film and microwave on Medium-High for 14–15 minutes. SERVES 6.

COMBINATION OVEN: Bake at 200 °C and Medium-Low microwave power level for 12–14 minutes (25–30 minutes if your oven alternates convection and microwave energy).

CHEESY BAKED AUBERGINE

1 onion
15 ml/1 tablespoon oil
3 tomatoes, peeled and chopped (see Hint, page 17)
pinch of sugar
salt and freshly ground black pepper to taste
30 ml/2 tablespoons shredded basil leaves
oil for frying
2 aubergines, unpeeled, sliced lengthwise and dégorged (see Hint, page 99)

CHEESE CUSTARD
200 g/7 oz ricotta cheese
75 g/2½ oz grated Parmesan cheese
3 eggs, beaten
250 ml/9 fl oz cream
pinch of paprika

Microwave the onion and oil in a large pie dish on High for 3 minutes. Add tomatoes, sugar and seasoning. Microwave on High for about 12 minutes until a thick purée is formed. Add basil. Preheat a browning dish on High for 6 minutes. Add oil and fry aubergine slices in batches for 1 minute on each side. Place on paper towels to absorb excess oil. Layer aubergine slices in a casserole, alternating with layers of tomato mixture.

To make the topping, combine ricotta and Parmesan cheeses, then stir in eggs and cream until mixture has a pouring consistency. Pour topping over the vegetables and dust with paprika. Microwave on Medium-High for 10–12 minutes, until topping has set. SERVES 4.

COMBINATION OVEN: Bake at 200 °C and Medium-Low microwave power level for 14–16 minutes (25–30 minutes if your oven alternates convection and microwave energy) until the topping is golden brown and firm.

Tomato Vegetable Curry (page 99), Apple and Celery Sambal (page 99) and Salsa (page 99).

CHEESY VEGETABLE CASSEROLE

1 potato, peeled and thinly sliced
1 red onion, thinly sliced
4 courgettes, sliced
2 large carrots, peeled and thinly sliced
4 small squash, sliced
freshly ground black pepper to taste
200–225 g/7–8 oz Cheddar or Gruyère
    cheese, grated
30 ml/2 tablespoons butter
125 ml/4½ fl oz plain yoghurt or soured cream

Layer the vegetables in a large casserole, sprinkle with black pepper and top with cheese. Dot with butter and pour yoghurt or cream over. Microwave, covered, on Medium-High for 17 minutes. Uncover and microwave on Medium-High for another 5 minutes. SERVES 4.

COMBINATION OVEN: Cook at 180 °C and Medium-Low microwave power level for 12-14 minutes (18-20 minutes if you oven alternates convection and microwave energy).

TOMATO VEGETABLE CURRY

2 large onions, sliced
4 cloves garlic, crushed
1 green or red pepper, seeded and diced
45 ml/3 tablespoons oil
20–25 ml/4–5 teaspoons curry powder
7.5 ml/1½ teaspoons garam masala
30 ml/2 tablespoons tomato paste
5 tomatoes, peeled, chopped and drained
    (see Hint, page 17)
1 bayleaf
100 ml/3½ fl oz hot Vegetable Stock (page 26)
    or yeast extract stock
2 large potatoes, peeled and diced
2 carrots, peeled and sliced
4 courgettes, sliced
2 small aubergines or 1 large, dégorged and
    cubed (see Hint, this page)

Microwave onion, garlic, green or red pepper and oil on High for 5–6 minutes, until onions are soft. Mix in curry powder and garam masala; microwave on High for 2 minutes. Stir in tomato paste, tomatoes, bayleaf, stock, potatoes and carrots, cover and microwave on High for 8–10 minutes, until potatoes and carrots are soft. Add courgettes and aubergines. Microwave, uncovered, on High for 5–6 minutes, until cooked. Serve with basmati rice (see Cooking Rice, page 118), Sambals (this page) and poppadums. SERVES 4–6.

SALSA

Serve as a side dish to a vegetable curry.

4 large tomatoes, peeled, seeded
    and chopped (see Hint, page 17)
45 ml/3 tablespoons spring onions,
    finely chopped
⅓ cucumber, seeded and diced
¼ green pepper, seeded and diced
¼ yellow pepper, seeded and diced
30 ml/2 tablespoons chopped fresh
    coriander, chives or parsley
salt and freshly ground black pepper
    to taste
5 ml/1 teaspoon sugar
1–2 green chillies, seeded and finely
    chopped, or a dash of Tabasco sauce
10 ml/2 teaspoons lemon juice
15 ml/1 tablespoon olive oil
1 avocado
fresh coriander leaves to garnish

Combine all ingredients except avocado. Cover and marinate for 1 hour in refrigerator. Drain off any liquid. Just before serving, peel and cube the avocado, and add to the dish. Garnish with coriander leaves. SERVES 6.

HINT
To dégorge an aubergine, peel and chop into cubes, then place in a colander. Sprinkle generously with salt and leave to stand for 30 minutes to draw bitter juices. Wash well under cold water, then pat dry.

SAMBALS

These side dishes add interest to a curried main dish, as well as providing some cooling relief to your palate!

♦ Cucumber: Chop one third of a cucumber into cubes. Sprinkle with salt and leave to drain for about 30 minutes, then rinse and pat dry with paper towels. Mix with enough yoghurt to bind and sprinkle with chopped mint.
♦ Banana: Slice bananas and toss in lemon juice.
♦ Onion, Green Pepper and Tomato: Finely chop 1 onion, 1 green pepper and 1 tomato and combine.
♦ Apple and Celery: Mix together 2 apples (with their skin, cored, cubed, and tossed in lemon juice), 2 sticks of celery, sliced, a handful of chopped dates, 30 ml/ 2 tablespoons plain yoghurt, and a pinch of ground nutmeg. SERVES 6.

NUT AND VEGETABLE LOAF

This crunchy loaf goes a long way, and leftover slices make wonderful lunch box fillers.

15 ml/1 tablespoon butter or oil
3 sticks celery, finely sliced
1 large onion, chopped
1 clove garlic, crushed
350 g/12 oz carrots, finely grated
60 g/2 oz fresh wholemeal breadcrumbs
50 g/1¾ oz ground almonds
150 g/5½ oz cashew nuts, finely chopped
salt and freshly ground black pepper to taste
2 eggs, beaten
250 g/9 oz smooth cottage cheese (see page 7)
15 ml/1 tablespoon chopped parsley
5 ml/1 teaspoon chopped fresh thyme or
    2.5 ml/½ teaspoon dried

Microwave butter or oil, celery and onion in a large glass bowl on High for 3 minutes. Stir in garlic and carrots. Cover and microwave on High for 4 minutes. Mix in remaining ingredients.

Grease a 1 kg/2¼ lb loaf pan and line the base with waxed paper. Spoon the mixture into the pan and microwave on Medium-High for 12–14 minutes until a metal skewer inserted in the middle comes out clear. Turn out on to a serving platter. Allow to cool slightly, then slice. SERVES 4–6.

COMBINATION OVEN: Bake at 200 °C and Medium-Low microwave power level for 12–14 minutes (20–25 minutes if your oven alternates convection and microwave energy).

HINT

To toast nuts, spread whole, chopped or flaked nuts in a shallow pie dish and microwave on High for 2–3 minutes (depending on the quantity and the kind of nut used), until they are a pale golden brown, stirring twice. Allow to cool before using.

SAVOURY BUCKWHEAT

1 onion, chopped
1 clove garlic, crushed
2 sticks celery, sliced
10 ml/2 teaspoons oil
pinch of ground cumin
10 ml/2 teaspoons garam masala
5 ml/1 teaspoon turmeric
150 g/5½ oz buckwheat
250 ml/9 fl oz hot Vegetable Stock (page 26)
2 carrots, peeled and diced
½ red pepper, seeded and diced
10 ml/2 teaspoons tomato paste
3 courgettes, sliced
salt and freshly ground black pepper
    to taste

Microwave onion, garlic, celery and oil in a glass bowl on High for 4 minutes. Stir in spices and microwave for a further 30 seconds. Stir in buckwheat, stock, carrots, red pepper and tomato paste. Cover and microwave on High for 12–15 minutes. Make sure mixture is not too dry — buckwheat should be soft and chewy. Add courgettes and seasoning. Cover and microwave for a further 5 minutes. Serve with a tossed salad. SERVES 4.

SUNFLOWER CASSEROLE

Add a touch of colour to this nutritious dish by serving it with a fresh green salad.

2 onions, chopped
15 ml/1 tablespoon oil
300 g/11 oz button mushrooms,
    roughly chopped
125 g/4½ oz chopped sunflower seeds
125 g/4½ oz bean sprouts
185 g/6½ oz canned butter beans, drained
200 g/7 oz millet, cooked (see Cooking
    Grains, page 118)
5 ml/1 teaspoon chilli powder

Microwave onions and oil in a large bowl on High for 5 minutes. Add mushrooms. Microwave for a further 3 minutes. Mix in sunflower seeds, bean sprouts, butter beans, millet and chilli powder, then spoon mixture into a casserole and microwave on High for 8 minutes. SERVES 4–6.

COMBINATION OVEN: Bake at 200 °C and Medium microwave power level for 12 minutes (20 minutes if your oven alternates convection and microwave energy).

CHEESY MUSHROOM AND RICE DISH

300 g/11 oz brown rice
5 ml/1 teaspoon salt
800 ml/1 pint 8 fl oz hot Vegetable Stock
   (page 26)
10 ml/2 teaspoons chopped fresh tarragon
   or 5 ml/1 teaspoon dried
300 g/11 oz brown mushrooms, sliced
1 green pepper, seeded and diced
10 ml/2 teaspoons oil
10 ml/2 teaspoons butter
30 ml/2 tablespoons soy sauce
freshly ground black pepper to taste
50 g/1¾ oz chopped fresh parsley
45 ml/3 tablespoons chopped spring onions
30 ml/2 tablespoons snipped fresh chives
75g/2½ oz Cheddar cheese, grated

Microwave rice, salt, stock and tarragon in a large
glass bowl, covered, on High for 12 minutes, then on
Medium for 25–30 minutes. Leave to stand for
10 minutes. The liquid should then be absorbed.

Microwave mushrooms, green pepper, oil and butter
on High for 3–4 minutes, until vegetables soften. Add
soy sauce and pepper. Cover and stand until rice is ready.

Fork through rice and fold in the mushroom
mixture, adding all the juices. Add the parsley, spring
onions and chives. Sprinkle the cheese on top and
microwave on High for 4–5 minutes, until heated
through. SERVES 4–6.

RICE MEDLEY

*Brown rice is rich in fibre and contains protein, calcium, iron
and vitamin B₁. With the addition of vegetables this is a
nutritious meal in itself, or serve it cold as a salad for a buffet.*

30 ml/2 tablespoons butter
1 onion, chopped
1 clove garlic, crushed
200 g/7 oz brown rice
700 ml/1¼ pints hot Vegetable Stock (page 26)
2 sticks celery, sliced
100 g/3½ oz button mushrooms, sliced
100 g/3½ oz whole kernel sweetcorn
   (fresh, frozen or canned)
15 ml/1 tablespoon butter
3 tomatoes, peeled and chopped
   (see Hint, page 17)
15 ml/1 tablespoon chopped parsley
50 g/1¾ oz dates, chopped
50 g/1¾ oz toasted cashew nuts, chopped
   (see Hint, page 100)

Microwave the 30 ml/2 tablespoons butter, onion and
garlic in a large glass bowl on High for 3 minutes. Stir
in rice and stock. Cover and microwave on Medium-
High for 25 minutes. Set aside — without uncovering!

Microwave celery, mushrooms, sweetcorn and the
15 ml/1 tablespoon butter on High for 3 minutes. Stir
into the rice with a fork. Stir in tomatoes, parsley and
dates. Sprinkle nuts on top. SERVES 4.

Cheesy Mushroom and Rice Dish (this page) and Nut and Vegetable Loaf (page 100).

NUTTY CHEESE DOLMADES

Serve these with a cheese and onion sauce. Delicious!

8 large Chinese cabbage leaves
100 ml/3½ fl oz Vegetable Stock (page 26)

FILLING
90 g/3¼ oz cooked brown rice
  (see Cooking Rice, page 118)
60 g/2 oz Cheddar cheese, finely grated
60 g/2 oz pecan nuts, chopped
15 ml/1 tablespoon chopped fresh parsley
15 ml/1 tablespoon snipped fresh chives
30 g/1 oz butter, melted
1 egg

SAUCE
1 onion, chopped
30 ml/2 tablespoons butter
30 ml/2 tablespoons plain flour
300 ml/11 fl oz milk mixed with liquid
  from the cabbage rolls
60 g/2 oz Cheddar cheese, grated
salt and freshly ground black pepper
  to taste

Wash the cabbage leaves and place them wet in a large plastic bag. Tie a loose knot to close the bag and microwave on High for about 2 minutes, until wilted. Reserve liquid for sauce.

Combine the filling ingredients, form into balls the size of golf balls, and place one in the middle of each cabbage leaf. Fold the sides over and roll leaves up so that the filling is enclosed. Place the rolls, seam-side down, in a casserole. Pour over the stock. Cover and microwave on High for 8–10 minutes. Drain off the liquid and use in the sauce.

To make the sauce, microwave the onion and butter in a medium-sized bowl on High for 3 minutes. Stir in the flour and blend well. Gradually stir in the milk and cabbage liquid, then microwave on High for 4–5 minutes, until the sauce has thickened, stirring a few times. Stir in the cheese and seasoning, pour the sauce over the cabbage rolls and reheat for 3–4 minutes on 100%. SERVES 4.

BARLEY AND VEGETABLE STEW WITH DUMPLINGS

30 ml/2 tablespoons butter
200 g/7 oz leeks, washed thoroughly
  and sliced
1 clove garlic, crushed
200 g/7 oz pearl barley, presoaked
  for 1 hour, drained and rinsed
200 g/7 oz potatoes, peeled
  and cubed
200 g/7 oz carrots, peeled and
  thinly sliced
200 g/7 oz courgettes, sliced
200 g/7 oz turnips, peeled and cubed
750 ml/1¼ pints hot Vegetable Stock
  (page 26)
200 g/7 oz button mushrooms, halved
200 g/7 oz broccoli florets
salt and freshly ground black pepper
  to taste
5 ml/1 teaspoon dried mixed herbs
15 ml/1 tablespoon cornflour

HERB DUMPLINGS
75 g/2½ oz butter
125 g/4½ oz wholemeal flour
45 g/1½ oz plain flour
5 ml/1 teaspoon baking powder
pinch of salt
5 ml/1 teaspoon dried mixed herbs
1 egg, beaten
125 ml/4½ fl oz milk

Microwave butter, leeks and garlic in a large bowl on High for 3 minutes. Stir in the drained pearl barley, potatoes, carrots, courgettes and turnips. Microwave on High for 5 minutes, stirring a few times during cooking time. Add half the stock. Cover and microwave on High for 10 minutes.

Add remaining stock, mushrooms, broccoli and pepper. Mix well, then cover and microwave on Medium-High for 10–15 minutes. While this is cooking, prepare the dumplings.

To make the dumplings, rub the butter into the dry ingredients until the mixture resembles fine bread-crumbs (for quicker results, you could use a food processor to do this). Mix in the herbs. Slowly add egg and milk until the mixture forms a soft dough. Drop spoonfuls of dumpling mixture, the size of golf balls, on to the stew, then microwave for a further 15 minutes on Medium-High.

When cooked, vegetables should be tender. Stir in salt and herbs. Mix cornflour to a paste with a little water and stir into the stew. Microwave for a further 2–3 minutes, until stew has thickened. SERVES 4.

Barley and Vegetable Stew with Dumplings (page 102).

BARLEY AND LENTIL DISH

1 onion, chopped
2 sticks celery, sliced
15 ml/1 tablespoon olive oil
2 potatoes, peeled and diced
2 carrots, peeled and diced
100 g/3½ oz pearl barley, presoaked
   for 1 hour
100 g/3½ oz split red lentils, washed
   and drained
250 ml/9 fl oz tomato juice
10 ml/2 teaspoons dried mixed herbs
salt and freshly ground black pepper
   to taste

Microwave the onion, celery and oil on High for
3 minutes. Stir in potatoes and carrots and microwave,
covered, on High for 5 minutes. Stir in the pearl
barley, lentils, tomato juice and herbs, cover and
microwave on High for 25–30 minutes, until tender.
Season. Leave to stand for 10 minutes, covered, then
serve. SERVES 4.

RICE AND LENTILS

200 g/7 oz brown rice
200 g/7 oz split red lentils
grated zest and juice of 1 lemon (see Hint,
   page 123)
1 litre/1¾ pints hot Vegetable Stock (page 26)
50 g/1¾ oz currants
100 g/3½ oz dried apricots, chopped
15 ml/1 tablespoon butter
5 ml/1 teaspoon curry powder
1 large red apple, cored and diced
50 g/1¾ oz pine nuts or cashews, chopped
30 ml/2 tablespoons chopped coriander leaves

Place rice and lentils in a deep dish with lemon zest,
juice and stock. Cover and microwave on High for
5 minutes, then on Medium High for 25 minutes.
Add currants and apricots. Microwave, covered, for
5 minutes on Medium-High. Microwave butter, curry
powder, apple and nuts in a small bowl on High for
2–3 minutes, stirring twice. Stir into rice mixture. Add
coriander leaves. Serve hot or cold. SERVES 4.

STIR-FRIED VEGETABLES

45 ml/3 tablespoons sesame seeds
15 ml/1 tablespoon sunflower oil
2 medium carrots, cut in julienne strips
2 sticks celery, cut diagonally
½ red pepper, seeded and cut in
    julienne strips
1 small onion, sliced
100 g/3½ oz broccoli florets
1 orange, cut into segments
30 ml/2 tablespoons soy sauce
10 ml/2 teaspoons freshly grated ginger
1 clove garlic, crushed
150 ml/¼ pint hot Vegetable Stock (page 26)
15 ml/1 tablespoon cornflour
30 ml/2 tablespoons bean sprouts

Preheat a large browning dish on High for 2 minutes. Spread sesame seeds in the dish and microwave on High for 1 minute, stirring twice, then remove. Wipe the dish clean, then heat it for a further 5 minutes. Add oil and microwave for another minute. Add carrots, celery, red pepper, onion and broccoli. Microwave on High for 4 minutes, stirring twice. Add orange segments, soy sauce, ginger and garlic. Mix stock and cornflour into a paste and add. Microwave on High for 3–4 minutes until mixture thickens. Stir in sesame seeds and bean sprouts. Serve on a bed of hot rice. SERVES 2.

POTATOES PROVENCALS

8 potatoes, peeled and thinly sliced
125 ml/4½ fl oz Chicken Stock (page 21)
2 onions, chopped
15 ml/1 tablespoon butter
3 cloves garlic, crushed
5 ml/1 teaspoon sugar
6 tomatoes, peeled and sliced (see Hint, page 17)
12 basil leaves
salt and freshly ground black pepper to taste
500 g/1 lb 2 oz spinach, tough stalks removed
25 ml/5 teaspoons butter
250 ml/9 fl oz double cream

Parboil potatoes with the stock in a medium-sized glass bowl, covered, on High for 8 minutes.

Microwave onions and butter in a small bowl on High for 3–4 minutes. Stir in garlic and microwave for another minute. Sprinkle sugar over the tomatoes.

Layer half the potatoes with the onions in a large, buttered casserole and sprinkle with salt and pepper. Layer tomatoes on top, cover with basil leaves and season. Cover with a thick layer of spinach. Layer the remaining potatoes and onions on top, dot with butter, and season. Cover and microwave on High for 10 minutes. Remove cover, then pour the cream over the vegetables and microwave for 15–20 minutes on Medium. SERVES 8.

Bean and Nut Loaf (page 105) and Stir-fried Vegetables (this page).

BEAN AND NUT LOAF

1 onion, chopped
15 ml/1 tablespoon butter
100 g/3½ oz fresh wholemeal breadcrumbs
10 ml/2 teaspoons chopped fresh sage or
   5 ml/1 teaspoon dried sage
salt and freshly ground black pepper to taste
125 ml/4½ fl oz low-fat milk
410 g/14 oz baked beans in tomato sauce
2 eggs, lightly beaten
30 ml/2 tablespoons low-fat plain yoghurt
100 g/3½ oz cashew nuts, chopped

Microwave the onion and butter on High for 3 minutes. Mix in the breadcrumbs, sage, seasoning and milk. Set aside for 10 minutes. Gently mix in the beans and their sauce, eggs, yoghurt and nuts.

Grease and line the base of a 1 kg/1 lb 2 oz loaf pan with waxed paper, pour in the mixture and level the top. Microwave on Medium-High for 14–15 minutes, until a metal skewer inserted in the middle comes out clean. Turn out carefully on to a serving platter. Serve hot or cold in slices. SERVES 6.

VARIATION: Instead of the nuts, use 100 g/3½ oz low-fat cheese such as Edam or mozzarella.

COMBINATION OVEN: Bake at 200 °C and on Medium microwave power level for 14–16 minutes (or for 25–30 minutes if your oven alternates convection and microwave power).

FRUITY VEGETABLE CURRY

1 onion, chopped
2 sticks celery, sliced
10 ml/2 teaspoons sunflower oil
10–15 ml/2–3 teaspoons curry powder,
   to taste
5 ml/1 teaspoon freshly grated ginger
10 ml/2 teaspoons lemon juice
100 g/3½ oz dried apricots, chopped
2 bananas, sliced
3 apples, peeled, cored and sliced
pinch of salt
200 ml/7 fl oz Vegetable Stock (page 26)
100 ml/3½ fl oz low-fat plain yoghurt

Microwave the onion, celery and oil on High for 3 minutes. Stir in the curry powder, ginger, lemon juice, fruit, salt and stock. Cover and microwave on High for 8–10 minutes. Stir in the yoghurt and serve on a bed of brown rice. SERVES 4.

VEGETABLE STROGANOFF

2 onions, chopped
1 clove garlic, crushed
2 sticks celery, sliced
2 carrots, peeled and thinly sliced
15 ml/1 tablespoon oil
300 g/11 oz button mushrooms, sliced
3 courgettes, sliced
100 g/3½ oz frozen peas
1 red pepper, seeded and sliced
100 g/3½ oz butternut squash, cubed
3 yellow patty-pan squash, sliced
250 ml/9 fl oz hot Vegetable Stock (page 26)
15 ml/1 tablespoon chopped fresh herbs or
   5 ml/1 teaspoon dried mixed herbs
salt and freshly ground black pepper
   to taste
10 ml/2 teaspoons cornflour
125 ml/4½ fl oz soured cream
15 ml/1 tablespoon sesame seeds and
   30 ml/2 tablespoons chopped parsley
   to garnish

Microwave the chopped onion, garlic, celery, carrots and oil in a large bowl on High for 5 minutes, stirring after 2–3 minutes. Stir in mushrooms, courgettes, peas, red pepper, butternut and patty-pan squash. Microwave on High for 3 minutes, stirring halfway through cooking time.

Pour the stock over the vegetable mixture and sprinkle with herbs. Microwave, covered, on High for 8 minutes, until vegetables are tender-crisp. Season. Mix cornflour to a paste with a little water and stir into vegetables. Microwave on High for 2 minutes, until thickened. Stir in soured cream. Microwave on Medium-High for 1½ minutes to heat through, and serve on a bed of brown rice (see Cooking Rice, page 118), topped with sesame seeds and parsley. SERVES 4.

HINT
If you wish to add salt to vegetables, add it after cooking otherwise the vegetables may become tough and lose their natural flavour.

BROCCOLI NUT BAKE

High in fibre and vitamin C, broccoli is an excellent food.

400 g/14 oz broccoli florets
30 ml/2 tablespoons water
30 ml/2 tablespoons butter
30 ml/2 tablespoons plain flour
300 ml/11 fl oz milk
salt and freshly ground black pepper to taste
200 g/7 oz Cheddar cheese, grated
3 eggs, beaten
5 ml/1 teaspoon chopped fresh tarragon
30 g/1 oz toasted flaked almonds (see Hint, page 100)
pinch of paprika

Microwave broccoli and water on High for 6 minutes. Leave to stand for 3 minutes then drain, reserving liquid.

Microwave butter for 30–40 seconds, until melted. Blend in flour. Gradually stir in milk and reserved broccoli liquid. Add seasoning. Microwave on High for 4–5 minutes, stirring halfway, until sauce thickens. Add half the cheese, the eggs, tarragon, nuts and broccoli. Pour into a casserole. Sprinkle with remaining cheese and dust with paprika. Microwave on Medium-High for 12–14 minutes, until centre is set. SERVES 6.

COMBINATION OVEN: Bake at 200 °C and Medium-Low microwave power level for 14–16 minutes (20–25 minutes if your oven alternates convection and microwave energy).

VEGETABLE CRISP

15 ml/1 tablespoon butter
2 potatoes, thinly sliced
1 red onion, thinly sliced
4 courgettes, sliced
2 large carrots, thinly sliced
4 patty pan squash, sliced
200 ml/7 fl oz hot Vegetable Stock (page 26)
5 ml/1 teaspoon chopped fresh mixed herbs or a pinch of dried
salt and freshly ground black pepper to taste
15 ml/1 tablespoon cornflour

TOPPING
75 g/2½ oz butter
60 g/2 oz fresh wholemeal breadcrumbs
75 g/2½ oz rolled oats
2.5 ml/½ teaspoon salt
15 ml/1 tablespoon chopped parsley
100 g/3½ oz Cheddar cheese, grated

Microwave butter, potatoes, onion, courgettes and carrots in a medium-sized bowl on High for 6 minutes, stirring a few times. Add squash, stock, herbs, salt and pepper. Cover and microwave on High for 8 minutes, until vegetables are tender-crisp. Thicken with corn-flour mixed to a paste with a little water; microwave for a further 2 minutes. Pour into a pie dish.

To make topping, microwave butter in a small bowl on High for 1 minute, then stir in remaining topping ingredients. Sprinkle over the vegetables and pat down gently. Microwave on High for 8 minutes. SERVES 4.

ORIENTAL VEGETABLES

A very tasty dish which is quick to cook. Serve on a bed of fluffy rice.

30 ml/2 tablespoons oil
1 onion, sliced
1 clove garlic, crushed
2 carrots, sliced
200 g/7 oz cauliflower florets
3 sticks celery, sliced
½ red pepper, seeded and sliced
½ yellow pepper, seeded and quartered
1 leek, sliced
10 ml/2 teaspoons cornflour
15 ml/1 tablespoon dry sherry
20 ml/4 teaspoons soy sauce
5 ml/1 teaspoon sugar
5 ml/1 teaspoon grated fresh ginger
150 ml/¼ pint Vegetable Stock (page 26)
410 g/14 oz canned lychees or mandarin oranges, drained
30 ml/2 tablespoons chopped parsley and 45 ml/3 tablespoons chopped nuts (such as cashews, peanuts or pecans) to garnish

Preheat a large browning dish on High for 8 minutes. Add oil and swirl around the dish. Add the vegetables and stir well to coat with oil. Microwave on High for 5–6 minutes, stirring every minute, until the vegetables are tender-crisp.

In a jug, mix the cornflour, sherry, soy sauce, sugar, ginger and stock, making sure that the cornflour is dissolved. Microwave on High for 2 minutes, stirring halfway, until the sauce thickens. Pour over vegetables. Add lychees or oranges, and microwave on High for 2–3 minutes to heat through. Pile on to a bed of rice (see Cooking Rice, page 118) and sprinkle with parsley and nuts. Serve immediately. SERVES 4.

VARIATION: Replace some or all of the cauliflower with broccoli.

Potatoes Provençals (page 104), Vegetable Crisp (page 106) and Broccoli Nut Bake (page 106).

CHAPTER NINE

PASTA

PASTA is a wonderful carbohydrate which can be combined with a variety of other ingredients, creating a filling and balanced meal that will satisfy all tastes. While you may think of pasta as 'family fare', the careful choice of sauce ingredients can turn it into a sophisticated dish too.

COOKING PASTA

Place 250 g/9 oz pasta in a large glass bowl. Pour 1 litre/1¾ pints boiling water over the pasta and add 5 ml/1 teaspoon salt and 5 ml/1 teaspoon sunflower oil. Stir, then microwave, uncovered, on High until cooked al dente — fresh pasta will cook in 3–4 minutes, while dried pasta takes 7–10 minutes, depending on the size and shape of the pasta (check the instructions on the label). Stir after 2 minutes to prevent sticking. Leave to stand for 5 minutes, covered, then drain.

PASTA WITH CURRIED CHICKEN

10 ml/2 teaspoons olive oil
10 ml/2 teaspoons freshly grated ginger
4 spring onions, sliced
1 clove garlic, crushed
½ green pepper, seeded and diced
5–10 ml/1–2 teaspoons curry powder
300 g/11 oz cooked chicken, diced (see Notes, page 79)
125 ml/4½ fl oz low-fat plain yoghurt
5 ml/1 teaspoon lemon juice
200 g/7 oz ribbon noodles
1 litre/1¾ pints boiling water
5 ml/1 teaspoon salt
5 ml/1 teaspoon sunflower oil

Microwave olive oil, ginger, spring onions, garlic and green pepper on High for 3–4 minutes, stirring halfway. Mix in curry powder; microwave for another minute. Add chicken, yoghurt and lemon juice. Microwave on High for 4–5 minutes to heat through.

Microwave noodles, water, salt and sunflower oil on High for 6–8 minutes, until cooked al dente. Leave to stand for 5 minutes, then drain. Toss with chicken sauce and heat through for a minute. SERVES 4.

ORIENTAL CHICKEN WITH NOODLES

4 chicken breasts, skinned and boned
10 ml/2 teaspoons sesame or sunflower oil
1 onion, sliced
1 clove garlic, crushed
10 ml/2 teaspoons freshly grated ginger
15 ml/1 tablespoon soy sauce
30 ml/2 tablespoons peanut butter
100 ml/3½ fl oz low-fat plain yoghurt
salt and freshly ground black pepper to taste
300 g/11 oz fresh Chinese egg noodles
1 litre/1¾ pints boiling water
5 ml/1 teaspoon salt
5 ml/1 teaspoon sunflower oil
15 ml/1 tablespoon snipped chives to garnish

Preheat a large browning dish on High for 6 minutes. Pat chicken pieces dry with paper towels. Cut on the slant into thin pieces. Place the chicken and oil in the hot dish. Microwave on High for 3 minutes, stirring after 1½ minutes. With a slotted spoon, remove the chicken and transfer to a plate.

Add onion, garlic and ginger to dish and microwave on High for 3 minutes. Return the chicken to the dish with the soy sauce. Microwave on High for 4 minutes, stirring after 2 minutes. Mix in the peanut butter until thoroughly combined. Stir in yoghurt and seasoning. Microwave on Medium for 3 minutes.

Microwave the Chinese egg noodles, water, salt and oil in a medium-sized bowl on High; follow the instructions given on the package for the cooking time — usually about 3 minutes (the time depends on how fresh they are and which kind you use). Leave to stand for about 3 minutes and then drain.

Serve chicken on a bed of Chinese noodles and sprinkle with chives. SERVES 4.

Oriental Chicken with Noodles (page 108) and Pasta with Curried Chicken (page 108).

SPAGHETTI WITH ASPARAGUS AND PRAWNS

250 g/9 oz fresh green asparagus spears
250 g/9 oz spaghetti
1 litre/1¾ pints boiling water
5 ml/1 teaspoon salt
5 ml/1 teaspoon oil
350 g/12 oz queen-size prawns, shelled
 and deveined (see Hint, page 62)
10 ml/2 teaspoons sunflower oil
2 cloves garlic, crushed
10 ml/2 teaspoons freshly grated ginger
30 ml/2 tablespoons dry sherry
30 ml/2 tablespoons toasted sesame seeds
 (see Hint, page 93)
15 ml/1 tablespoon chopped spring onion

Cut 1 cm/½ inch from the tough base of each asparagus spear with a sharp knife. Wash well, then lay top to tail in a large dish. Cover with cling film and microwave on High for 2½–3 minutes, until tender. Microwave spaghetti, water, salt and oil on High for 6–8 minutes. Leave to stand, covered, for 5 minutes, then drain.

When cool, cut each asparagus spear diagonally into three pieces. Preheat a large browning dish on High for 5 minutes. Pat prawns dry with a paper towel and microwave in the dish with oil, garlic and ginger on High for 2 minutes, stirring after a minute. Add sherry and asparagus pieces. Mix well. Microwave on High for 2 minutes. Stir in sesame seeds, spring onions and oil and combine thoroughly with the pasta. SERVES 4.

TAGLIATELLE WITH TOMATO AND MUSHROOM SAUCE

2 onions, chopped
1 clove garlic, crushed
1 stick celery, sliced
10 ml/2 teaspoons oil
410 g/14 oz canned tomatoes, chopped,
 liquid reserved
100 ml/3½ fl oz tomato purée (passata)
10 ml/2 teaspoons chopped fresh basil
salt and freshly ground black pepper to taste
5 ml/1 teaspoon sugar
5 ml/1 teaspoon Worcestershire sauce
1 bayleaf
300 g/11 oz brown mushrooms, sliced
10 ml/2 teaspoons butter
250 g/9 oz tagliatelle, cooked (see Cooking
 Pasta, page 108)
chopped parsley and grated cheese
 to garnish (optional)

Microwave onions, garlic, celery and oil for 5 minutes on High. Add tomatoes and their liquid, purée, basil, salt and pepper, sugar, Worcestershire sauce and bayleaf. Microwave on High for 12 minutes, stirring halfway.

Microwave mushrooms and butter in a medium-sized bowl on High for 4 minutes. Add to tomatoes. Mix well and spoon over the pasta. If you wish, sprinkle chopped parsley and grated cheese on top. SERVES 4.

VEGETABLE MACARONI CHEESE

This is a wonderful all-in-one pasta dish, which can be prepared a day in advance and cooked when required.

250 g/9 oz elbow macaroni
1 litre/1¾ pints boiling water
5 ml/1 teaspoon salt
5 ml/1 teaspoon oil
200 g/7 oz carrots, cut into slices
30 ml/2 tablespoons water
300 g/11 oz broccoli, presoaked for 30 minutes
250 g/9 oz courgettes, sliced
100 g/3½ oz frozen peas
100 g/3½ oz canned sweetcorn kernels
10 ml/2 teaspoons chopped fresh oregano
250 g/9 oz smooth cottage cheese (see page 7)
100 ml/3½ fl oz milk
10 ml/2 teaspoons Dijon mustard
dash of Tabasco
salt and freshly ground black pepper to taste
100 g/3½ oz Cheddar cheese, grated
100 g/3½ oz mozzarella cheese, grated
10 ml/2 teaspoons grated Parmesan cheese
pinch of paprika

Microwave macaroni in boiling water with salt and oil on High for 10 minutes, stirring after 5 minutes. Leave to stand for 5 minutes, then drain. Microwave carrots with the 30 ml/2 tablespoons water, covered, on High for 4–5 minutes, until soft. Remove carrots. Microwave broccoli on High for 3–4 minutes until soft. Reserve liquid. Combine pasta, carrots, broccoli, courgettes, peas, sweetcorn and oregano.

Blend together the cottage cheese, milk, reserved vegetable liquid, mustard, Tabasco, salt and pepper (a food processor works well). Mix into vegetables and pasta. Stir in Cheddar and mozzarella. Pour into a deep soufflé dish and sprinkle with Parmesan and paprika. Microwave on Medium for about 15 minutes. SERVES 6.

COMBINATION OVEN: Bake at 200 °C and Medium-Low microwave power level for 16–18 minutes (25–30 minutes if your oven alternates convection and microwave energy).

VEGETARIAN DELIGHT

5 ml/1 teaspoon yeast extract
5 ml/1 teaspoon peanut butter
250 ml/9 fl oz boiling water
60 g/2 oz fresh wholemeal breadcrumbs
salt and freshly ground black pepper to taste
3 tomatoes, peeled and chopped
15 ml/1 tablespoon tomato paste
2.5 ml/½ teaspoon lemon pepper
5 ml/1 teaspoon dried basil
1 large onion, chopped
10 ml/2 teaspoons butter
2 eggs, beaten
100 g/3½ oz Cheddar cheese, grated
100 g/3½ oz spaghetti or macaroni,
  cooked (see Cooking Pasta, page 108)
15 ml/1 tablespoon chopped fresh parsley

Combine yeast extract, peanut butter and water. Add breadcrumbs and seasoning. Stand for 15 minutes.

Add tomatoes, tomato paste, lemon pepper and basil to breadcrumb mixture. Microwave onion and butter on High for 3 minutes. Combine with tomato mixture. Add eggs and half the cheese. Combine with pasta.

Pour mixture into a pie dish and top with remaining cheese and parsley. Microwave on Medium-High for 12–14 minutes, then serve hot. SERVES 4–6.

COMBINATION OVEN: Bake at 200 °C and Medium-Low microwave power level for 14–16 minutes (25–30 minutes if your oven alternates convection and microwave energy).

SEAFOOD MACARONI

15 ml/1 tablespoon butter
1 onion, chopped
1 clove garlic, crushed
100 g/3½ oz canned smoked mussels,
  drained and oil reserved
410 g/14 oz canned tomatoes, chopped
10 ml/2 teaspoons tomato paste
45 ml/3 tablespoons dry white wine
5 ml/1 teaspoon anchovy paste
10 ml/2 teaspoons lemon juice
2.5 ml/½ teaspoon sugar
salt and freshly ground black pepper to taste
10 ml/2 teaspoons chopped fresh dill
15 ml/1 tablespoon chopped parsley
200 g/7 oz elbow macaroni
1 litre/1¾ pints boiling water
5 ml/1 teaspoon salt
5 ml/1 teaspoon oil
200 g/7 oz canned shrimps, drained

Microwave butter, onion, garlic and the oil from the smoked mussels in a large glass bowl on High for 3 minutes. Add tomatoes, tomato paste, wine, anchovy paste, lemon juice, sugar, salt, pepper and herbs. Microwave on High for about 12 minutes.

Microwave macaroni, water, salt and oil on High for 10–12 minutes, stirring halfway, until cooked al dente. Leave to stand for about 5 minutes, then drain.

Add mussels and shrimps to the tomato mixture. Microwave on High for 5 minutes. Pour over macaroni and serve. SERVES 4–6.

Spaghetti with Asparagus and Prawns (page 110) and Tagliatelle with Tomato and Mushroom Sauce (page 110).

Aubergine and Tomato Fusilli (page 113), Cheesy Wholemeal Pasta (page 114) and Vegetable Medley with Tagliatelle (page 113).

AUBERGINE AND TOMATO FUSILLI

10 ml/2 teaspoons olive oil
1 onion, chopped
3 cloves garlic, crushed
2 carrots, peeled and chopped into
    tiny cubes
410 g/14 oz canned tomatoes, chopped,
    liquid reserved
30 ml/2 tablespoons shredded basil leaves
salt and freshly ground black pepper
    to taste
pinch of cayenne pepper
1 medium aubergine, dégorged and cut in
    julienne strips (see Hint, page 99)
250 g/9 oz fusilli, cooked (see Cooking
    Pasta, page 108)
30 ml/2 tablespoons grated Parmesan
    cheese and 30 ml/2 tablespoons chopped
    parsley to garnish

Microwave oil, onion, garlic and carrots in a medium-sized glass bowl on High for 6–8 minutes, until carrots have softened slightly. Add tomatoes and their juice, basil, salt, pepper and cayenne pepper. Microwave on High for 6 minutes. Add aubergine and microwave for a further 5 minutes.

Spoon over the fusilli and sprinkle with cheese and parsley. SERVES 4.

LENTIL AND VEGETABLE LASAGNE

1 onion, chopped
2 sticks celery, finely sliced
200 g/7 oz finely grated carrot
15 ml/1 tablespoon olive oil
2 cloves garlic, crushed
2.5 ml/½ teaspoon cayenne pepper
15 ml/1 tablespoon garam masala
15 ml/1 tablespoon mustard seeds
250 g/9 oz red split lentils, washed
1 litre/1¾ pints Vegetable Stock
    (page 26)
410 g/14 oz canned tomatoes,
    chopped, liquid reserved
30 ml/2 tablespoons tomato paste
10 sheets precooked lasagne

TOPPING
300 ml/11 fl oz plain yoghurt
2 eggs, beaten
100 g/3½ oz Cheddar cheese, grated
30 ml/2 tablespoons grated
    Parmesan cheese

Microwave onion, celery, carrot and olive oil in a large bowl on High for 3 minutes. Stir in garlic, cayenne pepper, garam masala and mustard seeds. Cover and microwave for a further 2 minutes. Add lentils, stock, tomatoes with their juice and tomato paste. Mix well. Cover and microwave on High for 25 minutes until lentils are soft. Leave to stand for about 10 minutes.

Arrange layers of lasagne sheets and lentil mixture. Mix all the topping ingredients together in a jug and pour over the lentils. Microwave on Medium for 12–15 minutes, until topping has set. SERVES 4.

COMBINATION OVEN: Prepare as for microwave oven, then bake at 200 °C and Medium-Low microwave power level for about 18 minutes, until topping has set (30–35 minutes if your oven alternates convection and microwave energy).

NOTE: Although precooked lasagne is supposed to be ready to use, you may prefer to dip the sheets of lasagne in boiling water briefly to soften them slightly.

VEGETABLE MEDLEY WITH TAGLIATELLE

30 ml/2 tablespoons butter
250 g/9 oz broccoli florets
1 onion, chopped
3 carrots, peeled and diced
2 sticks celery, thinly sliced
1 clove garlic, crushed
100 g/3½ oz cherry tomatoes, peeled and
    halved (see Hint, page 17)
2.5 ml/½ teaspoon dried basil
salt and freshly ground black pepper to taste
250 g/9 oz tagliatelle, cooked (see Cooking
    Pasta, page 108)
100 g/3½ oz mozzarella cheese, grated, or
    45 ml/3 tablespoons grated Parmesan cheese
30 ml/2 tablespoons chopped parsley
a few fresh asparagus spears to garnish

Microwave butter, broccoli, onion, carrots, celery and garlic on High for 5–6 minutes, stirring once, until vegetables are tender-crisp. Add tomatoes, basil, salt and pepper and microwave for a further 3 minutes.

Reheat the tagliatelle on High for 2 minutes, if necessary, then pile on to a serving plate and spoon the vegetables over. Sprinkle with grated mozzarella or Parmesan cheese and parsley, and garnish with asparagus spears. SERVES 4.

VARIATION: For a richer dish, drain off butter and add 100 ml/3½ fl oz double cream. Microwave on Medium-High for 1½ minutes to heat through before serving.

TUNA LASAGNE

This delicious and economical dish really tests the elasticity of two cans of tuna!

8 sheets precooked lasagne
1 large onion, chopped
1 clove garlic, crushed
400 g/14 oz canned tuna in brine, drained
300 g/11 oz canned tomato soup
salt and freshly ground black pepper to taste
15 ml/1 tablespoon chopped parsley

CHEESE SAUCE
125 ml/4½ fl oz low-fat plain yoghurt
250 g/9 oz low-fat smooth cottage cheese
   (see page 7)
100 g/3½ oz ricotta cheese
100 g/3½ oz Cheddar cheese, grated

50 g/1¾ oz Cheddar cheese, grated, for topping

Precooked lasagne is supposed to be ready to use, but I usually dip the sheets into a bowl of boiling water for a minute to soften the pasta slightly as I assemble the dish.

Microwave onion and garlic, covered, on High for 3 minutes. Add tuna, soup, seasoning, and parsley. Microwave on High for 8 minutes. Blend the cheese sauce ingredients. Assemble the dish in layers: first the pasta, then the tuna mix, then the cheese sauce. Repeat layers. Sprinkle grated cheese on top and microwave on Medium-High for 10–12 minutes. SERVES 4–6.

COMBINATION OVEN: Bake at 200 °C and Medium-Low microwave power for 12–14 minutes (or for 25–30 minutes if your oven alternates convection and microwave energy).

CHEESY WHOLEMEAL PASTA

Serve with cooked spinach or a colourful salad of mixed lettuce leaves and vegetables sprinkled with bean sprouts.

250 g/9 oz wholemeal pasta shells
5 ml/1 teaspoon salt
5 ml/1 teaspoon oil
1 litre/1¾ pints boiling water
30 ml/2 tablespoons butter
2.5 ml/½ teaspoon curry powder
125 g/4½ oz smooth cottage cheese (see page 7)
150 ml/¼ pint plain yoghurt
30 ml/2 tablespoons grated Parmesan cheese
60 g/2 oz pecan nuts, coarsely chopped
bunch of watercress to garnish

Microwave the pasta, salt, oil and boiling water in a large bowl on High for 12–15 minutes until cooked al dente. Leave to stand for 5 minutes. Drain and keep hot.

Microwave butter and curry powder on High for 1 minute. Mix in cottage cheese and yoghurt. Fold in pasta, Parmesan cheese and nuts. Microwave on Medium-High for 3–4 minutes to heat through. Garnish with sprigs of watercress. SERVES 4.

MACARONI WITH PIZZA-STYLE TOPPING

Here pasta and vegetables are combined and layered in a colourful and tasty all-in-one dish.

300 g/11 oz macaroni or rigatoni, cooked
   (see Cooking Pasta, page 108)
200 ml/7 fl oz tomato purée (passata)
salt and freshly ground black pepper to taste
60 g/2 oz Gruyère or Cheddar cheese, grated
10 ml/2 teaspoons dried Italian herb mix or
   30 ml/2 tablespoons chopped fresh herbs
   (such as oregano, basil and parsley)
440 g/1 lb canned tomatoes, chopped, or
   5 tomatoes, peeled and chopped (see Hint,
   page 17)
60 g/2 oz cooked or canned chickpeas
   (see Cooking Chickpeas, page 86)
250 g/9 oz fresh vegetables (such as celery,
   courgettes, onion, spinach, red and green
   pepper), chopped
15 ml/1 tablespoon oil
8 black olives, pitted and halved
125 g/4½ oz mozzarella cheese,
   coarsely grated
pinch of paprika
15 ml/1 tablespoon chopped parsley

Place the macaroni in a large, round, greased casserole. Pour over the tomato purée. Season with salt and pepper. Sprinkle over the cheese and herbs. Place tomatoes on top. Spoon over the chickpeas. Set aside.

Microwave the mixed vegetables and oil in a medium-sized bowl on High for 4–5 minutes, stirring after 2–3 minutes, until tender-crisp. Spread vegetables on top of the tomatoes and chickpeas. Scatter the olives on top of the tomatoes, then sprinkle with mozzarella. Sprinkle over the paprika and parsley. Microwave on High for 8–10 minutes, until heated through thoroughly. SERVES 6.

COMBINATION OVEN: Cook at 200 °C and Medium-Low microwave power level for 14–16 minutes (25–30 minutes if your oven alternates convection and microwave energy).

Macaroni with Pizza-style Topping (page 114).

SPAGHETTI WITH PESTO SAUCE

PESTO SAUCE
60 g/2 oz chopped fresh basil
2 cloves garlic, crushed
30 g/1 oz pine nuts
30 ml/2 tablespoons extra-virgin olive oil
30 ml/2 tablespoons freshly grated
  Parmesan cheese
pinch of salt

300 g/11 oz spaghetti
1 litre/1¾ pints boiling water
5 ml/1 teaspoon salt
5 ml/1 teaspoon sunflower oil

Process the basil, garlic and pine nuts to a fine purée. With the machine running, slowly add the oil, pouring in a thin, steady stream. When thick, add the cheese and pulse briefly. Spoon into a bowl and check taste. Add salt if necessary.

Microwave the spaghetti, boiling water, salt and oil in a large bowl on High for 8–10 minutes, stirring after 4–5 minutes. Stand for 5 minutes. Drain and toss in pesto sauce. Serve hot or at room temperature. SERVES 4.

VARIATION: Serve over boiled new potatoes — delicious!

SLIMMER'S MACARONI CHEESE

15 ml/1 tablespoon butter
4 spring onions, sliced
30 ml/2 tablespoons plain flour
2.5 ml/½ teaspoon mustard powder
salt and freshly ground black pepper to taste
250 ml/9 fl oz low-fat milk
100 g/3½ oz low-fat cheese (such as Edam
  or mozzarella), grated
200 g/7 oz macaroni pieces
1 litre/1¾ pints boiling water
5 ml/1 teaspoon salt
5 ml/1 teaspoon sunflower oil
15 ml/1 tablespoon parsley to garnish
paprika

Microwave butter and spring onions on High for 2 minutes. Stir in flour, mustard powder and seasoning, and blend well. Gradually pour in milk, stirring well. Microwave on High for 4–5 minutes, until thickened, stirring twice. Add half of grated cheese to sauce and stir to melt. Microwave macaroni, water, salt and oil in a medium-sized glass bowl on High for about 10 minutes until cooked al dente. Leave to stand for 5 minutes, drain, then pour over sauce. Sprinkle over remaining cheese and top with parsley and paprika. SERVES 4.

CHICKPEAS AND VEGETABLES WITH WHOLEMEAL PASTA

300 g/11 oz broccoli
1 small onion, chopped
3 cloves garlic, crushed
10 ml/2 teaspoons virgin olive oil
410 g/14 oz canned chickpeas, drained
2 tomatoes, diced
salt and freshly ground black pepper to taste
200 g/7 oz wholemeal pasta
1 litre/1¾ pints boiling water
5 ml/1 teaspoon salt
5 ml/1 teaspoon sunflower oil
30 ml/2 tablespoons grated Parmesan cheese

Microwave broccoli with 30 ml/2 tablespoons water in a small bowl, covered, on High for 2 minutes. Drain and refresh under cold running water. Set aside. Microwave onion, garlic and olive oil on High for 2 minutes. Add chickpeas, tomatoes, seasoning and broccoli. Microwave pasta, boiling water, salt and sunflower oil on High for 8–10 minutes, until cooked al dente. Leave to stand for 5 minutes, then drain. Microwave vegetables on High for 3 minutes to heat through, and mix into pasta. Sprinkle over cheese. SERVES 4.

BROCCOLI AND PASTA BAKE

250 g/9 oz wholemeal spaghetti,
  broken into pieces
1 litre/1¾ pints boiling water
5 ml/1 teaspoon oil
5 ml/1 teaspoon salt
500 g/1 lb 2 oz broccoli
500 g/1 lb 2 oz tomatoes, peeled and
  chopped (see Hint, page 17)
1 large onion, chopped
1 clove garlic, crushed
10 ml/2 teaspoons chopped fresh
  oregano or 5 ml/1 teaspoon dried

TOPPING
250 ml/9 fl oz plain yoghurt
1 egg
125 g/4½ oz smooth cottage cheese
  (see page 7)
100 g/3½ oz Cheddar cheese, grated
pinch of paprika (optional)

Place the spaghetti in a large glass bowl. Pour over the boiling water and add the oil and salt. Microwave on High for 10 minutes, stirring after 3 minutes. Leave to stand for 3 minutes, then drain.

Cook the broccoli in a little water, covered, for 6 minutes, then drain. Place the tomatoes, onion, garlic and oregano in a bowl. Microwave on Medium-High for 10–12 minutes. To assemble, spoon a layer of tomato sauce into a casserole, followed by a layer of pasta, then broccoli. Repeat the layers.

To make the topping, beat together the yoghurt, egg and cheeses. Pour over the pasta and dust with paprika, if using. Microwave on Medium-High for 12–15 minutes. SERVES 4.

COMBINATION OVEN: Omitting the paprika, bake at 200 °C and Medium-Low microwave power level for about 12–14 minutes (20–25 minutes if your oven alternates convection and microwave energy).

TAGLIATELLE WITH COURGETTE AND TOMATO SAUCE

250 g/9 oz tagliatelle
1 litre/1¾ pints boiling water
5 ml/1 teaspoon salt
5 ml/1 teaspoon sunflower oil
30 ml/2 tablespoons butter
2 onions, sliced
300 g/11 oz courgettes, sliced
410 g/14 oz canned tomatoes, chopped
5 ml/1 teaspoon chopped fresh basil or
  2.5 ml/½ teaspoon dried
salt and freshly ground black pepper
  to taste
pinch of sugar
100 g/3½ oz mozzarella cheese, grated

Microwave the tagliatelle, water, salt and oil in a large glass bowl on High for about 8 minutes, until just tender, stirring after 3 minutes. Leave to stand for 5 minutes, then drain and set aside.

Microwave the butter and onions in a medium-sized glass bowl on High for 3 minutes. Stir in the courgettes and microwave for a further 2 minutes. Add the tomatoes and their liquid, basil, seasoning and sugar. Microwave on High for 8–10 minutes. If the sauce needs thickening, mix 15 ml/1 tablespoon cornflour to a paste with a little water, add to the vegetable mixture and microwave the sauce for a further 3 minutes to thicken. Leave to stand, covered, for 5 minutes, during which time you can reheat the tagliatelle on High for 3 minutes. Pile sauce on top of the tagliatelle and sprinkle with cheese. SERVES 4.

Tagliatelle with Courgette and Tomato Sauce (page 116) and Chickpeas and Vegetables with Wholemeal Pasta (page 116).

CHAPTER TEN

ACCOMPANIMENTS

SIDE dishes needn't be boiled and boring — with the judicious addition of herbs and spices or combination of flavours you can turn vegetable and rice dishes into real palate pleasers. Cooked in the microwave, they keep their flavour, colour and texture with minimal loss of nutrients.

COOKING RICE

To cook 200 g/7 oz rice:
♦ Brown rice: add 5 ml/1 teaspoon salt and 700 ml/1¼ pints boiling water. Microwave, covered, on High for 30–35 minutes.
♦ White rice: add 625 ml/1 pint 2 fl oz boiling water and 5 ml/1 teaspoon salt. Microwave, covered, on High for 12 minutes.
♦ Basmati rice: add 5 ml/1 teaspoon salt and 500 ml/18 fl oz boiling water. Microwave, covered, on High for 10 minutes.

COOKING GRAINS

♦ Presoak pearl barley for 1 hour. To cook 200 g/7 oz pearl barley, add 500 ml/18 fl oz boiling water and 5 ml/1 teaspoon salt, cover and microwave on High for 25 minutes.
♦ Barley needs to be presoaked, or use the quick method for pulses given on page 86. To cook 200 g/7 oz barley, add 625 ml/1 pint 2 fl oz boiling water and 5 ml/1 teaspoon salt, and microwave, covered, on Medium for 1 hour.
♦ Millet is cooked like rice, as follows: Microwave 200 g/7 oz millet, 5 ml/1 teaspoon salt and 625 ml/1 pint 2 fl oz boiling water in a bowl, covered, on Medium for 15–20 minutes. Leave to stand for 10 minutes. Fluff with a fork and add butter.

COCONUT BROWN RICE

1 onion, chopped
30 ml/2 tablespoons butter
200 g/7 oz brown rice
50 g/1¾ oz desiccated coconut
2 sticks cinnamon
a few cardamom seeds
5 ml/1 teaspoon salt
700 ml/1¼ pints boiling water

Microwave onion and butter on High for 3–4 minutes. Stir in rice and microwave for 3 minutes on High. Stir in remaining ingredients. Cover and microwave on High for 30–35 minutes. SERVES 4.

PEARL BARLEY AND MUSHROOM BAKE

250 g/9 oz pearl barley, presoaked for 1 hour
1 litre/1¾ pints boiling water
5 ml/1 teaspoon salt
1 large onion, chopped
30 ml/2 tablespoons butter
250 g/9 oz button mushrooms, chopped
30 g/1 oz plain flour
60 g/2 oz mushroom soup powder and
   500 ml/18 fl oz milk or
   410 g/14 oz canned mushroom soup and
   250 ml/9 fl oz milk
15 ml/1 tablespoon yeast extract
5 ml/1 teaspoon dried mixed herbs
3 eggs, beaten
250 ml/9 fl oz Cheese Sauce (page 93)
100 g/3½ oz blue cheese

Rinse pearl barley, then microwave, covered, with water on High for 10 minutes and on Medium for 40 minutes. Add salt and leave to stand, covered, for 15 minutes. Drain, reserving liquid for Cheese Sauce. Microwave onion and butter on High for 3–4 minutes. Add mushrooms and microwave for 2 minutes. Stir in flour and soup powder and gradually blend in milk, or stir in flour then canned soup and milk. Microwave for 4 minutes on High, stirring halfway. Add yeast extract, herbs, barley and eggs. Pour into a greased casserole. Microwave on Medium-High for 22 minutes, until cooked in centre.

When cool, cut into wedges. Place on an ovenproof serving plate. Surround with Cheese Sauce and crumble blue cheese on top. Grill until browned (or microwave for 1½ minutes on High to melt the cheese, but note that it will not brown this way). SERVES 6–8.

COMBINATION OVEN: Bake at 200 °C and Medium-Low microwave power level for about 25 minutes (35 minutes if your oven alternates convection and microwave energy).

Brown Rice and Mushroom Bake (this page) and Rice and Lentils (page 103).

BROWN RICE AND MUSHROOM BAKE

45 ml/3 tablespoons butter
1 onion, finely chopped
300 g/11 oz mushrooms, thinly sliced
1 clove garlic, crushed
200 g/7 oz brown rice, cooked
   (see Cooking Rice, page 118)
10 ml/2 teaspoons soy sauce
juice of ½ lemon (see Hint, page 123)
2 drops Tabasco sauce
125 g/4½ oz mature Cheddar cheese, grated
salt and freshly ground black pepper to taste
15 ml/1 tablespoon chopped parsley
   or chives to garnish

In a deep casserole, microwave butter and onion on High for 3 minutes. Add mushrooms and garlic, mixing well. Microwave on High for 3 minutes.

Mix in remaining ingredients. Smooth the top. Microwave on Medium-High for 8–10 minutes. Sprinkle with parsley or chives and serve. SERVES 4.

SAVOURY PEARL BARLEY

A colourful and tasty way to serve pearl barley.

225 g/8 oz pearl barley, rinsed well
800 ml/1½ pints hot Vegetable Stock
   (page 26)
2.5 ml/½ teaspoon salt
1 small onion, chopped
50 g/1¾ oz frozen peas
100 g/3½ oz button mushrooms, sliced
15 ml/1 tablespoon butter
5 ml/1 teaspoon garlic-and-herb seasoning

Microwave pearl barley, stock and salt in a medium-sized glass bowl, covered, on High for 10 minutes and on Medium-High for 30 minutes, until cooked and soft. Leave to stand for 10 minutes.

Microwave the onion, peas, mushrooms and butter in a small bowl on High for 5 minutes. Stir into pearl barley with the garlic-and-herb seasoning. Combine well and serve. SERVES 4.

SPRING VEGETABLE MEDLEY

200 g/7 oz new potatoes, peeled
45 ml/3 tablespoons water
8 pickling onions, peeled (see Hint, page 76)
30 ml/2 tablespoons water
30 ml/2 tablespoons butter
10 baby carrots, peeled
6 yellow patty-pan squash, sliced,
  or if very small, left whole
125 g/4½ oz baby French green beans
250 g/9 oz peas
1 bunch parsley, tied together
30 ml/2 tablespoons water
salt and freshly ground black pepper to taste

DRESSING
10 ml/2 teaspoons lemon juice
5 ml/1 teaspoon prepared mustard
2.5 ml/½ teaspoon tarragon, chopped
salt and freshly ground black pepper to taste
15 ml/1 tablespoon butter

Parcook potatoes with 45 ml/3 tablespoons water, covered, on High for 5 minutes. Cook onions in 30 ml/2 tablespoons water, covered, on High for 2–3 minutes. Microwave butter, carrots, patty-pan squash, beans, peas, parsley and the remaining 30 ml/ 2 tablespoons water, covered, on High for 8 minutes. Add potatoes and onions. Stir well and microwave for a further 5 minutes. Add seasoning. Set aside. Microwave the dressing ingredients on High for 30–40 seconds, covered, and pour over the vegetables. SERVES 4–6.

NOTES
♦ Cut vegetables to the same size for even cooking.
♦ Vegetables cooked whole in their skins, like butternut squash, aubergines, soft-skinned squash and so on, should be pierced before cooking to prevent bursting.
♦ Cook vegetables in a small quantity of water — about 30 ml/2 tablespoons — so that the nutrients are not lost.
♦ Salt dries out vegetables during cooking, so where necessary, add to vegetables afterwards.

SPINACH DREAMS

A colourful addition to your meal that is simple to make.

1 small onion, grated and drained
10 ml/2 teaspoons butter
250 g/9 oz frozen spinach, thawed and drained
45 ml/3 tablespoons single cream or plain
  yoghurt
1.25 ml/¼ teaspoon French mustard
30 ml/2 tablespoons grated Cheddar cheese
pinch of freshly grated nutmeg
salt and freshly ground black pepper to taste
1 egg, beaten

Microwave the onion and butter in a bowl on High for 2 minutes. Stir in the remaining ingredients until thoroughly mixed. Spoon the mixture into greased ramekins. Cover with pierced cling film and microwave on Medium for 5–7 minutes, until firm and set. Leave to stand for a few minutes, then invert on to a serving plate and serve. SERVES 2.

BEANS ALMANDINE

125 g/4½ oz green beans, trimmed
30 ml/2 tablespoons water
45 ml/3 tablespoons flaked almonds
30 ml/2 tablespoons butter
salt and freshly ground black pepper to taste

Microwave the beans and water in a small bowl, covered, on High for 5–6 minutes, until slightly tender but still crisp. Leave to stand, then drain. In another small bowl, microwave the almonds and butter on High for 3 minutes, until the almonds are brown. Stir the almonds into the beans. Season and serve. SERVES 2.

LEMON AND THYME MUSHROOMS

300 g/11 oz mushrooms
30 ml/2 tablespoons butter
5 ml/1 teaspoon chopped fresh lemon thyme
5 ml/1 teaspoon lemon juice

Wash mushrooms well and dry with a paper towel. Microwave all ingredients on High for 3–4 minutes. Serve as an accompaniment to a meal. SERVES 4.

VARIATION: Stir in 45 ml/3 tablespoons soured cream and microwave on Medium for about 2 minutes to heat through.

SWEET AND SOUR CARROTS

500 g/1 lb 2 oz carrots, diced
100 ml/3½ fl oz water
30 ml/2 tablespoons oil
1 onion, sliced
2 sticks celery, sliced
10 ml/2 teaspoons cornflour
10 ml/2 teaspoons soy sauce
15 ml/1 tablespoon light brown sugar
15 ml/1 tablespoon cider vinegar
10 ml/2 teaspoons lemon juice

Microwave the carrots with the water in a small bowl, covered, on High for 6 minutes. Drain the carrots, reserving cooking liquid.

Microwave the oil, onion and celery on High for 4 minutes. Add carrots and stir well. Blend cornflour, soy sauce, sugar, vinegar and lemon juice. Add the liquid from the carrots, stir well and pour over the vegetables. Microwave on High for 3–4 minutes, stirring twice. SERVES 4.

COURGETTES PROVENCALES

450 g/1 lb courgettes
45 ml/3 tablespoons boiling water
1 onion, chopped
1 clove garlic, crushed
10 ml/2 teaspoons chopped fresh marjoram
   or 5 ml/1 teaspoon dried
2.5 ml/½ teaspoon sugar
10 ml/2 teaspoons butter
2 tomatoes, chopped

Top and tail courgettes, cut in half lengthwise and scoop out the flesh. Place courgette shells in boiling water and microwave on High for 3–4 minutes. Drain. Chop courgette flesh finely.

Microwave the chopped courgette flesh, onion and garlic in a bowl on High for 3–4 minutes. Add marjoram, sugar, butter and tomatoes. Microwave on High for 2 minutes and spoon into courgette shells. Place on a serving platter. Just before serving, heat through on High for 5 minutes. SERVES 6.

Courgettes Provençales (this page), Sweet and Sour Carrots (this page) and Spring Vegetable Medley (page 120).

Savoury Squash Bake (this page), Vegetable and Chive Fritters (page 123) and Carrots with Minty Pineapple Sauce (this page).

CARROTS WITH MINTY PINEAPPLE SAUCE

A simple and unusual side dish to serve to guests.

> 400 g/14 oz baby carrots
> 15 ml/1 tablespoon lemon juice
> 15 ml/1 tablespoon butter
> 100 ml/3½ fl oz pineapple juice
> 45 ml/3 tablespoons water
> 10 ml/2 teaspoons cornflour
> 30 ml/2 tablespoons honey
> salt and freshly ground black pepper to taste
> 5 ml/1 teaspoon chopped fresh mint

Microwave carrots, lemon juice and butter in a medium-sized bowl, covered, on High for 6–8 minutes, until tender-crisp. Blend pineapple juice, water and cornflour until dissolved. Add honey and microwave on High for 3–4 minutes, until thickened. Add mint and seasoning and pour over the carrots. SERVES 4.

VARIATION: Replace the pineapple juice with an equal quantity of orange juice.

SAVOURY SQUASH BAKE

> 6 small round squash
> 100 g/3½ oz cheese, grated
> 125 ml/4½ fl oz Chicken Stock (page 21)
> 15 ml/1 tablespoon brandy
> 30 ml/2 tablespoons cream or plain yoghurt
> 1 egg, beaten
> 5 ml/1 teaspoon chopped fresh thyme or
>   2.5 ml/½ teaspoon dried
> salt and freshly ground black pepper to taste
> 100 g/3½ oz savoury biscuits, crushed
> pinch of paprika

Cut squash in half and place in an oven roasting bag. Microwave on High for 10 minutes, then leave to stand for 5 minutes. Remove the pips and scoop out the flesh. Place in a casserole.

Add half the cheese, as well as the stock, brandy, cream or yoghurt, egg, thyme and seasoning. Sprinkle the crushed biscuits on top of the squash with the remaining cheese and paprika. Microwave on High for 7–8 minutes. SERVES 4.

CITRUS RICE

15 ml/1 tablespoon butter
½ onion, finely chopped
1 stick celery, chopped
2.5 ml/½ teaspoon turmeric
100 g/3½ oz rice
grated zest and juice of 1 orange (see Hint, below)
5 ml/1 teaspoon lemon juice
2.5 ml/½ teaspoon grated lemon zest
250 ml/9 fl oz hot Chicken Stock (page 21)

Microwave the butter, onion, celery and turmeric on High for 2–3 minutes. Stir in the remaining ingredients. Cover and microwave on High for 8–10 minutes. Leave to stand for 10 minutes before serving. SERVES 2.

HINT
The best way to get all the juice out of a lemon (or orange or lime) is to prick the skin all over, then microwave the lemon on High for 10–15 seconds. Halve the lemon, then squeeze the juice out.

CARROTS JULIENNE

125 g/4½ oz carrots, cut in julienne strips
15 ml/1 tablespoon soft brown sugar
30 ml/2 tablespoons fresh orange juice (see Hint, above)
15 ml/1 tablespoon butter
salt and freshly ground black pepper to taste

Combine all the ingredients except the seasoning, in a covered casserole. Microwave on High for 5–6 minutes, stirring often. Add seasoning and serve. SERVES 2.

NEW POTATOES WITH BLUE CHEESE

250 g/9 oz new potatoes, pierced
20 ml/4 teaspoons water
15 ml/1 tablespoon butter
salt and freshly ground black pepper to taste
45 ml/3 tablespoons crumbled blue cheese

Microwave the potatoes and water in a bowl, covered, on High for 5–6 minutes, until a skewer goes right through the middle. Drain, then add the butter, seasoning and cheese. Microwave on Medium-High for 1 minute. Serve hot. SERVES 2.

BRUSSELS SPROUTS AU GRATIN

500 g/1 lb 2 oz fresh or frozen Brussels sprouts
100 ml/3½ fl oz water

SAUCE
30 ml/2 tablespoons butter
30 g/1 oz plain flour
375 ml/13 fl oz milk
45 ml/3 tablespoons single cream
110 g/4 oz Cheddar or Gruyère cheese, grated
salt, freshly ground black pepper, nutmeg and mustard to taste

TOPPING
45 ml/3 tablespoons dry breadcrumbs
30 ml/2 tablespoons grated Parmesan cheese
15 ml/1 tablespoon chopped parsley
pinch of paprika

Place Brussels sprouts and water in a medium-sized glass dish, cover and microwave on High for 10 minutes, until tender. Rinse with cold water and drain.

To make the sauce, microwave butter in a jug on High for 40 seconds, until melted. Stir in the flour and milk. Microwave on High for 5 minutes, stirring twice. Stir in the cream and cheese. Season well and pour over the Brussels sprouts.

Combine topping ingredients and sprinkle over the sprouts. Microwave on Medium-High for about 5 minutes, until piping hot. SERVES 4.

VEGETABLE AND CHIVE FRITTERS

2 large potatoes, grated
2 large carrots, grated
30 ml/2 tablespoons snipped fresh chives
salt and freshly ground black pepper to taste
30 ml/2 tablespoons rice flour or potato flour
2 eggs, beaten
oil for frying

Combine all the ingredients except the oil. Preheat a browning dish on High for 6 minutes. Add 15 ml/1 tablespoon oil. Add half a cup of mixture. Microwave on High for 1 minute. Turn over and microwave for a further minute.

Keep fritter warm and continue making up the rest of the batter. Wipe out the dish after each fritter, then reheat it for 3 minutes, add a little oil and proceed as before. SERVES 4.

SWEET AND SOUR COURGETTES

6 courgettes, sliced
15 ml/1 tablespoon water
1 onion, chopped
10 ml/2 teaspoons oil
45 ml/3 tablespoons plain yoghurt
5 ml/1 teaspoon soy sauce
30 ml/2 tablespoons honey
45 ml/3 tablespoons apple cider vinegar

Place courgettes and water in a small bowl and microwave, covered, on High for 2½ minutes. Drain and refresh under cold water. Microwave onion and oil on High for 3 minutes, then combine with courgettes. Combine yoghurt, soy sauce, honey and vinegar and pour over courgettes and onions. SERVES 4 AS A SIDE DISH.

STIR-FRIED MUSHROOMS

300 g/11 oz button mushrooms
15 ml/1 tablespoon butter
1 clove garlic, crushed
30 ml/2 tablespoons dry white wine
15 ml/1 tablespoon soy sauce
30 ml/2 tablespoons medium dry sherry
10 ml/2 teaspoons honey
10 ml/2 teaspoons cornflour

Microwave mushrooms, butter and garlic in a glass bowl on High for 3 minutes. Mix remaining ingredients in a jug until cornflour has dissolved. Add to the mushrooms and microwave on High for 2 minutes, stirring halfway. SERVES 4 AS A SIDE DISH.

BAKED BUTTERNUT SQUASH

500 g/1 lb 2 oz butternut squash, peeled
   and sliced into rounds
5 ml/1 teaspoon ground cinnamon
25 ml/5 teaspoons soft brown sugar
20 ml/4 teaspoons butter

Layer the butternut squash rounds, overlapping, in a shallow casserole. Sprinkle with cinnamon and brown sugar. Melt the butter on High for 20 seconds in a small jug and pour over the butternut squash. Microwave, covered, on High for 10 minutes. Leave to stand for 2–3 minutes, then serve. SERVES 4.

VARIATION: Use pumpkin instead of butternut squash.

SPINACH PATTIES

300 g/11 oz fresh spinach, washed, drained
   and finely chopped
1 medium potato, peeled and coarsely grated
1 small onion, coarsely grated
pinch of ground nutmeg
1 egg, beaten
salt and freshly ground black pepper to taste
10 ml/2 teaspoons oil
10 ml/2 teaspoons butter
45 ml/3 tablespoons yoghurt to serve

Combine all ingredients except oil and butter (mixture should be very sloppy). Preheat a browning dish on High for 4 minutes. Add oil and butter and microwave for 20 seconds. Drop spoonfuls of mixture in dish and microwave on High for 2–3 minutes, turning patties halfway. Serve each with a dollop of yoghurt. SERVES 4.

VARIATION: Add 50 g/1¾ oz button mushrooms, finely chopped, to the mixture.

POTATO AND CARROT CREAM BAKE

750 g/1lb 10 oz potatoes, peeled and
   thinly sliced
4 carrots, peeled and thinly sliced
250 ml/9 fl oz hot Vegetable Stock
   (page 26)
100 ml/3½ fl oz milk
250 g/9 oz low-fat smooth cottage cheese
   (see page 7)
1 clove garlic, crushed
salt and freshly ground black pepper
   to taste
50 g/1¾ oz Cheddar cheese, grated
30 ml/2 tablespoons chopped parsley
pinch of paprika

Microwave the potatoes and carrots with the vegetable stock in a deep, round dish, covered, on High for 8–10 minutes. Leave to stand. Mix the milk, cottage cheese, garlic, seasoning and half the Cheddar cheese. Drain the vegetables and place in a serving dish. Pour the cheesy mixture over vegetables and stir in to combine. Sprinkle the remaining cheese, parsley and paprika on top. Microwave on Medium for 20–25 minutes, until vegetables are soft. SERVES 6.

COMBINATION OVEN: Bake at 200 °C and Medium-Low microwave power level for 18–20 minutes (25–30 minutes if your oven alternates convection and microwave energy).

MUSHROOMS AND TOMATOES

1 onion, chopped
1 clove garlic, crushed
10 ml/2 teaspoons butter
5 ml/1 teaspoon lemon juice
2.5 ml/½ teaspoon dried mixed herbs
300 g/11 oz button mushrooms, sliced
300 g/11 oz tomatoes, peeled and
   chopped (see Hint, page 17)
salt and freshly ground black pepper to taste

Microwave onion, garlic and butter in a medium-sized glass bowl on High for 3 minutes. Stir in lemon juice, herbs, mushrooms, tomatoes, salt and pepper. Microwave on High for 6 minutes. If mixture needs thickening, mix 10 ml/2 teaspoons cornflour to a paste with water and add to mushroom and tomato mixture, stirring well. Microwave on High for 2 minutes. SERVES 4 AS A SIDE DISH.

VARIATION: Top with a little grated cheese before last 2 minutes of microwaving.

VEGETABLE KEBABS

12 new potatoes, washed and pierced
20 ml/4 teaspoons water
4 large courgettes
12 baby sweetcorn
12 large button mushrooms
12 cherry tomatoes
100 ml/3½ fl oz ready-made Italian
   salad dressing

Microwave the potatoes and water in a small bowl, covered, on High for 5–6 minutes, until a skewer goes through the potatoes easily. Leave to stand for a few minutes, then drain.

Cut courgettes and baby sweetcorn into chunks. Place all the vegetables in a dish. Pour dressing over, and marinate for a few hours. Drain vegetables, pierce with a wooden skewer, and make up the kebabs.

Place in a flat-bottomed dish and microwave on High for 6–8 minutes, until all the vegetables are cooked.

Serve on a bed of rice (see Cooking Rice, page 118) with a green salad. MAKES 6.

Oriental Vegetables (page 106) and Vegetable Kebabs (this page).

BARLEY AND MUSHROOM CASSEROLE

60 g/2 oz butter
2 onions, chopped
300 g/11 oz mushrooms, sliced
200 g/7 oz pearl barley, presoaked for
    1 hour, then rinsed and drained
5 ml/1 teaspoon salt
freshly ground black pepper to taste
5 ml/1 teaspoon chopped fresh thyme
300 ml/11 fl oz hot Vegetable Stock
    (page 26)
10 ml/2 teaspoons soy sauce

Microwave butter and onions in a medium–sized glass bowl on High for 5 minutes. Add mushrooms and microwave for a further 3 minutes. Stir in pearl barley, salt, pepper, thyme, vegetable stock and soy sauce. Cover and microwave on High for 10 minutes, then on Medium for 25 minutes, until pearl barley is cooked. Leave to stand for 10 minutes. SERVES 4.

VARIATIONS: Top with chopped parsley and grated cheese before standing time, or make a chopped salad topping using ingredients such as spring onions, tomato, avocado and cucumber mixed together and placed on top of the cooked casserole.

RICE AND VEGETABLES IN RED WINE

200 g/7 oz white rice
30 ml/2 tablespoons butter
2 tomatoes, peeled and chopped
    (see Hint, page 17)
250 g/9 oz mushrooms, sliced
1 onion, finely chopped
125 ml/4½ fl oz red wine
650 ml/1 pint 3 fl oz hot Vegetable Stock
    (page 26)
5 ml/1 teaspoon salt
freshly ground black pepper to taste
5 ml/1 teaspoon chopped fresh oregano
125 g/4½ oz peas, cooked
30 ml/2 tablespoons grated Parmesan cheese

Microwave rice, butter, tomatoes, mushrooms and onion on High for 6 minutes, stirring occasionally. Add wine, stock and seasoning. Cover and microwave on Medium-High for about 15 minutes, until rice is tender and liquid nearly absorbed. Add oregano and peas and stir. Cover and leave to stand for 10 minutes. Sprinkle with Parmesan cheese. SERVES 6.

VARIATION: For a healthier dish, use brown rice and increase cooking time to about 25 minutes.

Vegetable and Rice Timbales (page 127), Gingered Carrots with Coriander (page 127) and Vegetable Variety (page 127).

VEGETABLE VARIETY

　350 g/12 oz green beans, cut into
　　5 cm/2 inch lengths
　1 aubergine, unpeeled, cubed and
　　dégorged (see Hint, page 99)
　1 onion, chopped
　50 g/1¾ oz carrots, sliced
　2 sticks celery, sliced
　1 tomato, peeled and chopped (see Hint, page 17)
　½ green pepper, seeded and chopped
　½ red pepper, seeded and chopped
　½ yellow pepper, seeded and chopped
　250 ml/9 fl oz tomato juice
　5 ml/1 teaspoon oil
　salt and freshly ground black pepper to taste
　5 ml/1 teaspoon sugar
　10 ml/2 teaspoons chopped fresh basil or
　　5 ml/1 teaspoon dried
　4 courgettes, cut in julienne strips
　100 ml/3½ fl oz plain yoghurt

Combine all the vegetables except the courgettes in a large casserole. Combine tomato juice, oil, seasoning, sugar and basil and pour this mixture over the vegetables. Cover and microwave on Medium-High for 20 minutes. Add courgettes and microwave for a further 8 minutes. Pour the yoghurt over the vegetables and serve with rice or couscous. SERVES 4.

COMBINATION OVEN: Cook at 180 °C and Medium-Low microwave power level for 20 minutes plus 8 minutes for the courgettes (35–40 minutes plus 10 minutes if your oven alternates convection and microwave energy).

GINGERED CARROTS WITH CORIANDER

　400 g/14 oz whole baby carrots
　peel and juice of 1 tangerine
　10 ml/2 teaspoons butter
　5 ml/1 teaspoon honey
　5 ml/1 teaspoon soy sauce
　1 small piece fresh ginger, crushed
　salt and freshly ground black pepper to taste
　5 ml/1 teaspoon fresh coriander leaves

Scrub the carrots and break the tangerine peel into pieces. Place the carrots in a glass dish with the tangerine peel and juice, butter, honey, soy sauce and ginger. Cover and microwave on High for 10 minutes, until tender-crisp. Uncover and microwave on High for 5 minutes to reduce liquid to a syrup. Season and sprinkle with coriander leaves. SERVES 4.

LAYERED AUBERGINE CASSEROLE

　1 large onion, chopped
　2 cloves garlic, crushed
　1 large aubergine, unpeeled, cubed and
　　dégorged (see Hint, page 99)
　450 g/1 lb courgettes, sliced
　1 red pepper, seeded and diced
　450 g/1 lb tomatoes, peeled and chopped
　　(see Hint, page 17)
　10 ml/2 teaspoons chopped fresh mixed herbs
　　(such as basil, oregano or rosemary) or
　　5 ml/1 teaspoon dried
　salt and freshly ground black pepper to taste

Microwave the onion and garlic in a small glass bowl, covered, on High for 3–4 minutes.

Layer vegetables in a serving dish — first aubergine, then courgettes, red pepper, tomatoes and onion mixture. Season layers with herbs and pepper. Keep layering until all the vegetables have been used.

Cover and microwave on High for 15 minutes, then uncover and microwave for a further 5 minutes. Add salt to taste. Cover again and leave to stand for about 5 minutes. SERVES 4.

VEGETABLE AND RICE TIMBALES

Use leftover rice to make these colourful accompaniments.

　15 ml/1 tablespoon butter
　1 small red pepper, seeded and finely diced
　1 small green pepper, seeded and finely diced
　100 g/3½ oz mushrooms, finely chopped
　160 g/5½ oz cooked white rice (see Cooking
　　Rice, page 118)
　salt and freshly ground black pepper to taste
　5 ml/1 teaspoon chopped fresh oregano or
　　2.5 ml/½ teaspoon dried

Microwave butter, peppers and mushrooms in a medium-sized bowl on High for 3–4 minutes. Stir in rice, seasoning and oregano. Microwave on High for 1½–2 minutes to heat through. Press mixture into four moulds. Leave to stand for a few minutes, then turn out on to a serving platter. SERVES 4.

NEW POTATOES WITH LOW-FAT YOGHURT DRESSING

For those people who enjoy baked potatoes with cream cheese, here is a healthy alternative using low-fat plain yoghurt.

500 g/1 lb 2 oz new potatoes
45 ml/3 tablespoons water
pinch of salt

YOGHURT DRESSING
125 ml/4½ fl oz low-fat plain yoghurt
2.5 ml/½ teaspoon salt
2.5 ml/½ teaspoon prepared mustard
dash of Tabasco sauce
5 ml/1 teaspoon chopped parsley
45 ml/3 tablespoons cold-pressed
  sunflower oil

Microwave the potatoes, water and salt in a small bowl, covered, on High for 10 minutes, until the potatoes are soft. Leave to stand for 10 minutes, then drain and allow to cool.

Process all the ingredients for the dressing, slowly adding the oil through the feeder tube. Pour into a container, cover and refrigerate. Pour over potatoes when cold. SERVES 4.

BROCCOLI BAKE

500 g/1 lb 2 oz broccoli florets
30 ml/2 tablespoons water
100 g/3½ oz self-raising flour
pinch of salt and freshly ground black pepper
pinch of nutmeg
100 ml/3½ fl oz low-fat plain yoghurt
3 eggs, beaten
200 g/7 oz Cheddar cheese, grated
pinch of paprika

Microwave broccoli and water in a medium-sized glass bowl, covered, on High for 6–8 minutes until tender-crisp. Leave to stand for 3 minutes and drain, then process to a smooth purée.

Sift flour into a large bowl, add salt, pepper, nutmeg, yoghurt and eggs, and stir to combine. Add broccoli and cheese. Sprinkle with paprika and microwave on Medium-High for 12–14 minutes until a metal skewer inserted comes out clean. SERVES 6.

COMBINATION OVEN: Bake at 200 °C and Medium-Low microwave power level for 12–14 minutes (or 25–30 minutes if your oven alternates convection and microwave energy).

OKRA WITH TOMATOES

400 g/14 oz okra, sliced and stems removed
30 ml/2 tablespoons butter
½ green pepper, seeded and chopped
1 onion, chopped
3 tomatoes, peeled and chopped (see Hint,
  page 17)
2.5 ml/½ teaspoon sugar
2.5 ml/½ teaspoon chopped basil

Microwave okra and butter on High for 4 minutes. Add all remaining ingredients. Cover and microwave on High for 5 minutes, then on Medium for 8 minutes. Serve on a bed of rice. SERVES 4.

GARDEN VEGETABLE BAKE

1 medium head of cauliflower
15 ml/1 tablespoon water
salt and freshly ground black pepper to taste
500 g/1 lb 2 oz young spinach leaves,
  shredded
250 g/9 oz carrots, sliced
15 ml/1 tablespoon water
pinch of sugar

WHITE SAUCE
30 ml/2 tablespoons butter
30 ml/2 tablespoons flour
250 ml/9 fl oz low-fat milk
seasoning
pinch of nutmeg

Break cauliflower into florets and soak in water for 30 minutes. Drain and microwave, covered, with 15 ml/1 tablespoon water on High for 8 minutes. Drain, reserving liquid, season and set aside. Microwave spinach, covered, on High for 4 minutes, then season and set aside. Microwave carrots, covered, on High with remaining 15 ml/1 tablespoon water for 5 minutes. Drain, reserving liquid, add sugar and set aside.

To make the sauce, microwave butter for 30 seconds on High until melted. Stir in flour and gradually blend in milk and reserved cooking liquid from vegetables. Season and microwave on High for 3 minutes, stirring once, until sauce thickens. Add nutmeg.

Layer vegetables in a casserole in order of preparation, pouring sauce over each layer. Microwave on High for 4–5 minutes to heat through. SERVES 4–6.

VARIATIONS:
♦ Top with chopped toasted pine nuts or almonds.
♦ Sprinkle with grated cheese and grill for a minute.

Garden Vegetable Bake (page 128), New Potatoes with Low-fat Yoghurt Dressing (page 128) and Okra with Tomatoes (page 128).

CHAPTER ELEVEN

DESSERTS

For those watching their weight and for hostesses with 'health nut' friends, here are some ideas for wholesome, fruity desserts as well as some rich, creamy, sugary ones. Also included are a couple of unusual sauces to pour over puddings or ice cream for a quick sweet treat.

PASSION FRUIT FLUFF

15 ml/1 tablespoon powdered gelatine
75 ml/2½ fl oz water
100 g/3½ oz caster sugar
100 g/3½ oz canned passion fruit pulp
350 ml/12 fl oz low-fat passion fruit yoghurt
3 egg whites
2.5 ml/½ teaspoon cream of tartar

Sprinkle gelatine on to water in a large bowl. Allow to sponge. Microwave on High for about 40 seconds until bubbles start forming. Gradually beat sugar into gelatine, then beat in passion fruit pulp and yoghurt. Leave to stand at room temperature for about 10 minutes to thicken slightly. Whisk egg whites with cream of tartar until stiff and fold gently into the passion fruit mixture. Pour into a glass serving bowl or individual glass dessert bowls and refrigerate until set. SERVES 4.

VARIATIONS:
♦ Replace the passion fruit pulp with the same quantity of puréed strawberries and the passion fruit yoghurt with low-fat strawberry yoghurt.
♦ Use 4 ripe bananas puréed with 30 ml/2 tablespoons lemon juice in place of the passion fruit pulp, and low-fat plain yoghurt instead of the passion fruit yoghurt.

CREAM SUBSTITUTE

1 egg white
15 ml/1 tablespoon clear honey
175 ml/6 fl oz low-fat plain yoghurt

Beat egg white until stiff. Microwave honey on High for 10 seconds, then pour on to egg white. Continue beating until very thick. Fold in the yoghurt gently and serve immediately with dessert instead of cream.

YOGHURT AND BANANA FRIDGE TART

CRUST
200 g/7 oz digestive biscuits, crumbled
60 g/2 oz butter, melted (see Hint, page 13)

FILLING
5 ripe bananas
175 ml/6 fl oz low-fat plain yoghurt
30 ml/2 tablespoons lemon juice
10 ml/2 teaspoons sugar
175 ml/6 fl oz evaporated milk, chilled
10 ml/2 teaspoons powdered gelatine
30 ml/2 tablespoons water
5 ml/1 teaspoon grated lemon zest

banana slices, dipped in lemon juice, and
mint sprigs or lemon leaves to decorate

Mix crumbs and butter together and press into the base and sides of a 23 cm/9 inch pie dish. Microwave on High for 2 minutes. Allow to cool.

Process bananas, yoghurt, lemon juice and sugar until smooth. Beat evaporated milk until thick and fold into banana purée. Sprinkle gelatine on to water in a ramekin dish, allow to sponge, and microwave on High for about 30 seconds until liquid just starts to boil. Pour in a thin stream into the banana mixture. Fold in the lemon zest. Pour into prepared crust and chill for a few hours until set. Decorate as suggested. SERVES 6.

HONEY

Honey, used as a sweetener for millennia, is often thought to be healthier than sugar. However, it has almost as high a calorie count, so is hardly slimming. If you do not want its distinctive flavour to dominate, use a paler, milder variety. To liquidize honey that has crystallized, microwave on High for a few seconds.

BUTTERMILK CHEESECAKE WITH BERRY SAUCE

750 g/1¾ lb ricotta cheese
4 eggs
250 ml/9 fl oz buttermilk
150 g/5½ oz caster sugar
10 ml/2 teaspoons lemon juice

BERRY SAUCE
450 g/1 lb raspberries or youngberries
100 g/3½ oz icing sugar, sifted
10 ml/2 teaspoons kirsch or lemon juice

Beat ricotta cheese with an electric mixer, adding eggs one at a time. Add buttermilk, caster sugar and lemon juice and mix in gently. Pour mixture into a pie dish. Microwave on Medium-Low for 18–20 minutes until set. Allow to cool, then refrigerate.

To make the sauce, purée berries (reserving a few for decoration), icing sugar and kirsch or lemon juice, then strain and pour into an attractive jug. Decorate cheesecake with whole raspberries or youngberries and serve with berry sauce. SERVES 6.

POACHED PEARS WITH STRAWBERRY PUREE

1 litre/1¾ pints apple juice
2 sticks cinnamon
4 pears

STRAWBERRY PUREE
300 g/11 oz strawberries, washed,
    hulled and halved
30 ml/2 tablespoons apple juice

In a small, deep dish (a soufflé dish would be best) microwave apple juice and cinnamon sticks on High for 10 minutes until boiling. Peel the pears and add to the hot apple juice so that they are submerged. Cover and microwave on High for at least 6 minutes, until the pears are tender but not mushy. Uncover and allow pears to cool in the liquid.

To make the strawberry purée, process strawberries with apple juice until smooth. If they aren't sweet enough you may wish to add a little sweetener to taste.

Remove pears from liquid, refrigerate and serve, fanned, with strawberry purée. SERVES 4.

Poached Pears with Strawberry Purée (this page) and Buttermilk Cheesecake with Berry Sauce (this page).

APPLE TANSY

4 Granny Smith apples
45 ml/3 tablespoons water
1 sprig tansy
150 ml/¼ pint cream
2 egg yolks
15 ml/1 tablespoon honey

Core, peel and slice the apples. Microwave them with the water and tansy in a medium-sized glass bowl, covered, on High for 6 minutes. Remove tansy.

Stir in the cream and egg yolks. Microwave on Medium for 6 minutes, stirring after 3 minutes. Stir in honey, and serve warm or cold. SERVES 4.

VARIATION: If you can't obtain tansy, replace this with a sprig of lemon verbena.

RICE PUDDING

500 ml/18 fl oz milk
4 stalks lemon grass, bruised
225 g/8 oz cooked brown or white rice
  (see Cooking Rice, page 118)
60 g/2 oz sultanas
3 eggs
75 ml/2½ fl oz honey
ground cinnamon

Microwave the milk and lemon grass in a jug on High for 3 minutes. Cover and leave to infuse for 30 minutes. Place the rice and sultanas in a flat dish. Beat together the eggs and honey, strain the milk and blend in. Pour the milk mixture over the rice. Dust with cinnamon, then microwave on Medium-Low for about 12 minutes, until set. SERVES 4.

Strawberry Honey Cream (page 133) and Lemon Creams with Berry Sauce (page 133).

LEMON CREAMS WITH BERRY SAUCE

A light, tangy, refreshing dessert which is ideal to serve after a rich meal.

250 ml/9 fl oz milk
2–3 fresh lemon verbena leaves
5 ml/1 teaspoon grated lemon zest
300 ml/11 fl oz cream
3 eggs, separated
45 ml/3 tablespoons caster sugar
12.5 ml/2½ teaspoons powdered gelatine
45 ml/3 tablespoons lemon juice

BERRY SAUCE
250 g/9 oz raspberries or youngberries
425 ml/¾ pint hot water
200 g/7 oz sugar

whipped cream and lemon verbena flowers
and sprigs to decorate

Microwave the milk, lemon verbena and lemon zest on High for 1 minute. Set aside, covered, for 30 minutes, then strain. Stir in the cream and blend. Beat the egg yolks and caster sugar together until light and creamy. Microwave on Medium for 1½ minutes, stirring every 30 seconds with a wooden spoon. Beat again, gradually adding the milk mixture, then microwave on Medium for 2 minutes, stirring every 30 seconds until the mixture thickens. Set aside to cool. (Place the bowl in a larger bowl of ice blocks if you are in a hurry.)

Sprinkle gelatine on to the lemon juice in a small dish and leave to sponge. When the lemon juice is thick and rubbery, microwave on High for 30 seconds until the mixture just starts to boil. Pour the gelatine mixture in a thin stream into the lemon cream mixture and blend quickly. Refrigerate.

Beat the egg whites until stiff and fold into the lemon cream. Spoon the mixture into six greased moulds and refrigerate.

To make the berry sauce, wash the raspberries or youngberries and set aside in a sieve to drain. Microwave the water and sugar on High for 5 minutes, stirring twice to dissolve sugar, then microwave for a further 5 minutes. Add berries to the syrup (reserving a few for decoration) and microwave for another 4 minutes, until the berries soften. Allow to cool.

Turn out lemon cream moulds on to individual plates. Surround with berry sauce and decorate with cream, fresh berries and lemon verbena sprigs and flowers. SERVES 6.

NOTE: If you cannot find fresh raspberries or youngberries in your area, replace them with another berry of your choice or use canned ones to make the sauce.

STRAWBERRY HONEY CREAM

500 g/1lb 2 oz strawberries
45 ml/3 tablespoons honey
2–3 rose-scented geranium leaves
250 g/9 oz marshmallows

Microwave strawberries, honey and geranium leaves in a medium-sized glass bowl, covered, on High for 4 minutes. Remove leaves. Stir in marshmallows and microwave, uncovered, on High for 3 minutes. Stir. Allow to cool, then refrigerate, or serve hot over scoops of ice cream — wow! SERVES 6.

LEMON CHEESECAKE

This cheesecake is best made a day ahead — leave in the refrigerator for 12 hours.

BASE
75 g/2½ oz butter
175 g/6 oz digestive biscuits, crushed
50 g/1¾ oz caster sugar

FILLING
500 g/1lb 2 oz cream cheese
75 g/2½ oz caster sugar
2 eggs
vanilla essence to taste
12.5 ml/2½ teaspoons cornflour
5 ml/1 teaspoon chopped fresh lemon verbena
25 ml/5 teaspoons lemon juice
200 ml/7 fl oz cream

sprigs of lemon verbena and violets to decorate

Place butter, crushed biscuits and caster sugar in a 23 cm/9 inch pie dish. Microwave on High for 1–2 minutes, until butter has melted. Combine and press down firmly on to base and sides of pie dish. Microwave on High for 2½ minutes.

Beat the filling ingredients together until smooth. Pour into the base and microwave on Medium-Low for 18–20 minutes until the centre wobbles slightly. Serve on a platter, decorated with sprigs of lemon verbena and violets for an elegant look. SERVES 8–10.

TANSY
Well-known in Europe, tansy is a hardy and versatile herb. Young leaves, chopped, can be used sparingly in salads, omelettes, cakes and puddings.

TROPICAL FRUIT PLATTER

This is a lovely summer dessert to serve at a brunch or weekend lunch party. Attractively garnished, it looks very elegant, but is simplicity itself. You need a large, round, white tray or platter to serve it on.

2 papinos or mangoes
4 oranges
1 pineapple
3 bananas
juice of ½–1 lemon (see Hint, page 123)
4 yellow clingstone peaches
1 small watermelon
1 cantaloupe melon
1 honeydew melon
mint sprigs to decorate

YOGHURT MIX
10 ml/2 teaspoons clear honey
300 ml/11 fl oz low-fat plain yoghurt
5 ml/1 teaspoon ground cinnamon

Peel all the fruit. Slice papinos or mangoes thinly. Cut oranges into segments. Cut pineapple into very thin slices, core and cut each slice into six wedges. Slice bananas across diagonally and dip the slices in lemon juice to prevent them from becoming discoloured. Cut peaches into slices. Cut watermelon into thin slices and cut each slice into wedges. Cut cantaloupe melon and honeydew melon into crescents. Keep all the fruit covered in refrigerator until ready to serve.

Place honey in a serving dish. Microwave on High for 5 seconds to make it runny. Add the yoghurt and cinnamon and mix well. Place on the edge of the serving tray and then arrange the fruit in concentric circles or in rows leading from the bowl. Decorate with mint sprigs and serve immediately. SERVES 10–12.

VARIATION: Scoop the flesh of two fresh passion fruits into the yoghurt and omit the cinnamon. If you have a passion flower creeper growing in your garden, decorate the outer edge of the serving tray with long fronds of this attractive plant.

SWEETENERS

Fructose, available from health food shops, is a natural substitute for sugar, with double the sweetness and half the calories; add sparingly to desserts. Artificial sweeteners are available as tablets or granules, and have barely any calories, but while they are great for adding to drinks and cold desserts, many cannot be used in cooking as they break down when heated and lose their sweetness.

FRUITY YOGHURT DESSERT

Served beautifully, this simple, healthy dessert can look rather elegant!

410 g/14 oz canned pineapple chunks
   in natural juice
300 g/11 oz canned mandarin oranges
   in natural juice
20 ml/4 teaspoons cornflour
200 ml/7 fl oz low-fat plain yoghurt
100 g/3½ oz seedless grapes, halved
1 pear, peeled and diced
1 banana, sliced
50 g/1¾ oz strawberries, quartered
mint sprigs to decorate

Drain the canned fruit, reserving juice separately. Pour the pineapple juice into a jug and make up to 150 ml/¼ pint with the mandarin juice. Blend cornflour and a little of the drained juice into a paste. Add the 150 ml/¼ pint juice and microwave on High for about 3 minutes, until thickened, stirring after 1½ minutes. Cool, then stir in yoghurt. Combine all the fruit in a bowl. Stir in the yoghurt mixture gently until fruit is coated. Serve in chilled, long-stemmed glass dessert bowls. Decorate with sprigs of mint. SERVES 4.

MANGO MOUSSE

100 ml/3½ fl oz water
15 ml/1 tablespoon powdered gelatine
500 ml/18 fl oz mango pulp (preferably fresh)
125 ml/4½ fl oz pineapple and mango
   or apple and mango juice
30 ml/2 tablespoons Grand Marnier liqueur
125 ml/4½ fl oz low-fat plain yoghurt
2 egg whites
30 ml/2 tablespoons sugar
mango cubes and mint to decorate

Pour water into a small bowl. Sprinkle gelatine on to water and leave to sponge. Combine mango pulp, juice and liqueur in a bowl. Microwave gelatine on High for about 1 minute or until mixture just starts to boil. Remove immediately from microwave, pour into the mango mixture in a thin stream and mix in with a fork. Chill for 30 minutes.

Blend in yoghurt. Beat egg whites until stiff. Adding sugar gradually, beat until thick and glossy, then fold into mango mixture. Pour into a serving bowl or individual glass bowls. Decorate with small cubes of mango piled in the centre and top with a fresh mint sprig. SERVES 4.

Strawberry Cream (this page), Apricot Ice (this page) and Mango Mousse (page 134).

APRICOT ICE

15 ml/1 tablespoon powdered gelatine
45 ml/3 tablespoons water
250 ml/9 fl oz apricot juice
410 g/14 oz canned apricot halves
   in natural juice
2 egg whites
45 ml/3 tablespoons flaked almonds,
   toasted (see Hint, page 100)

Sprinkle gelatine on to water in a ramekin dish. Leave to sponge, then microwave on High for 30 seconds, until just beginning to boil. Pour apricot juice into a medium-sized bowl and stir in gelatine mixture.

Purée apricots in a food processor until smooth. Slowly pour in the apricot juice mixture. Freeze overnight in a metal container until quite firm. Cut the frozen mixture into cubes. Beat the egg whites in a processor until stiff. Slowly drop in the frozen cubes, processing all the time. When apricot mixture is smooth and light, transfer to a freezer container, cover and freeze until required. Serve garnished with toasted almonds. SERVES 4.

STRAWBERRY CREAM

300 g/11 oz strawberries
30 ml/2 tablespoons kirsch
300 ml/11 fl oz low-fat plain yoghurt
30 ml/2 tablespoons low-fat milk
30 ml/2 tablespoons sugar
5 ml/1 teaspoon powdered gelatine
10 ml/2 teaspoons water
1 egg white

Wash and hull strawberries, and marinate in kirsch for 1 hour. Place four strawberries in each of four long-stemmed dessert dishes.

Blend remaining strawberries with yoghurt, milk and sugar until smooth. Sprinkle gelatine on to water in a small ramekin dish, allow to sponge, then microwave on High for 15–20 seconds until just starting to boil. Pour in a thin stream into the strawberry cream and mix well. Beat the egg white until stiff, then fold into the strawberry purée.

Pour mixture on to the strawberries in the dessert dishes. Refrigerate for a few hours. Decorate with a whole strawberry and leaves if possible. SERVES 4.

ROSE-SCENTED GERANIUM CUSTARD SAUCE

This mouthwatering custard is wonderful with ice cream or apple pie, and can be made the day before you need it and stored in the refrigerator.

500 ml/18 fl oz milk
30 ml/2 tablespoons roughly chopped
  rose-scented geranium leaves
4 large egg yolks
37.5 ml/2½ tablespoons sugar

Microwave the milk and rose-scented geranium leaves on High for 3 minutes. Cover and leave to stand for 20 minutes, then strain.

Beat the egg yolks and sugar together in a medium-sized bowl until the mixture is a pale lemon colour. Slowly stir in the milk. Microwave on Medium-Low for 5–6 minutes, stirring every minute with a wooden spoon, until sauce thickens. Cover and allow to cool. Serve over scoops of home-made vanilla ice cream. MAKES ABOUT 550 ML/19 FL OZ.

VARIATION: To make a mint custard sauce, use double the quantity of sugar, add a little vanilla essence (to taste) and replace the rose-scented geranium leaves with 30 ml/2 tablespoons chopped mint leaves. Serve hot or cold with chocolate ice cream and decorate with sprigs of mint.

APPLE SPONGE PUDDING

60 g/2 oz butter
30 ml/2 tablespoons brown sugar
120 g/4 oz caster sugar
2 eggs
160 g/5½ oz self-raising flour
125 ml/4½ fl oz low-fat milk
1 large apple, peeled and thinly sliced
  (about 200 g/7 oz)
5 ml/1 teaspoon cinnamon
50 g/1¾ oz sultanas
50 g/1¾ oz walnuts, chopped

Cream butter and sugars until light and fluffy. Beat in eggs, then fold in flour and milk. Pour half of the mixture into a lightly greased pudding basin, cover with apples, cinnamon and sultanas, and pour remaining cake mixture over. Sprinkle with nuts and, if you wish, a little extra brown sugar. Microwave the pudding on Medium-High for 10–12 minutes, until a skewer inserted in the centre comes out clean. Serve hot with custard or Cream Substitute (page 130). SERVES 4.

WINTER LEMON BAKE

As well as lemons, this recipe uses the more unusual lemon verbena to give the dessert a distinctive and different flavour.

SYRUP
30 ml/2 tablespoons apple juice
10 ml/2 teaspoons apple cider vinegar
100 g/3½ oz sugar
250 ml/9 fl oz water
30 ml/2 tablespoons lemon juice
5 ml/1 teaspoon grated lemon zest
5 ml/1 teaspoon chopped fresh lemon verbena

BATTER
125 g/4½ oz plain flour
pinch of salt
5 ml/1 teaspoon bicarbonate of soda
2.5 ml/½ teaspoon ground ginger
pinch of ground nutmeg
60 g/2 oz butter
50 g/1¾ oz sugar
1 large egg, beaten
15 ml/1 tablespoon smooth apricot jam
125 ml/4½ fl oz buttermilk or plain yoghurt

lemon verbena sprigs for decoration

Microwave syrup ingredients in a large bowl on High for 10 minutes. Cover and set aside.

Sift the dry ingredients together. Cream the butter and sugar until pale. Beat in the egg and jam, then gently mix in the dry ingredients alternately with the buttermilk or yoghurt.

Strain the hot syrup into a large, deep casserole. Spoon batter into the syrup. Microwave on Medium-High for 15 minutes until cooked (it should have the texture of cake). Decorate with lemon verbena sprigs and serve with custard, cream or ice cream. SERVES 4.

LEMON VERBENA
Lemon verbena is a small, deciduous shrub that grows well in regions with a warm climate. The strongly scented leaves fill the air with a marvellous lemon scent. They may be used in place of lemon grass, which is one of the key ingredients in Thai cooking.

Winter Lemon Bake (page 136) and Lemon Cheesecake (page 133).

CHAPTER TWELVE

CAKES AND BREADS

THESE recipes are ideal for the microwave as the cakes, breads and muffins turn out wonderfully moist. Fruit, corn, cheese and herbs add interesting flavours and textures to the recipes in this chapter, which are full of goodness.

NOTES

♦ Take care not to overcook cakes and breads as they will become dry — remember that they continue cooking after you have removed them from the microwave oven.
♦ The cake or bread is done as soon as it pulls away from the side of the dish.
♦ Alternatively, test by inserting a metal skewer in the centre, down to the bottom. If the skewer comes out clean, the cake or bread is ready. If it is sticky, bake for a further 30 seconds and test again.
♦ It's best to use plastic containers for microwave baking. Make sure that you use heatproof microwave cookware for combination baking.

YOGHURT AND BANANA LOAF

125 g/4½ oz butter
200 g/7 oz caster sugar
1 egg
2 bananas, mashed
50 g/1¾ oz pecan nuts, chopped
250 ml/9 fl oz granadilla or mocha yoghurt
125 g/4½ oz plain flour
125 g/4½ oz wholemeal flour
7.5 ml/1½ teaspoons baking powder
pinch of salt

Cream butter and sugar until light and creamy. Stir in egg, bananas, nuts and yoghurt. Mix in sifted flours, baking powder and salt. Pour into a greased loaf pan. Microwave on Medium-High for 12–14 minutes, until a metal skewer inserted in the centre comes out clean.

COMBINATION OVEN: Bake at 200 °C and on Medium-Low microwave power level for 14–16 minutes (25–30 minutes if your oven alternates convection and microwave energy).

FRUIT MUFFINS

These muffins are delicious served with tea or as a breakfast treat!

185 g/6½ oz mixed dried fruit, finely chopped
250 ml/9 fl oz hot water
5 ml/1 teaspoon bicarbonate of soda
20 ml/4 teaspoons butter, softened
200 g/7 oz light brown sugar
2 eggs
250 g/9 oz wholemeal flour
2.5 ml/½ teaspoon baking powder
50 g/1¾ oz nuts (such as pecans), chopped
15 ml/1 tablespoon light brown sugar
pinch of ground cinnamon

Microwave the dried fruit and water on High for 2 minutes. Add the bicarbonate of soda, and allow to cool slightly.

Cream butter and the 200 g/7 oz sugar. Beat in the eggs. Sift in flour and baking powder, then add to the fruit mixture and blend. It is important not to overmix the batter — a light stirring of about 20 seconds should be sufficient. The batter should be lumpy.

Pour the mixture into a microwave patty pan dish, lined with paper cup cases. Sprinkle a few nuts, sugar and cinnamon on top. Bake six at a time on Medium-High for 2–3 minutes, until a metal skewer inserted through the centre of the muffin comes out clean. MAKES ABOUT 24 MUFFINS.

VARIATIONS: Substitute any of the following for the mixed dried fruit:
♦ 75 g/2½ oz chopped dried apricot
♦ 150 g/5½ oz chopped dates
♦ 150 g/5½ oz chopped dried figs
♦ 100 g/3½ oz mashed ripe bananas
♦ 125 g/4½ oz grated apple and 5 ml/1 teaspoon grated lemon zest

Wholemeal Apple Cake (page 140), Fruit Muffins (page 138) and Yoghurt and Banana Loaf (page 138).

MAIZE BREAD

440 g/1 lb canned sweetcorn kernels, drained,
   or 400 g/14 oz cooked corn kernels
150 g/5½ oz butter
200 g/7 oz sugar
2.5 ml/½ teaspoon vanilla essence
3 eggs
250 g/9 oz plain flour, sifted
5 ml/1 teaspoon baking powder
2.5 ml/½ teaspoon bicarbonate of soda
salt to taste
75 g/2½ oz yellow cornmeal
45 ml/3 tablespoons buttermilk

Process the sweetcorn in a food processor. Strain to remove the liquid.

Cream the butter and sugar until light and fluffy. Add vanilla essence and the eggs, one at a time, beating constantly. Add sifted flour, baking powder, bicarbonate of soda and salt. Mix in the cornmeal alternately with the buttermilk. Spoon the mixture into a greased 1 kg/2 lb loaf pan, lined on the base with waxed paper. Level the top of the mixture. Microwave on Medium-High for 12–14 minutes.

COMBINATION OVEN: Bake at 200 °C and Medium-Low microwave power level for 16–18 minutes (25–30 minutes if your oven alternates convection and microwave power).

WHOLEMEAL APPLE CAKE

250 g/9 oz self-raising flour
5 ml/1 teaspoon bicarbonate of soda
5 ml/1 teaspoon salt
5 ml/1 teaspoon mixed spice
5 ml/1 teaspoon ground cinnamon
pinch of ground cloves
350 g/12 oz light brown sugar
125 g/4½ oz wholemeal flour
375 ml/13 fl oz oil
3 eggs
5 ml/1 teaspoon vanilla essence
375 g/13 oz canned pie apples, drained
   and chopped
40 g/1½ oz raisins
40 g/1½ oz sultanas
100 g/3½ oz pecan nuts, chopped

FRUITY GLACE ICING
185 g/6½ oz icing sugar, sifted
15–20 ml/3–4 teaspoons apple juice
30 ml/2 tablespoons chopped pecan nuts

Sift the self-raising flour, bicarbonate of soda, salt and spices together into a large mixing bowl. Mix in the brown sugar and wholemeal flour.

Beat together oil, eggs and vanilla essence. Fold into the dry ingredients with a spatula. Mix in apples, raisins, sultanas and nuts. Pour into a large, greased ring mould. Microwave on Medium-High for 23–25 minutes.

Let the cake stand, covered with a tea-towel, for 10 minutes before turning out on to a platter. Cover with a tea-towel until cold. Dust cake with sifted icing sugar or spread with Fruity Glacé Icing.

To make the icing, combine the icing sugar and apple juice in a 1 litre/1¾ pint plastic or Pyrex jug. Microwave this mixture on High for 20 seconds, then stir well with a fork and pour over the cake. Sprinkle nuts over the top.

COMBINATION OVEN: Bake cake at 200 °C and Medium-Low microwave power level for 18–20 minutes (25–30 minutes if your oven alternates convection and microwave energy).

WHOLEMEAL BREAD

90 g/3¼ oz crushed wheat
125 g/4½ oz self-raising flour
200 g/7 oz wholemeal flour
60 g/2 oz bran
90 g/3¼ oz oats
75 g/2½ oz sunflower seeds or
   pecan nuts, chopped
5 ml/1 teaspoon salt
50 g/1¾ oz brown sugar
5 ml/1 teaspoon bicarbonate of soda
500 ml/18 fl oz plain yoghurt
15 ml/1 tablespoon oil
15 ml/1 tablespoon sesame seeds

Combine all the dry ingredients except bicarbonate of soda in a large bowl. Add the bicarbonate of soda to the yoghurt. Add this, with the oil, to the dry ingredients. Mix well.

Spoon the dough into a greased loaf pan and level the mixture with a wooden spoon. Sprinkle with sesame seeds, then press them into the dough. Bake on a low rack on Medium-High for 14–16 minutes, until a metal skewer inserted through the centre comes out clean. Leave to stand for 10 minutes, then turn out on a rack to cool.

COMBINATION OVEN: Bake bread at 220 °C and Medium-Low microwave power level for 20–22 minutes (30–35 minutes if your oven alternates convection and microwave energy).

Herb Cheese Bread (this page), Tomato Soup (page 16) and Maize Bread (page 140).

HERB CHEESE BREAD

500 g/18 oz self-raising flour
5 ml/1 teaspoon salt
100 g/3½ oz Cheddar cheese, grated
10 ml/2 teaspoons chopped fresh herbs or
  5 ml/1 teaspoon dried
2.5 ml/½ teaspoon celery salt
10 ml/2 teaspoons onion flakes
500 ml/18 fl oz buttermilk
1 egg, beaten

Sift dry ingredients together, then add cheese and herbs. Soak onion flakes in buttermilk for 10 minutes. Mix in egg. Add buttermilk mixture to dry ingredients, and mix to a stiff dough. Line the base of a greased loaf pan with waxed paper. Spoon in mixture. Microwave on Medium-High for 14 minutes, until a metal skewer inserted in the centre of the loaf comes out clean.

COMBINATION OVEN: Bake bread at 200 °C and Medium-Low microwave power level for 14–16 minutes (25–30 minutes if your oven alternates convection and microwave energy).

SORGHUM BREAD

250 g/9 oz fine sorghum flour
  (obtainable from health food shops)
30 ml/2 tablespoons sugar
10 ml/2 teaspoons salt
15 ml/1 tablespoon baking powder
50 g/1¾ oz butter
125 ml/4½ fl oz hot water
4 eggs, lightly beaten

Sift the sorghum flour, sugar, salt and baking powder together and mix well. Melt the butter in the hot water. Make a well in the centre of the flour mixture and pour in the melted butter and water; add the eggs. Mix well. Place dough in a greased 1 kg/2 lb loaf pan. Microwave on Medium-High for 12–14 minutes, until a skewer inserted in the centre of the loaf comes out clean.

COMBINATION OVEN: Bake bread at 220 °C and Medium-Low microwave power level for about 15 minutes (25–30 minutes if your oven alternates convection and microwave energy).

INDEX

NOTES AND HINTS